ASPECTS OF THE PRESIDENCY

ALSO BY JOHN HERSEY

The Walnut Door (1977)
The President (1975)
My Petition for More Space (1974)
The Writer's Craft (1974)
The Conspiracy (1972)
Letter to the Alumni (1970)
The Algiers Motel Incident (1968)
Under the Eye of the Storm (1967)
Too Far to Walk (1966)
White Lotus (1965)
Here to Stay (1963)
The Child Buyer (1960)
The War Lover (1959)
A Single Pebble (1956)
The Marmot Drive (1953)
The Wall (1950)
Hiroshima (1946)
A Bell for Adano (1944)
Into the Valley (1943)

ASPECTS OF THE
PRESIDENCY

JOHN HERSEY

Introduction by Robert A. Dahl

New Haven and New York

TICKNOR & FIELDS

1980

Material from chapters 1 through 6 first appeared in the *New Yorker* between December 16, 1950 and May 5, 1951. The Gerald R. Ford foreword and chapters 8 through 13 first appeared, in somewhat different form, in the *New York Times Magazine* April 20, 1975 and, later, as *The President,* published 1975 by Alfred A. Knopf, Inc. Used by permission.

Grateful acknowledgment is made to Annandale Music Co. for permission to quote from "Send the Girls Over There," words and music by Richard M. Sherman & Milton P. Larsen; from the record album "Smash Flops/ Sing a Song of Sickness," produced by Oliver Berliner; copyright 1960 by Hall of Fame Music Co., assigned to Annandale Music Co. All rights reserved.

Library of Congress Cataloging in Publication Data

Hersey, John Richard, 1914–
    Aspects of the presidency.

    Contains 2 pts.: Harry S. Truman, first published
in The New Yorker, 1950–1951; and Gerald R. Ford, which
was originally published in 1975 under title: The
President.
    1. United States — Politics and government —
1945–1953 — Addresses, essays, lectures. 2. Truman,
Harry S., Pres. U.S., 1884–1972 — Addresses, essays,
lectures. 3. United States — Politics and government —
1974–1977 — Addresses, essays, lectures. 4. Ford,
Gerald R., 1913–   —Addresses, essays, lectures.
I. Hersey, John Richard, 1914–   Harry S. Truman.
1980. II. Hersey, John Richard, 1914–   President.
1980. III. Title.
E813.H45   353.03'1'0922   79-27694
ISBN 0-89919-012-X

Printed in the United States of America

V 10 9 8 7 6 5 4 3 2 1

For my brothers,
Arthur and Roscoe Hersey

CONTENTS

INTRODUCTION

Robert A. Dahl

Twice in the years after World War II, John Hersey had a unique opportunity to observe the American Presidency in action. As a special visitor to the White House, first to Harry S. Truman and later to Gerald Ford, he was privileged day after day to watch and listen as these particular holders of that office carried out their duties and then, as a trained reporter and a talented writer, to relate what he had heard and observed.

The Hersey accounts make timely reading at a stage in our history when the Presidency has come through a new period of change and difficulty. They also provide a chance to reflect on how the post has evolved since it was first conceived by the Framers of our Constitution, for Hersey clearly reveals aspects of the Presidency the Framers never foresaw — and would have found worrisome if they had.

In the first instance, they would have been worried by the thought that in order to perform well in the office they created, a President would one day have to possess an almost superhuman range of capacities. Yet this is what the modern Presidency appears to demand.

Hersey portrays Dean Acheson, Truman's Secretary of State, counting off some of the President's tasks to Truman himself:

> "First of all, you have to be a glorified Grover Whalen; you have to receive delegations of Indian chiefs and high-school essay winners and officers of the American Society of Bigger and Better Goat Farmers presenting you with their prize goat. Second, you have to keep on good terms with Congress — and who knows better than I what that means? Third, you have to deal with

the press. Fourth — a small matter — you have to run the country's economy and war effort, enough work in itself for twenty Chief Executives!"

"And don't forget he is also Commander-in-Chief of the armed forces," Truman said, making a characteristic switch to the third-person-singular pronoun.

"And you're Commander-in-Chief," Acheson said. "Otherwise, you're an idle man."

"It *is* a tremendous job, Dean," the President said. "A really huge job. One to make a person stop and think . . ."

One searches the words of the Constitution in vain for a job description of the office as Truman had found it. The Framers had obviously decided it would be folly to describe an office requiring moral and intellectual qualities beyond the normal range. They intended their document to fit the dimensions of men, not supermen, and they were decidedly unromantic in the judging of human nature. Benjamin Franklin probably voiced the general view when he said at the Constitutional Convention that "there are two passions which have a powerful influence on the affairs of men. These are ambition and avarice; the love of power and the love of money." Clearly a constitution had to be designed on the postulate of human frailty.

One remedy was to parcel out power, not concentrate it, and to pit one part of the government against another. In grade school, we all learn the civics lesson that Hersey heard President Ford deliver to a group of students assembled in the Cabinet Room: "This Government of ours has three coequal branches. . . . We have a system of checks and balances." The Framers intended this system to create constitutional barriers to the lust for power which they assumed would be among the inherent frailties of those who occupied public office.

But when it came to the Presidency, the Framers really did not know what the chief magistrate of a republic should look like. The model they knew best — and on the whole admired — was the British constitution. Yet clearly monarchy was out, so they faced the task of designing a constitution that would provide the functions of a monarch and his chief ministers in a republican framework. Unable to specify the tasks of the chief magistrate they had to create, they assigned the office a few powers in brief and cryptic language and left it to history to write the rest. An office the Framers left largely unfinished was completed by those who held it. In John Hersey's chapters we can perceive the directions the completion has taken in recent decades. The Imperial Presidency, for instance, was obviously in force in some ways under Truman — and headed for extinction under Ford, following the Nixon excesses. But what is revealed most distinctly is how much there is to the modern Presidency and how little of this the authors of the Constitution were able, or wished, to anticipate.

Every President does indeed spend a good many hours serving as the country's chief greeter. At such times, the President takes on a role that was created at the outset by Washington, who played it almost flawlessly. But as head of state, the President also serves as a symbolic representative of the nation; he rises above partisanship and, at his best, exhibits in conduct and personality a moral model for Americans to emulate. In most other modern democracies, this function is separate from the office of chief executive; the effective head of government is the prime minister or chancellor, while the symbolic head of government is a monarch or a president who possesses only nominal authority. However, struggling in 1787 to invent a design, the Framers decided in the first weeks of the convention that the chief executive was to be one office and one person. On that aspect of the office, as on few others, they never wavered. So the American President has to be both prime minister *and* monarch.

Yet how folksy, how "democratic" our American monarch tends to be! Where else would the head of state follow Bob Hope in a banquet speech, as we see Ford doing here, armed with gags supplied by Presidential speechwriters and already rehearsed?

If the President is expected to rise above partisanship

when functioning as the symbolic head of the whole country, he must nonetheless descend into partisan battle if he is to get much done. It was Jefferson who added this function to the tasks of the President; he shaped and superbly played the role of political manager, party leader, organizer of majority coalitions in the Congress and the country. The task has always been difficult, and it grows more so. American parties are much more fragmented than major parties in other countries; and unlike party leaders elsewhere, a President is often unable to hold his own party together. Thus we see Ford confronted by a divided party: the Republican leader in the House insists that House Republicans should develop their own legislative program, separate from the President's, while other Congressional Republicans circulate a statement indicating their loyalty to the chief.

To rally their followers, most Presidents advance a claim that Ford, who succeeded to the office from the Vice-Presidency, could not make, as Truman could not in his first term. This is the claim that, by virtue of his election, the President uniquely represents the people, or at least a national majority. In this view, election by a national majority provides the President with a mandate to carry out his policies. Once again, the Framers would have been uncomfortable with the idea of a special Presidential mandate, for in their Whiggish view only the legislature could represent the people, while the President was merely the chief executive officer (at the convention they often referred to the office as "the Chief Magistracy"), who was obliged to carry out the will of the people as interpreted by Congress. Even Jefferson, who in actuality exerted strong control over Congress, never explicitly challenged the assumption that the authentic reflection of the people's will was Congress.

It was Jackson, our first populist President, who advanced the audacious claim that the President is the sole elected official who represents *all* the people, and who thereby has a superior legitimacy as the spokesman *for* the people. In the Jacksonian view, the Congress represents only bits and pieces of the people, Congressional districts or, at most, single states. Thus was born the mystique of the popular mandate of the President. Today the Framers' Whig view of the executive office is, for all practical purposes, dead. If Ford had won the election in 1976, almost surely he would have claimed that the election had given him a popular mandate for his conservative policies.

Another aspect of the Presidency that everyone takes for granted, though the Framers did not, is the responsibility for initiating policy. For example, at Hersey's first session, Truman considers making public his "memo for the leaders in Congress on things we want to have done." A little later, his Special Counsel offers a brief glimpse of how policies are formulated in the executive branch:

> "Well, Mr. President, in mapping the legislative program for the next Congress, it seems evident that we're going to have to reexamine the existing legislation on manpower. It's a matter that will need considerable groundwork and talking around and coordination between the various departments and agencies of the government."

Truman's Fair Deal required a large volume of legislation that, in the main, he failed to extract from Congress, even when the 1948 elections replaced the famous "do-nothing" Republican Congress with Democratic majorities in each house. Yet by pressing Congress to adopt his policies, he helped to build support for a legislative program that would come to fruition nearly a generation later under Johnson's leadership.

In Hersey's account, we expect to find Ford, like Truman, busy with policy and legislation. Yet by early afternoon of his first day with Ford, Hersey has reason to ask himself, "When was policy made? When was thinking done?" At a speechwriting session late in the day, he is still wondering. Perhaps domestic policy just happened to be low on the agenda during Hersey's week at the White House, but another explanation may be that a conservative Republican President confronted by a relatively liberal Democratic Congress can afford to be less innovative and more reactive. As Hersey points out, Ford was "the most veto-prone President since Grover Cleveland, the all-time record holder." Although Ford could not get a Democratic Congress to enact the conservative policies he preferred, he could use the veto to prevent the Democrats from adopting their more liberal policies.

That the President will present a legislative program to Congress is a twentieth-century assumption. The standard view until this century is nicely reflected in the statement of a youthful Whig Congressman in the 1840s: "Were I President, I should desire the legislation of the country to rest with Congress, uninfluenced in its origin or progress by the veto unless in very special and clear cases." The young Congressman was, of all people, Abraham Lincoln. It took Theodore Roosevelt and, even more, Woodrow Wilson to add this task to the Presidency — although as late as Truman's years in the White House, Republican spokesmen were sometimes still heard to denounce this activity as a usurpation of Congressional functions.

It was also Theodore Roosevelt and Woodrow Wilson who developed — though they did not create — the role of the President as manager of foreign affairs, including the use of the military to back up Presidential policies in the conduct of international relations. Probably nothing in the entire history of the Presidency has contributed more to the growth of Presidential power than the authority conveyed by the sixteen words of Article II, "The President shall be Commander in Chief of the Army and Navy of the United States," together with about fifty innocuous words allotted to his authority in foreign affairs.

For every President since Franklin Roosevelt, foreign policy has been a major preoccupation, often dominating everything else. By chance, Hersey's first morning with Truman culminates in a moment of exceptional gravity, drama, and emotion when, following routine business through which Truman has exercised incredible self-control, the President announces that the Chinese have intervened in Korea with a quarter million troops. Suddenly we are made aware of how much authority accrues to the President by virtue of being the country's prime leader in foreign policy and Commander-in-Chief of the armed forces. Truman had already committed our military forces to Korea almost singlehandedly. What would the Commander-in-Chief do in the face of this new Chinese attack? Use nuclear weapons? Later, at his press conference, he is asked whether such action is under consideration, and his off-hand response sets off shock waves around the world.

If we see little of foreign policy, except for the comings and goings of Henry Kissinger, during Hersey's week with Ford, there is a very good reason: from these sessions, the writer is barred. Yet it is Ford's handling of foreign policy that causes Hersey most concern:

> And now this idea suddenly bothered me, and even alarmed me — not the idea of my own exile, I mean, but that United States foreign policy should have been transacted man-to-man between Henry Kissinger and Gerald Ford. I had seen endless meetings of six, eight, ten advisers sitting with the President to hammer out policy on the economy and energy and Congressional tactics and everything else under the sun; there the President had heard numerous advisory voices. But foreign policy was apparently of a different order. . . . This President, who had had a minimal exposure to foreign affairs before he came to office, heard, I was told, only one voice, and a mercurial voice it was, Henry Kissinger's. Yes, this was the most alarming thought I had had all week.

Less dramatic than the supervision of foreign policy, and therefore more easily overlooked, is the President's management of the federal bureaucracy. Although this was small potatoes before the Presidency of Franklin Roosevelt, the expansion of federal agencies set in motion by the New Deal now makes Presidents more or less responsible for guiding the activities of a huge, fragmented collection of organizations, each of which has its own aims, frequently enjoys special ties with its own clienteles and with a crucial Congressional committee or subcommittee and, in practice, as all Presidents since Roosevelt have discovered, is not very responsive to the White House. Few Presidents seem to enjoy the job of overseeing the federal bureaucracy. Elizabeth Drew reports that a White House aide said of Carter during his second year in office, "The President doesn't run things. No one here does. The President doesn't like to call people on the phone or into his office and chew them out." Yet without close supervision from the White House, Presidential policies may languish in the agencies. Many people picture the President giving orders and being obeyed, like a general. But things rarely happen that way. Richard Neustadt says that Truman liked to imagine how Eisenhower would act in the White House: "He'll sit here, and he'll say, 'Do this! Do that!' *And nothing will happen.* Poor Ike! It won't be a bit like the Army. He'll find it very frustrating." And so it proved to be.

Another function worth mentioning, one that shows up again and again in Hersey's accounts, is the President as a prime source of public information, propaganda, news. As monarch and prime minister rolled into one, the President ordinarily has a built-in advantage in getting his views before the public. Thus a member of Ford's staff assures him, with reference to Vietnam and Cambodia, that "the public believes the President gets all the information and others only partial information." But the role has its risks, especially when reporters are sharply adversarial, as many were with Nixon, particularly as Watergate unravelled. Functioning as the nation's chief public information officer can be risky even with friendly reporters if they happen to catch the President off guard, as they did with Truman on the question of the nuclear option in Korea. Since anything the President says will be scrutinized for explicit or hidden meanings, a Presidential slip of the tongue, especially on foreign and military affairs, can have grave consequences.

Is there really a candidate out there who can perform well, or even satisfactorily, *all* the roles the President must now discharge? To think so seems to me to defy human experience. Perhaps the one thing we can count on is that a President's performance will measure badly or well along one or another dimension of the office, depending on his prior experience, temperament, inner needs, and ways of understanding the world.

The difficulties a President faces in performing all his roles satisfactorily are compounded by the larger political system in which he plays his part. As the Framers well understood, if executive and legislature were *too* independent, governing would be impossible. What they sought was a design that would make President and Congress simultaneously independent and interdependent. In the end, they succeeded: the basic theory of the Constitution insured that while the President could not always count on the support of Congress, neither could Congress replace a President in the event of a deadlock. As the system evolved — and it continues to evolve even today — it came to provide an opportunity for resistance and even veto by well-entrenched minorities located in a Congressional subcommittee, a committee, a majority of one house, a Senate filibuster, or less openly but just as effectively, in an executive department or agency — and sometimes, for a final stand, in the Supreme Court. In the system of government the Framers helped to create, majorities are weak, while minorities are comparatively strong. In this respect, they got the constitution they intended.

What the Framers did not accurately foresee is how the evolution of the Presidency, within their system of constitutionally separated centers of power, each capable of checking the other, might increase the chances of conflict and deadlock between President and Congress. We may fantasy that if the Framers had foreseen the way the two systems of democratic government, parliamentary and Presidential, would evolve, they might have chosen the first rather than the second. For in a parliamentary system, deadlock between executive and legislation will not long persist because the prime minister and cabinet could not have attained their offices to begin with unless they already had the support of a majority in the parliament, and also because if they should lose that majority, a new prime minister and cabinet would have to be found, through new elections if need be. This, anyhow, is the theory, and in many countries practice is tolerably close to theory. Little good our fantasy does us, however, for what emerged from the anguish of the Framers during the convention, less by definite intention than from uncertainty, was Presidential government.

It is tempting to suggest that the problems of this Presidential government might be solved if we were now to make the choice that the Framers did not: that is, to change ours to a parliamentary system with a chief executive directly responsible to Congress. Though this alternative ought to be explored, I doubt whether one should support it, given the state of our current knowledge. Making a good constitution is among the noblest of the arts, but it is a highly imperfect science. More frequently than not, the important consequences of a change in political structures cannot accurately be foreseen. For better or worse, after nearly two hundred years, the American Presidency is part of an organic whole. We cannot be sure how transplants from other systems would work, though we can be reasonably sure that they would not function here the way they might work elsewhere.

Yet some of the aspects of the Presidency displayed in these Hersey accounts leave me with a sense of uneasiness. For one thing, given the theory and practice of the American Constitution and political system, the Presidency seems to be better suited to the goals of a conservative like Ford, who does not intend to rock the boat, than to an innovator and activist like Truman, who needs legislation in order to change the status quo. Consequently, reformist Democrats — F.D.R. after his first term, Truman, Kennedy — have been more handicapped than Republican Presidents like Eisenhower, Nixon, and Ford, who were less ambitious for change in domestic policies.

We are also reminded in this book that the office allows an exceptional amount of freedom for any President who wants to be an activist in the domain of foreign affairs. Truman's Fair Deal was blocked by a Republican Congress in 1946 and fared little better when the Democrats took over in 1948, but he was able to commit our military forces to war in Korea. Later, when he discovered that he lacked the power to control General MacArthur, he showed that he still had enough power to sack him. When the steel industry shut down as a result of a strike and thereby threatened war production, he used his executive authority to take over the industry. By the time the Supreme Court got around to slapping his wrists, he had already gained the settlement he wanted.

Thus under Truman the Imperial Presidency had already begun: he exercised his authority in foreign and military affairs without significant interference from the legislative and judicial branches. Indeed, the Imperial Presidency had begun even earlier, under Franklin Roosevelt, the first President to play all the roles which have accumulated in the evolution of that office. Or did it begin with Wilson, or with Theodore Roosevelt? Or earlier yet, with Jackson, who first introduced the concept of a Presidential mandate, thus creating the potential for a sort of elective monarchy not restrained by the national legislature?

In any event, this stage in the history of the Presidency came to an end when Nixon, who carried the Imperial Presidency to its outermost limits, fled from Washington barely in time to head off conviction on charges of impeachment. The concept of the Imperial Presidency was disgraced, and Gerald Ford, colorless and decent, helped the country to close one chapter in the American Presidency and begin another.

Where that chapter will take the Presidency and what its main aspects will be remain to be seen. We are probably as shielded from that knowledge as were the Framers, who would read with astonishment and fascination John Hersey's accounts of Truman and Ford in the office created by their Constitution.

HARRY S. TRUMAN

FOREWORD

In the first days of 1950, William Shawn, the managing editor of the *New Yorker,* called me and asked if I would like to write a profile of the President of the United States. I had seen Harry Truman in the flesh just once — on the rear platform of a railroad observation car in the station at Norwalk, Connecticut, during a whistle-stop late in the 1948 election campaign. I took my two older sons, then seven and five, with me that evening to give them a look at a President who, all the wise men and poll takers were saying, was soon to be humiliated by Thomas E. Dewey, the stiff little Republican nominee with the toothbrush mustache and the pablum speeches. When we arrived at the Norwalk railroad station, well before the Presidential train pulled in, I was astounded, first of all, by the size of the crowd, which packed the platforms and lined the tracks for hundreds of yards, and, second, by its nature: these were not the people who usually showed up at political rallies, these were laboring people, many still in their work clothes, and they were in a quickened, picnic-like mood: crackling chatter, sharp bursts of laughter. The train pulled in. Out onto the back platform came the big-eyed bantam. I lifted one son, then the other, up to see. The President had a prepared speech in his hand, but he said he guessed he'd just talk a little straight talk to these folks off the top of his head — and he began, with relish and a raunchy energy, to lay into the "do-nothing 80th Congress." The crowd exploded with cheers and laughter and shouts of "Give 'em hell, Harry!" This was not a beaten man — and what came through so clearly was that under the brass there was steel; yet also that under the exuberant, cocky joshing was a deep, unfeignable concern for these very people who crowded the tracks. My sons and I went home convinced that this man would be hard to beat.

I told Shawn I would like very much to write about Truman, provided I could get permission to do an inside job; if

I could, for instance, observe him in a staff conference or a cabinet meeting, sit in on some appointments, see him through some hard decisions, go for a morning walk with him, perhaps attend one of Margaret's concerts with him; if I were able, in other words, to picture him not simply as a journalistic biographee but rather as a living and working President, an entire man in office.

Harold Ross, founder and editor of the *New Yorker,* was acquainted with his namesake, Charles G. Ross, the President's Press Secretary, and in mid-January he wrote a letter proposing that I be permitted to write a series on "the President as a Human Being," and he enclosed a memorandum from Shawn which, besides outlining the proposal in greater detail, said that "Hersey could get Truman down" for history, and added that "possibly Truman has some sort of obligation to let himself be got down." We realized that there were all sorts of obstacles to this plan, such as the conventions of confidentiality and secrecy surrounding the President, to say nothing of the flat rule of those days which constrained the press from quoting the President directly on any matter. Still, the proposal seemed worth a try.

The reply, two weeks later, was discouraging. Ross answered Ross:

> "I hate to say 'no' to anything that you want. But 'no' it must be, at least to the request that John Hersey be allowed to spend a day with the President. I have had a dozen such requests, both from newspapers and from magazines. If I should now favor the *New Yorker,* I should get myself into one hell of a mess. Anyway, whatever I might recommend, I doubt very much whether the President would be willing to break down a rule he has had to make for himself."

Ross went on to say, however:

> "It seems to me that Hersey, even though denied special access to the President, would still find it possible to get plenty of material for the series you have in mind — the President as a Human Being. I would help him in

any way possible. I could put him in touch with others who could help him. I cannot guarantee it, but I think I could get him in to see the President, not for an interview but for a first-hand impression of him at his desk. We could work out together how any material gathered in this way might be used. Hersey could, of course, attend any regular or special press conferences. If he cared to come to Key West (it looks as if we might be going down there in the middle of March) he might be able to get some intimate stuff . . ."

I did not much relish what Charles Ross had offered; the prospect, for example, of jostling the entire seasoned White House press corps at Key West in a quest for "some intimate stuff" did not seem promising — for anything like history. I told them I'd like to think it over. Shortly afterward I took a trip to Europe; somewhere along the way I decided I simply had to gamble, with this proposal, that I could eventually work out some way to write more than a straightforward journalistic profile. And on my return I told Harold Ross I would like to lay that bet.

On June 27 I talked at length with Charles Ross at the White House, and then for four months I worked intensively, within the ground rules he had staked out, on research for whatever was to come. I spent several weeks in Washington, interviewing Truman's former colleagues in the Senate and House, his current cabinet members and staff, and his friends: Fred Vinson, Clinton Anderson, Sherman Minton, Charles Ross, Clark Clifford, Matthew Connelly, Harry Vaughan, and many others. After a most helpful conference with Margaret Truman, I went to Kansas City and Independence and delved into Truman's past.

It did not take long for the remnants of the picture I had retained of Harry Truman, even after his victory in 1948, to come tumbling down — the more or less popular picture, sketched, I suppose, during his unsure and bumbling years, 1946 and 1947: the hack politician who succeeded the great F.D.R.; alumnus of the notorious Pendergast machine; shelterer of second-rate cronies; spunky, crass, impulsive, and slightly rattled party loyalist. What I now began to see in him was pungent, to be sure, and perhaps a bit harum-scarum; but I became very much more aware of the moral texture underlying all his vagaries, a texture as strong and durable as brake lining. Framed behind his desk, in Mark Twain's hand, were the words, "Always do right — this will gratify some and astonish the rest." I discovered in Independence the nature of the steel under the brass — a frontier probity, sorely toughened in pain and conflict; his ancestors were pioneers, westward-removed Kentuckians, and every family in his Scotch-Irish-German-Dutch Independence circle had had some relative who had been killed by redlegs or bushwhackers. There had been much Bible — Old and New Testament — in his youth, and humility had been drummed into him, without, however, depriving him of the capacity for feeling pleased with himself a lot of the time. Praise, he said, made him swell up "like a pizened pup," and he often quoted Luke 6, xxvi: "Woe unto you, when all men shall speak well of you, for so did their fathers to the false prophets." This man wouldn't pose for pictures in Indian headdress when campaigning, and wouldn't kiss babies (he always told the mothers he had a cold). Politically, as far as I could dig to find, he was clean as a whistle; the formidable Pendergasts must have regarded him as some kind of mascot. He had a Jacksonian anti-intellectual bias — said he wore double-breasted suits because he didn't happen, like some single-breasted fellows he knew, to own "a watch chain with a Phi Beta Kappa key on one end and no watch on the other"; yet he knew a whale of a lot about Hammurabi, Ramses III, David, Alexander the Great, Hannibal, Caesar, Mark Antony, Marcus Aurelius, Justinian, Charles Martel, Charlemagne, Saladin, Genghis Khan, the Black Prince, Tamerlane, Hunyadi, Elizabeth I, Henry IV of Bourbon, Peter the Great, Gustavus Adolphus, George Washington, Napoleon, Jackson, Lee, Sherman, Sheridan. I was told that he had recently been reading *Lee's Lieutenants*, by James Southal Freeman; that he had given a lecture at the War College on Napoleon's marshals; and that one day he bet his Correspondence Secretary, Bill Hassett, five dollars that

Charles I of England (1601–1649) was a contemporary of
Louis XIII of France (1601–1643) and told Hassett to pay
off "to Bess's church fund, so they can buy some tinware."
He was a little weak on spelling, particularly of *ie* and *ei*
words, but he had an orderly mind: Dryden and Mozart
were favorites. He remembered. "I've almost never come
across a case," the Assistant to the President, John Steelman,
told me, "in which the President gave me something to do
which, or even part of which, he had given to someone else."
He liked things to be in their proper place and to know
where they came from; he always referred to the Ten Com-
mandments as Exodus 20 and the Sermon on the Mount as
St. Matthew 5 to 7. He got seasick on the Presidential yacht.
He never forgave an enemy, and he wrote intemperate notes
late at night. "He's one tough son of a bitch of a man," his
pal Harry Vaughan told me. But his friend John Snyder
said, "He's the Great Ameliorator." He had written in longhand at the bottom of the draft of his State-of-the-Union
message the year before, "All I want is to see that everyone
gets a fair deal."

By mid-autumn I was ready to test my bet with myself
about this man. I asked Charles Ross for the session with the
President which he had half-promised, and he arranged it; I
was summoned to a three-thirty appointment on October 30.
My wager with myself about Truman revolved around what
Charles Ross had written Harold Ross: "I doubt very much
whether the President would be willing to break down a rule
he has had to make for himself." My appeal, when I was
seated opposite the President in the Oval Office, was to history. I told him that after my several months' work I was
now prepared to write a routine profile of him, but that I
was convinced that I could do something much more to his
taste, and might even be able to contribute a fragment to the
history of his Administration, if he would let me do what we
had earlier asked Charles Ross permission to do — walk with
him for a few days, as it were, in various chambers of the
Presidency. I reminded him that though he loved history, he
had not surrounded himself, as Roosevelt had, with histo-
rians, and I repeated Shawn's earlier point to Ross — that

perhaps he had some sort of obligation to let himself be glimpsed, from time to time, for history.

This appeal, valid or not, carried the day for me, much more easily than I had imagined possible; Truman heard me out and then simply said he thought we could arrange what I'd proposed.

And so began three months' work, from which the episodes recorded in this book emerged. Charles Ross died while the work was under way, and William Hassett, Truman's Correspondence Secretary and, besides Acheson, his most literate friend — a former newspaperman, a reader, a wit, and a history buff — became my intermediary with the President. I worked without benefit of a recording machine. My long period of research now came in good stead. On the morning walk, for example, I had already heard from others most of the stories he told me, and I could concentrate my attention on *how* he told them. I took sketchy notes during each session, and then immediately afterward wrote down everything I could remember, and I supplemented and, if necessary, revised my own recall by checking it as soon as possible, individually, with those who were present at each occasion. When the pieces were written, I submitted them to Hassett. The issue of direct quotation, about which I had had considerable trepidation, was simply never raised. The firmness of the decisions that came from Hassett — not a word, by the way, was censored — convinced me that the President had read the pieces, but after the article about the morning walk came out, and the wire services had a heyday with his line about saving up some good hard punches in the nose for gossip columnists, which he was going to deliver personally when he was out of the White House, and papers all over the country picked up the story, and reporters at a press conference questioned him about those hoarded blows, he blithely said he had not read the article and didn't intend to read it; but he added with a grin, keeping open the possibility of delivering those punches one day, "People have a right to write anything they please about me." One reporter, wanting to push the matter further, asked if he would deliver the punches after the 1952 election or after 1956, and

Truman, joining in the general laughter, suggested that everyone wait and see.

It may be necessary to ask whether these pictures of Truman in office are "accurate" for history's sake. It is obvious that my mere presence, with notebook in hand, brought about distortions in each episode, just as the presence of a television camera or a recording machine would also distort, today, no matter how it might be argued that the protagonist eventually would lose consciousness of the machine's eye or ear. In this sense all oral history is slightly distorted; the weight of historical consequence hangs on every word.

In one rather important area, the episodes in this book give a different picture of Truman from that given in Merle Miller's *Plain Speaking,* some tape-recorded interviews with the ex-President, made in 1961 and 1962 for a television series that never came off. That "oral biography" shows Truman as not only feisty and often funny, which he had certainly been as President, but also profane, abusive, vulgar, and sometimes just plain lowdown. During my work on these pieces I never heard such a Truman. I believe this difference cannot be accounted for simply by the distortion of my presence and my notebook's, as opposed to Miller's, and his tape machine's, or even by the fact that Truman was a decade older and crankier when Miller interviewed him than when I observed him, but rather by something that had struck me as my view of Truman shifted and enlarged during the months of my research, and especially during the weeks of closer touch with him. President Truman seemed to think of himself sometimes in the first person and sometimes in the third — the latter when he had in mind a personage he still seemed to regard, after nearly four years in office, as an astonishing tenant in his own body: the President of the United States. Toward himself, first-personally, he was at times mischievous and disrespectful, but he revered this other man, his tenant, as a noble, history-defined figure. Here was a separation of powers within a single psyche, and a most attractive phenomenon it was, because Harry Truman moved about in constant wonder and delight at this awesome stranger beneath his skin. And to some de-

gree this wonder and delight must have elevated and purged
the mere man.

One further note: In its original version the press conference piece, which appears here as Chapter 3, was rendered
in indirect quotations, according to the rules of those days.
For this record I have restored what the President actually
said, as it was transcribed for the archives at the time.

1. TEN O'CLOCK
MEETING

At ten o'clock on Tuesday morning, November 28, 1950, President Truman, who had evidently never learned to ring summoning buzzers, appeared at the door between his office, in the West Wing of the White House, and its anteroom to call his staff in to their daily conference with him. Eleven members of the staff were waiting in the outer room for his summons: his Appointments, Press, and Correspondence Secretaries; his Assistant; his Special Counsel; three Administrative Assistants; his Military and Air Force Aides (his Naval Aide, Rear Admiral Robert Lee Dennison, was sick at the time); and his Executive Clerk. "Now, gentlemen," the President said, "I'm ready for you if you're ready for me." He put his hands on his hips, in an attitude of mock impatience he often adopted, but the exuberant, defiant mien he would normally have worn under such circumstances was absent; he was grinning, but the grin was faint and formal.

The staff straggled into the President's office, and each man took his customary seat. The President sat in a swivel chair at his massive desk, within the southern arc of the Oval Office. Behind him, between the slats of a Venetian blind in a high French window, bars of cheery, haze-softened sunlight stacked up, as if on glorious, tiny shelves. Facing him, on the curving north wall about thirty feet away, portraits of three American liberators — Simon Bolivar, George Washington, and José de San Martín — glistened in the pleasant light. On a hearth beneath the trio of portraits stood a terrestrial globe, nearly a yard in diameter, which Eisenhower used at SHAEF and later gave to his Commander-in-Chief and which the President would occasionally pat just before he showed a visitor out, saying, "We won the war on this old globe; I hope we can win the peace on it, too." From where he was sitting, Truman could cast his eye at any one of eight timepieces: three ship's clocks on the mantel and walls, four clocks on his desk, and on his wrist a chronometer that Winston Churchill gave him, accurate not only as to second and hour but also as to phase of the moon and year under the sun. Furthermore, the President was surrounded by mementos that could tell him where he stood in his century and in history: on one end of the mantel, in a small case, stood, as a reminder of the hazards and the continuity of his station and nation, a piece of wood that had been built into the original White House, in 1793, and had been licked at by flames the redcoats touched off in 1814; on a pedestal, off to his left, reared a small equestrian statue of Andrew Jackson, Truman's favorite President and his political lodestar; all across a console table behind his desk were ranged photographs of his family, holding his every act under their vigilant stares; on the wall, to his right, to make him feel the weight of the mantle on his shoulders, was a portrait of Roosevelt, caped for the sea and storm-blown; while before him on his desk, as a hedge against lapses in the wisdom of his own viziers, were various magic charms — a tiny totem pole, some monkeys shunning evil, a model of a French seventy-five, and a miniature electrotype plate of the *Chicago Tribune's* jubilant banner headline "DEWEY DEFEATS TRUMAN." Four of the staff took chairs grouped close around the executive desk. The seven others sat against the wall, flanking the President — three in chairs beside a television set, to his left, and the rest on a leather sofa and, nearer him, in a chair against the opposite curve, under the portrait of F.D.R.

When the members of the staff were all settled, the President, without calling for order, began handing out papers from a huge folder on his desk to various men. He murmured a sentence or two in a low voice as he passed each document out: "John, here's some stuff for you that has accumulated. . . . Look this over, will you, Murph? . . . This is much too long, Elsey. Boil it down to a page. . . . Do you know what we did with that thing the Attorney General gave me, Matt?"

Then suddenly the President turned to Charles G. Ross,

his Press Secretary, and said, "What've you got, Charlie?"

Ross was sitting close to the desk, at the President's left. Eighteen months younger than the President, Ross was born and brought up in Truman's home town, Independence, Missouri. They were both in the Independence High School class of 1901. Ross was the valedictorian and all-round big man of that class, and from high school he went on, as Truman was unable to do, to college. (Truman passed examinations for West Point but was rejected because of poor eyesight.) After graduating from the University of Missouri, Ross taught journalism there for ten years; then he practiced it for twenty-eight on the *St. Louis Post-Dispatch.* Truman took him on as his Press Secretary in May, 1945. Ross was a tall, slender man with a long and weary face, so thin that instead of circles or puffs under his eyes, he had curious little purses perched on his cheekbones; these made him look sadder than he ever was. Besides handling the President's press relations, Ross, a gentle and quiet man who had long suffered from arthritis and heart trouble, considered it his duty — and he had the ability — to make his friend feel comfortable, to ease the tautness of office. He always carried into staff meetings, together with his regular business, two or three trivial, entertaining items that he might or might not bring up, depending on how the President was feeling. This morning apparently mindful of the wan grin with which Truman had greeted the staff, Ross shuffled his papers, picked out a clipping from the *Washington Post,* and said, "Mr. President, did you see this item this morning? It's the column called 'Town Topics,' and it has one delightful bloomer in it that I thought you might enjoy. It describes a cocktail party given yesterday by Mr. and Mrs. Morris Cafritz, and it says here, 'It was good to see Secretary of the Treasury John W. Snyder and Mrs. Snyder in silver blue mink.' "

The staff all laughed. So did the President, but without much heart. It almost seemed as if he were trying to please Charlie Ross, who was trying to please him. "That's a good one, Charlie," the President said.

Now Ross got down to work. "Is there anything that can

be said about the appointment of an Ambassador to Spain?"
he asked. "Smitty [Merriman Smith, the White House correspondent of the United Press] was questioning me about it
yesterday, and I promised to check up."

"We're going to appoint Stanton Griffis on January 15th,"
the President said, "but we don't want to announce it just
now."

"Then there is no information on that subject?" Ross said.

"Not a word," the President said.

Truman seemed preoccupied. In staff conferences, he
usually spoke in a low, patient, easy voice, and not with the
brisk, belligerent stridence of his press-conference utter-
ances or with the earnest, primer-reading care of his radio
speeches; this morning he was speaking quietly and with his
customary grave politeness, but he was obviously thinking
about something else. Ross came up, therefore, with another
playful triviality. "Did you see, in the column of Roosevelt's
letters the *Post* is running," he asked, "that one complaining
to Sumner Welles about leaks in the State Department and
telling him to tighten up over there?"

At this, the President brightened a little. "Did it cure the
situation permanently?" he asked with faint irony.

"Oh, but did you see the next one?" said William D. Hassett, the President's erudite Correspondence Secretary, who
was then seventy years old. Hassett was sitting by the television set, and the President swung slightly to the left in his
swivel chair to face him. Hassett, the only holdover from
Roosevelt's staff among the men in this meeting, had under
Truman — as he had also had under F.D.R. — two important functions: he nourished and delighted the President's
aesthetic side, and he tried, manfully and humorously, to
persuade the President to let his Correspondence Secretary
do all his corresponding for him. "The next letter," he said,
in his granitic Vermont accent, "concerned a matter of some
import that F.D.R. sent over to Sumner with *instructions* to
leak it."

"In other words," the President said, smiling, "it was one
of those two-way streets that don't really lead both ways —

was that it, Bill?" Then Truman turned back to Ross. "Go on, Charlie," he said.

Ross picked up a document and began, "I have this memorandum —"

"Yes," the President said, interrupting; he had looked at the papers in Ross's hand and had evidently seen what they were — a list of legislative recommendations for the lame-duck session of the Eighty-first Congress, which had just convened. "I'd like to put that out. That's the memo for the leaders in Congress on things we want to have done. They're the matters I discussed yesterday with the Big Four [the Vice President, the Speaker of the House, and the Majority Leaders of the Senate and the House, with whom the President conferred on Congressional strategy once each week]. I think we ought to let the public know what we're trying to do. Those things are listed in the order in which we want to see them done. Yes, I'd like to make all that available."

The President swung around to his right, toward Charles S. Murphy, his Special Counsel, who was sitting on the chair beside the sofa. "Murph," Truman said, "can you see any reason why we shouldn't put that out?"

Murphy, who was, in effect, the President's lawyer, was charged mainly with helping to prepare plans and recommendations for legislation — an assignment to which he brought the benefit of twelve years' experience in the office of the Legislative Counsel of the Senate. He had, however, like every member of the President's staff, other duties by the dozen; they included, most importantly, the supervision of speech- and message-drafting. A forty-one-year-old North Carolinian, Murphy was husky, nearly bald, stolid, cautious, unhurried, and systematic, and he talked a jurisprudential language slowly, with a mild Southern accent. "Sir," he now said, "there are two categories of legislation on that list — matters of considerable urgency and others that are less pressing. The only trouble I can see in releasing the list might come in the second category. That matter of education benefits for disabled veterans, so far as I know, hasn't been made public in any way."

"We could leave that item out," the President said. "Anything else?"

"I wouldn't like to be too definite about it in an offhand way," Murphy said. "That's a long list."

"I can get together with Murphy," Ross suggested, "and go over it with him."

The President said, "You do that — but let out everything you can on that list."

Ross shuffled his papers again. "We have a long draft of a proposed statement on the naming of a Point Four Committee —"

"It's terrible!" the President said. "I read it last night and I wanted to tell you to redraft it. You can cut out every other paragraph without losing anything."

George McK. Elsey, one of the President's Administrative Assistants, an alert Jack-of-all-trades who, at thirty-two, was the youngest man on the staff, sitting now on the sofa, to Murphy's right, said, "Mr. President, I ran across that draft, saw it was unsuitable for you, and briefed it into a more concise statement for you to work on." He handed up two typewritten pages.

"That's much better," the President said after glancing at Elsey's draft. "I'll go over this. All we need to say about Point Four is that I've been for it, I'm still for it, and I'm going to stay for it."

"That's all I have," Ross said.

The President turned to Dr. John R. Steelman, his Assistant, who had pulled his chair right up to the desk and spread out a folder and a number of papers on its outer edge. Steelman, who was born in Arkansas, was a professor at Alabama College before he entered the United States Conciliation Service, in 1934. He helped Truman out in the lacklustre days of late 1945 and early 1946 as a special assistant on labor matters, and in December, 1946, was given the title The Assistant to the President; he now still kept his "The," though W. Averell Harriman had since been made "Special" Assistant to the President. Steelman served mainly as the President's liaison man with Cabinet members, but his many other functions made him the closest thing to an alter ego that Truman could tolerate. Although Steelman was fifty, he maintained an eager, hyper-cheerful, undergraduate look. He now handed a document of several pages across the desk to the President and said, "Here's something to look at when you get a chance."

The President, glancing at the document, saw that it was a digest of the opinions of labor leaders as to why the Democratic Party had suffered such reverses in the Congressional elections earlier in the month. "I'll be glad to read this," he said. "Say! Did you fellows see the ad on the back of the *Post* this morning? That gives one answer to why we lost in some places."

This was an instance of the inconvenience to his staff of the President's industrious use of the early-morning hours. Most of the staff members had to go out after the conference and look for the ad the President spoke of: it was a full page paid for by the pro-Taft *Toledo Blade,* warning Senator Taft not to take his victory in Ohio as a sign that he was now the undisputed leader of his party — or even that he was particularly popular in his home state. His victory, said the *Blade,* was due largely to the circumstance that the Democrats had put up such a pitiful hack against him.

Steelman began his next point: "On that price-increase matter —" (He was referring to the fact, previously discussed in a staff meeting, that the big steel companies had asked authorization to raise their prices, in anticipation of future wage raises. At the time of the present staff meeting, wage and price controls had not been decided on. The companies had alleged that general wage increases, when they came, would have many immediate, costly secondary effects — increased prices of materials, for instance — but that their own price increases would not recompense them for the labor costs for a long time, since they habitually operate on future orders and would not make collections on orders at the new prices for several months.)

The President broke in quickly. "Stu [W. Stuart Symington, then Chairman of the National Security Resources

Board] started to talk with me about that, and I expressed such a violent opinion" — Truman smiled — "that I don't think he dared go any further with the thing."

Steelman, seeing that the President's mind was made up, dropped the matter. He then said, "Senator Kilgore [of West Virginia] is very worried about the big snow-and-ice storm these last few days in the Alleghenies. He says if we get a sudden thaw there'll be a dreadful flood — the worst we've known."

Elsey spoke up. He said, "Does he propose that we turn off the sun?"

The President laughed and said, "I think maybe the Senator places too much confidence in the powers of the Chief Executive. Anyway, that's one power the Congress hasn't ceded me." Truman, who had worked closely with Harley M. Kilgore on the Truman Committee and remained intensely loyal to him, broke off the levity. "But the Senator has a point there," he said. "Will you see that we take whatever precautionary steps we can, John?"

"That's all," Steelman said, squaring off and putting away in a folder several memoranda on other points he might have raised but now had apparently decided to hold for some other day.

"Matt?" The President had turned to Matthew J. Connelly, his Appointments Secretary, who was seated at the right end of the desk.

Connelly, a Massachusetts man, spent several years working as an investigator for the W.P.A. and then for a number of Congressional committees; it was when he was an investigator for the Truman Committee that he caught Truman's eye. He had been secretary to the Boss, as he and the other staff members called Truman, since 1945. He was slender, dark, quick, neat, witty and shrewd. His job was to arrange the President's schedule and make sure it was adhered to. He saw more of Truman, face to face, than anyone else, and, like Ross, he was sensitive to the President's moods. Seeing that the President was oppressed this morning, and knowing that friendly ribbing was one of the President's principal amusements and that Hassett was a goodhumoredly cantankerous goat for pranks, Connelly now said, "Mr. President, Bill Hassett has got you in for a full-blown production on this Wilson deal." The "Wilson deal" was that Truman was soon to receive the Woodrow Wilson Foundation Award for efforts to achieve a lasting world peace, which had been given in previous years to Lord Robert Cecil, Elihu Root, Cordell Hull, Thomas Masaryk, Henry L. Stimson, Jan Smuts, and Bernard M. Baruch; the award to Truman, the first President to receive it, was to be, in the tentative words of the citation, "in recognition of his wisdom, courage, and leadership, by his action of June 25, 1950, in strengthening the United Nations as an effective instrument of world law." "Thanks to Mr. Hassett," Connelly went on, his eyes twinkling with malice, "they're all set for an evening broadcast, with a reception for some two hundred people, and now they have come in with a proposal for a big dinner."

Hassett snorted. "I wish to be heard," he said, "and I will express myself in language as restrained as I can command. When this whole business first came up, I let loose the opinion upon Louis Brownlow that it might be possible to set up a dignified ceremonial of some nature here on these premises. 'Who shall be present,' I then said, 'shall be mutually decided between your group and Mr. Matthew Connelly.' Next, Arthur Sweetser came to me with a more ambitious plan. Assuming that you share my detestation of banquets —"

"I do! I do!" the President said. Now he seemed to be enjoying himself a little.

"— I told Sweetser that we'd better start all over again, for it was one thing to honor a private citizen with a public spread; such formalities for a busy President, even considering the exceptional honor of this award, would be unbecoming in these times. I urged him to consider a simple ceremonial in this room — something that wouldn't require the use of a flying trapeze."

"In daylight hours," Connelly put in.

"In daylight hours," the President agreed, already serious again. "That'll be all right."

"I'm very glad I happened to be here to defend myself this morning," Hassett said.

Connelly then said, "A—— says you have made him a commitment to see B——"

"I made no such commitment," the President said.

"That's good," Connelly said. Then he handed across a letter from a friend of the President's in Missouri, and said, "This will interest you."

Truman looked at the signature, said "What's biting C——?," and tucked the letter into his folder for later reading.

"You won't forget," Connelly said, "that you're to make a speech on December 5th, at ten in the morning, to the Mid-Century White House Conference on Children and Youth."

"Oh, yes," Ross said. "I've been asked whether radio facilities would be available, and I've made tentative arrangements. I assume that is your wish."

"That'll be all right," the President said.

"I suppose that it will be a prepared speech," Ross said.

"Yes," Truman said, "it will have to be a prepared speech. I think we'll have a chance then to discuss public morals a little bit. I think we could say something on that subject, and it certainly is needed. I was talking to Scott [Senator Scott W. Lucas, of Illinois, then Majority Leader of the Senate, who had been defeated in the November election] the other day, and he was telling me what a dirty, rotten, lying campaign the D—— E—— [an organization] and F—— [a man] put on against him out there in Illinois. It was a vicious, libellous campaign. It seems that candidates for public office and their followers in this country won't stop at saying anything. I tell you, it's pretty bad. Look at what happened to Tydings, with that scurrilous, fraudulent composite photograph his opponents put out that made it seem as if he'd been talking as a friend to Earl Browder. And look at the lies and hints and all that they used on Graham and Myers and Elbert Thomas and the others. I tell you, we're liable to run into a situation where we'll repeat the mistakes our people made, beginning with the eighteen-thirties, in the anti-Masonic campaign and all the Know-Nothing business that led to the line of weak Presidents we had up until the Civil War. It's exactly the same kind of thing. We ought to learn by our mistakes. We've repeated this sort of hysteria over and over in our history — in 1692, 1798, 1832, 1855, 1866, and again in 1920 to '22. Those were waves of ignorance and prejudice and anti-religion." (The dates referred to the Salem witch hunts, the Alien and Sedition Acts, the year the Anti-Masonic Party ran a Presidential candidate, the height of the anti-Catholic Know-Nothing movement, the organization of the Ku Klux Klan, and the Red scare and reappearance of the Klan after the First World War.)

Hassett, like the President a lover of the past, chimed in, "The reign of D. C. Stephenson all over again!"

"That's right," the President said. "With Stephenson you had the revival of the Klan. I think we ought to try to put some of that into a speech, and try to help people keep level heads. We have to recognize subversion for what it is, and stamp it out when it appears, but that doesn't mean we should turn on each other with a lot of hatred and lies. I tell you, we've got to stop this name-calling. It weakens us here in this country. What we've got to do is persuade people to lay off personalities and talk about issues. Anything else, Matt?"

"That's all," Connelly said.

The President swung to the right again and asked, "What do you say, Murphy?"

"Well, Mr. President," Murphy said, "in mapping the legislative program for the next Congress, it seems evident that we're going to have to reëxamine the existing legislation on manpower. It's a matter that will need considerable groundwork and talking around and coördination between the various departments and agencies of the government. John [Steelman] and Dave [David H. Stowe, an Administrative Assistant] and I have talked the question over, and we agreed that Dave would be admirably qualified to receive your appointment as informal coördinator on manpower problems."

"Yes," said the ebullient Dr. Steelman. "We three settled on Dave. It was unanimous, by two to one."

"That's all right," the President said, not laughing. "I guess Dave can handle that."

"Now, as to the present Congress, Mr. President," Murphy went on, "I'd like to ask how you feel about the advisability of meeting the principal members of both parties in Congress, especially the foreign-relations people, in the near future. It would give those gentlemen an opportunity to blow off some steam before we go at them with our proposals for this session. It appears that next Monday morning might be a suitable time to have a meeting. That's when you'll be seeing the Big Four; then you could take the Big Four in and talk with the others. Both Mr. Harriman and Senator McMahon have called to say that it would be helpful to convene such a meeting as soon as possible."

"The main value of having them in here," the President said, embodying assent in his comment, "is to have people from both parties come down to the White House, so they'll feel we all belong to one country, after all." A shadow crossed his face, and he added, "But I want to say something more about that a little later on. Hold your horses on that."

"That's all I have," Murphy said.

"Dave?" the President said, turning to Stowe, who was sitting at the far end of the sofa.

Stowe, a native of Connecticut who was for some time a college professor, and then a civil servant in North Carolina, went to work in Washington, in the Federal Bureau of the Budget, in 1941, and eventually became Chief Budget Examiner. Truman, who keeps as close and anxious a watch on the federal budget from month to month as most men do on their own domestic accounts, liked Stowe's work. Steelman took Stowe into his office, and in 1949, the President made Stowe an Administrative Assistant. Stowe, who was now forty, had a talent for detail work, and the President gave him, for the most part, complicated operational assignments — like the coördinating of manpower problems, which had landed in his lap just a few minutes before.

"We have a problem in civil defense," Stowe said. Because of Murphy's slow speech, Stowe seemed to have the loquacity of a flock of starlings; his sentences and facts were run tightly together in a rapid murmuration. "You may be aware that we've had a barrage of adverse editorials coming down on us, making invidious comparisons between what we've done in civil defense and what they've done in Great Britain, but don't forget that the British were making plans from 1927 onward, and then they had the breathing spell of the phony war, from 1939 forward, and then they had several years of unpleasant laboratory experience, with the blitz and all, while we're building on mere plans and theories, and have only recently had our first realization that this isn't just fancy dancing. Up to now, our main troubles have been vagueness and generalization. Symington and Lawton [Frederick J. Lawton, director of the Bureau of the Budget] and I met at nine this morning to put some specificity into the setup." And Stowe went on to outline, at some length, details the three had agreed upon. The most important decisions had to do with the division of cost between federal and local governments on such things as stockpiles of medical supplies.

"That's all right, Dave," the President said when Stowe had finished. Truman had hardly seemed to be listening. Members of the staff told me later, however, that the President, who had trained himself to listen carefully, very likely had absorbed ninety per cent of this swift lecture, and that they confidently expected him to purl out most of Stowe's facts on some occasion when they would be needed — at a meeting of the Cabinet, or of the National Security Council, two or three months later.

"What do you say, Elsey?" Truman then asked.

Elsey said, "The letter to Congress on the appropriation for assistance to Yugoslavia will be ready this afternoon. The over-all requests for supplemental appropriations won't be ready until tomorrow morning. The supplemental-appropriations message is a cat-and-dog message that doesn't include defense requirements; the Yugoslav appropriation will be the most important part of these requests. Should the letter go up ahead of the message?"

"No," the President said. "The supplemental message ought to go up at the same time the letter does. Hold the letter until morning."

"That's all," Elsey said.

The President turned next to Donald S. Dawson, another Administrative Assistant, who was charged with screening and liaison work on Truman's governmental appointments. Before the President put him into this delicate job, Dawson had worked for fourteen years on the administration of government loans; for some time he had been Director of Personnel of the Reconstruction Finance Corporation. Dawson, who was sitting on the sofa with Stowe and Elsey, had returned the day before from a week in Florida, and his tanned face, framed in silver sideburns and split by a habitual, handsome grin, made him look like a prosperous banker among a number of pale, workaday, cage-dwelling tellers and clerks. He began to discuss some intricate maneuvers on important appointments. An implication of the conversation between Dawson and the President that followed was that it had proved hard to persuade prominent men to go to work for the government, even in crucial times — partly, it seemed, because so many important men were Republicans, and partly because so many were distinguished liberals who, whichever their party, were jealous of their reputations and their privacy and were unwilling to subject themselves to the humiliations of the Congressional investigation preceding confirmation. At one point, the President, speaking of his own current efforts to get one extremely famous American, who happened to be a Republican, to take a very big job, said, "I tried to get him on the phone for two days, but he was always out, so last night, at one o'clock in the morning, I sat down and wrote him a longhand letter and mailed it right away, special delivery. He ought to have it on his desk today. I expect I'll hear from him tomorrow." At another point, speaking of a far lesser, bureaucratic post, the President said, "I think I'll reappoint G———. He's always been right." Then he smiled, and added, "He's always been on our side."

Next, the President called on Hassett.

"I hold in my two hands," Hassett said, lifting a bundle of papers from his lap, "some material from the H——— I——— [an organization]. It contains recommendations on how to dispose of the Communists. I have no idea how this matter reached my lowly desk, unless it was by the White House belt conveyor. I would like to take this occasion to pass it along, as it was passed to me, to the Messrs. Murphy, Steelman, Ross, Elsey, and others. As far as I'm concerned, they can forward it to each other for the rest of their born days."

The President and the staff laughed. Evidently thinking back to the way Murphy and Steelman had unloaded manpower onto Stowe, the President said, "Well! There seems to be a fair amount of buck-passing going on here this morning."

"Seriously, though, Mr. President," Hassett said, "I've studied this material, and it's not for you. I have also one thing to pass on to you. Yesterday, you handed me this book, offering to endorse it over to me as a Christmas gift." Hassett laid on the television set beside him a huge, boxed volume — *The Mystery of Hamlet, King of Denmark,* by Percy MacKaye, four neo-Elizabethan plays written in the twentieth century in Shakespearean blank verse, set in Elsinore, Denmark, and concerned with events preceding those of *Hamlet.* "I have perused, though sketchily, the eight hundred pages of this work," Hassett said, "and I'd like to turn it in for a new model."

"All right," the President said. "I have something else for you. I brought it in specially for you this morning." He picked up and handed to Hassett a copy of *Kon-Tiki,* by Thor Heyerdahl.

Hassett opened the front cover and smiled when he saw, on the end paper, in the President's hand, this inscription:

HARRY S. TRUMAN
Bought and Paid For.

"It's not going to be easy for you to endorse *this* over to me, I see," Hassett said.

"You seem to have the idea that everything I own has

been given to me," the President said. "But you're wrong. Every once in a while, the Madam and I will order a book that we've read about in the *Saturday Review of Literature* or in one of the Sunday book sections, if it looks interesting. I think you'll like that one, Bill."

"I thank you," Hassett said.

"Anything this morning, Harry?" The President addressed this question to Major General Harry H. Vaughan, his Military Aide and old friend, who was sitting next to Hassett. Vaughan made Truman's acquaintance during the First World War, in which Vaughan ultimately commanded a battery of the 130th Field Artillery Regiment, while Truman had a battery in the 129th Regiment. They became close friends as fellow reserve officers, along with John Snyder, now Secretary of the Treasury, in summer training camps in the twenties and thirties. As Military Aide, Vaughan's function was mainly social; he was really a kind of court jester. He seldom spoke at staff meetings except to crack jokes. This morning, responding in his own way to the President's serious mood, he was subdued and matter-of-fact as he said, "Frank Pace [Secretary of the Army] tells me they announced the decision on that Gilbert case yesterday."

"I know," the President said. "That's the colored officer in Korea who ran away in the face of the enemy. First they were going to shoot him. Then they were going to give him life. Then they were going to give him thirty years. What did they finally decide to do?"

"They've reduced the sentence to twenty years," Vaughan said. "Here are the final orders for you to sign." He put some papers before the President.

"I know one thing —" Truman said. Then he broke off and stared into space for a moment. (He might have been thinking — since the parallel was so close — of the first important test of his own courage, the episode that in reunions of his Battery D is now known as the Battle of Who Run. On the night of August 29, 1918, on a mountain called Herrenberg, in the Vosges, some near misses by German artillery caused Captain Truman's battery to panic and flee for cover under the screaming leadership of a terrified sergeant. Only

Truman's rare virtuosity in Missouri cursing drove the men back to the guns. Afterward, Truman refused to courtmartial, but tried instead to salvage the disgraced sergeant as a private.) "I know one thing," he resumed. "If this had happened in the other war, and if I'd been this fellow's commanding officer, we wouldn't have needed any trial at all; we would have handled it in our own way. That's a serious thing, to run away in the face of your country's enemy." The President hesitated, then quickly took a pen, signed the order, and handed it back to Vaughan.

"Do you have anything, Bob?" Truman asked, turning to Brigadier General Robert B. Landry, his Air Force Aide, who was in the chair next to Vaughan's. Landry, who was forty-one, had commanded groups of both fighters and heavy bombers in Doolittle's Eighth Air Force in England. "Nothing," Landry said, "except Nick Bez sent you some fresh salmon, but the plane was held up and the fish spoiled. He just wanted me to tell you that he would try to send some more along to you, and he'd hope it would get through."

"That's too bad," the President said. "Thank Nick for me."

Now, having gone once around the figurative council table, the President centered himself at his desk. For a few moments, he shifted papers back and forth and straightened a pair of scissors and two paper cutters lying on the leather margin of his desk pad. He had suddenly drooped a little; it appeared that something he would have liked to forget was back in his mind, close behind his hugely magnified eyes.

"We've got a terrific situation on our hands," Truman said in a very quiet, solemn voice. "General Bradley called me at six-fifteen this morning. He told me that a terrible message had come from General MacArthur. MacArthur said there were two hundred and sixty thousand Chinese troops against him out there. He says he's stymied. He says he has to go over to the defensive. It's no longer a question of a few so-called volunteers. The Chinese have come in with both feet."

The President paused. The shock of this news — for this was the first that any of the other men in the room had heard of the all-out intervention of the Chinese Communists in the Korean war — made everyone sit stiff and still. The success in Korea that had seemed to be so nearly achieved was abruptly snatched away by that word "defensive." The entire policy since June, which had seemed to be turning out for the best, was now to be more heavily tested than ever; hopes of imminent peace were gone; the willingness of the Chinese Communists, and therefore, obviously, of the Russian Communists, to risk a general war for the stake in Korea was suddenly palpable. All of the staff must also have realized instantly what this news meant to the President, who would be answerable, quite alone and inescapably, for the outcome in Korea. The decision to order American forces north of the 49th parallel had been his, and the Chinese incursion was clearly a response to that provocation.

"Now," the President went on, "I'm going to meet with the Cabinet this afternoon. General Bradley will be there to discuss the situation. General Marshall is going to meet with the State and Treasury people. Acheson is informing the Congressional committees. It may be necessary to deliver a special message in a few days declaring a national emergency. When things are settled down a bit and we know exactly what our policy in answer to this thing will be, we'll talk to the people — a simple, four-network hookup from right here, about ten days from now, I would say. I want to have that meeting with the Congressional leaders you were talking about, Murphy. Let's not wait till Monday; let's arrange it for Friday. I don't think a personal appearance before the Congress would be desirable just now; the military-appropriations message will give us a chance to say whatever needs to be said to the Congress."

In outlining his concrete plans and acts, the President had hidden, as indeed he had all through the staff meeting up to this point, his feelings about this new development, with which he had lived for only about four hours. Now he paused for a few seconds, and suddenly all his driven-down emotions seemed to pour into his face. His mouth drew tight, his cheeks flushed. For a moment, it almost seemed as if he would sob. Then, in a voice that was incredibly calm and quiet, considering what could be read on his face — a voice of sorely tested conviction — he said, "This is the worst situation we have had yet. We'll just have to meet it as we've met all the rest. I've talked already this morning with Bradley, Marshall, Acheson, Harriman, and Snyder, and they all agree with me that we're capable of meeting this thing. I know you fellows will work with us on it, and that we'll meet it."

Quickly, again, and characteristically, the President brought himself back to thoughts of concrete plans. "I'll have to ask you all to go to work and make the necessary preparations — the declaration of emergency, if we decide to go ahead with it; the appropriations message; the speech to the people. Matt, I may have to cancel all my appointments tomorrow. You be ready for that, will you?"

"Sure," Connelly said.

"Did you say two hundred and sixty thousand Chinese troops?" Landry asked incredulously.

"That's right," the President said. "They have something like seven armies in there. Of course, what they call an army isn't the same as ours. Their armies are about the same as our corps."

"I don't suppose you want me to announce anything yet," Ross said.

"Charlie, there's nothing to announce," the President said. "I don't know what can be said. We don't have to say anything about the Cabinet meeting, because it's our regular Tuesday meeting."

"That's true," Ross said. "We wouldn't want to call special attention to it, since it's a regular meeting."

The President nodded to William J. Hopkins, his Executive Clerk, who was sitting next to Steelman, and Hopkins, a self-effacing, taciturn man of forty who has been a clerk in the White House since 1943, stood up and handed across the desk to the President a pile of documents for signature. Truman pulled out the left leaf of the desk, put the papers on it, and began to sign them. (Most of them were letters drafted by Hassett, answering expressions of regret at the assassination attempt, which had taken place not long before; there was one official document, on a public-housing matter.) While the President was signing the papers, he said, "Well, the liars have accomplished their purpose. The whole campaign of lies we have been seeing in this country has brought about its result. I'm talking about the crowd of vilifiers who have been trying to tear us apart as this country. *Pravda* had an article just the other day crowing about how the American government is divided, and how our people are divided, in hatred. Don't worry, *they* keep a close eye on our dissensions. We can blame the liars for the fix we are in this very morning. It's at least partly the result of their vicious, lying campaign. What has appeared in our press, along with the defeat of our leaders in the Senate, has made the world believe that the American people are not behind our foreign policy — and I don't think the Communists would ever have dared to do this thing in Korea if it hadn't been for that belief. Why, J——— [a newspaper publisher] had an editorial just yesterday claiming that he was personally responsible for the defeat of our foreign policy. He *boasts* about it! And the result is this news we got this morning."

The President handed the papers he had signed back to Hopkins. Then he sat squarely in his chair again, and again his mood quickly changed. He suppressed every sign of the anguish that had been so visible on his face a few minutes before and of the irritability and disgust he had shown during his last remarks; his voice, though still quiet, took on a confident tone, and as he spoke now he struck an intensely personal note, seeming by his use of the first-person-plural pronoun to be remembering and resummoning the deep loyalty of these men around him. "We have got to meet this thing just as we've met everything else," he said. "And we will. We will! Let's go ahead now and do our jobs as best we can."

Then the President, with still another sudden shift of mood, closed the meeting with a playful formula he was then using, with slight variations, nearly every day, and as he did so he appeared to have recovered at least a measure of the exuberance with which he normally confronted life. "Well!" he exclaimed pleasantly. "If none of you gentlemen have any more non-controversial items, I'll declare myself satisfied, and the meeting can adjourn."

2. QUITE A HEAD OF STEAM

Before dawn one chilly morning a few days later, I stood in an alley behind Blair House, across Pennsylvania Avenue from the White House, waiting, along with some Secret Service agents, for the President; he had invited me to go along with him on one of his famous early morning walks. The White House was being renovated then, and the President and his family were living in Blair House for the time being. Because some Puerto Rican Nationalists had, not long before, made an attempt to storm the house and assassinate the President, the Secret Service was no longer allowing him to take casual strolls straight from the executive mansion down past the Ellipse and around the Washington Monument, or out along the Mall, or through Lafayette Square into the heart of town, as he had done all the previous months of his Presidency, walking wherever his whim took him, tipping his hat gravely to other early citizens. Now, in spite of his protests (for he hated precautions on his behalf and spoke sometimes of his honorable station as "this jail I'm in"), the agents were taking him by car to places here and there around the city's edges where he could still stir up his blood but would probably not be accosted, or even encountered, and where, because of a daily change of locale, his brisk matutinal presence could not be counted on. We waited, each man hugging and pounding himself to keep warm, while near us the Presidential limousine fogged the air with its rapid breath. Another car, for some of the agents, stood not far away. The agents joshed each other, checked certain weapons with which they were supplied, and now and then looked at their watches. The Boss, as they called Truman when they spoke of him, was due to come out, and they asserted to me that he would appear promptly, at six-forty. The sun was due to rise that morning, and they assumed that *it* would likewise appear on time, at six-forty-nine.

At the turn of six-forty, the agents, as if called to order by the blow of a gavel, fell silent. A few seconds later, the Blair House door opened, and the President, accompanied by two more agents, came out. He smiled the unforced smile of a man with an already revved-up metabolism, and, looking at us, he said, "Good morning, gentlemen." He was carrying a yellowish walking cane with a rubber tip.

Various agents answered, saying, "Good morning, sir," or "Morning, Mr. President." One of the men opened the rear door of the limousine.

"A little zip in the air this morning!" the President said, and then stepped into the car and sat down on the right side.

"Yes, sir," the agent at the door said. "It's snappy out."

"You hop right in here," the President said to me, patting the seat beside him. The driver and that morning's senior agent, a man named Henry Nicholson, got into the front seat (which was not separated from the back by a glass partition), and the rest of the agents boarded the other car. As I bent over to get into the limousine, I noticed that a small rubber foot pad, something like a shower mat, had been waiting for the President's feet on the right side of the floor, and that now his feet were planted tidily side by side in the middle of the mat. The President had settled himself back in the seat. He was wearing a heavy dark-blue double-breasted overcoat, gray suède gloves, and a wide-brimmed, string-banded light-gray felt hat.

Truman turned to me, when I was seated, and said, "Sorry to get you out so early. From what I hear of writers, this must be a strain on you."

I answered, as the cars began to move, that one of the agents had told me the President would make a farmer of me if I stayed around long enough.

"That's right!" the President said. "I've been up since five-thirty. I get up at five-thirty every morning. Most people don't know when the best part of the day is: it's the early morning."

The cars started out on Pennsylvania Avenue. On the far side of the avenue, we could just make out, in the first gray of dawn, that huge architectural cranberry bush, the old State Department Building. The limousine moved slowly.

I asked the President what he had been doing since he got up.

He said, as if he were talking about someone else, "A President has a lot of chores to do."

I said, "Charlie Ross told me that you carry home a briefcase five inches thick every night. Is that what you've been doing — going through your briefcase?"

"That's right," the President said. "I've already read a stack of secret papers. Reports from the military people, from the National Security Council, from Central Intelligence — from Cloak and Dagger, I call them. All kinds of papers that pile up on the desk."

I asked him if he had eaten breakfast.

"Not a bite yet," he said. "I'll go walking, then go to the gym and sweat off a pound or two, then take a swim. After that, I'll eat half the breakfast I want and then go hungry all day long."

"What will half the breakfast you want be?"

"A strip of bacon, a scrambled egg, a piece of toast, and a glass of milk."

"No coffee?"

"I don't crave coffee. It hurts the peculiar talent I have for lying down and dropping right off to sleep in two minutes. Doc Graham [Brigadier General Wallace Graham, the President's physician] won't let me eat the way I'd like to. If it weren't for the Doc, I could eat a whole side of beef for breakfast. I think I could."

The limousine stopped for a red light. We had been going past rows of boxlike government buildings, some of them of the sort that has been called "temporary" for more than thirty years. The day was coming on fast. A few blocks ahead, at the end of the street we were on, we could make out one of the capital's many monuments to heroes of the past. The President called my attention to it. The lights changed, and we started up again.

Having heard that during the earliest morning hours the President takes a surprisingly thorough gallop through the *New York Times* and *Herald Tribune,* the *Washington Post* and *Star,* the *Baltimore Sun,* and occasionally a day-old Missouri paper as well, and having taken a hurried preparatory look at the morning's *Post* myself, only to be rewarded with the gloomy news that the Chinese had the United Nation armies in full rout, I remarked stupidly, "The news was pretty bad again this morning."

Truman turned his head, looked at me rather pityingly, and said, "People who don't know military affairs expect everything to go well all the time. They don't understand. A general can't be a winner every day of the week. The greatest of generals have had to take reverses. I advise you to study the lives of Alexander the Great, Tamerlane, Gustavus Adolphus, Hunyadi — and Robert E. Lee and Stonewall Jackson. You'll find they all won most of the time, but they all had their troubles, too. I'm not upset, like most people, about these reverses MacArthur is taking."

The President went on to make other observations about that morning's news — about a speech by Acheson, and about some new attacks on the Secretary of State by Republican senators. Then suddenly he broke off and asked Nicholson, "How's your family, Nick?"

Nicholson turned around in the front seat and said, "They're all fine, sir. Nick Junior saved my life this morning. My alarm didn't go off; I guess I forgot to pull the button. He came running in and alerted me. 'You better get up, Pop,' he says "It's five minutes to six!' "

"Well, good for him!" Truman said. "He's going to be as smart as his old man. I can see that now."

"He's a fine boy," Nicholson said.

"Oh, he's smart," the President said emphatically.

Now the road swung out beside a body of water and followed its curving shore. The limousine moved at an easy pace. The air was quiet. Below the lightening sky, out over the edges of the city, a low night mist still hovered. The water near us looked like monel metal. On it, not far from us, a cluster of sitting waterfowl black-dotted the slick gray surface.

"Look at those ducks!" the President exclaimed. "Wouldn't you think they'd get cold feet sitting out there? B-r-r-r!"

The limousine began to meet traffic hurrying into the city from the suburbs. Not far beyond the place where we had seen the ducks, a District of Columbia police car pulled out into our path and drove along in front of us. Truman sat forward in his seat and looked rather pleased at having acquired a police escort. "They told me he was going to pick us up along about here," he said. "The regular road is blocked by repairs up ahead. He's going to lead us around a detour."

The President's caravan drove to its destination deviously, as he had predicted. At one point, near some water again, the ground was littered with driftwood and broken branches, which had been washed up there during a windstorm a few days before. As we drove along, the President spoke of that storm and the clutter it had caused. In the distance, while he talked, the roar of a takeoff from one of the city's airports began to build up, like the roll of a huge kettledrum. In the motionless air, the noise was insistent and ominous, and all of us in the limousine looked toward its source, hidden in a sullen bank of mist, out of the top of which hangars humped up into the clear air above. Suddenly, startling close, there emerged from the low-lying vapor, headed straight our way and slowly rising, a Constellation.

"Look at that thing lift up!" the President said, speaking loudly, to be heard above the plane's rumbling. "I don't believe it yet. It's one of the miracles of our age how a big, heavy thing like that will lift up off the ground. I estimate that the machine weighs thirty tons. Think of what it takes to lift thirty tons of machinery off the ground! I can hardly believe my eyes when I see it."

For a moment, the plane throbbed directly above our heads, and then very quickly it was gone, and unheard. We looked out from the leisurely-moving limousine over the now silent landscape. The bank of mist and the brightening

sky above it were reflected in shifting patterns on the na-
creous water near us.

I said it was a pretty sight.

The President said, in a voice that seemed very soft after
his speech in competition with the plane's noise, "Out here's
one place where there's peace." Then, briskly again, he said,
"This is a nice morning for walking, isn't it, Nick?"

"Looks fine. Yes, sir," Nicholson said.

After we had driven a little farther, the car slowed down
and stopped, and the President said, "Well, here's where we
get onto shanks' mares."

We stepped out of the limousine and began at once to
walk along a concrete pathway that ran more or less parallel
to the road. Nicholson and the driver walked close behind
us. The other agents took up various more distant convoy
duties. I walked on the President's left. The President carried his cane, swinging it high, in the near — his left —
hand.

I remarked on the fact that his pace was lively.

"This is just the regular Army marching speed," he said.
"One hundred and twenty paces to the minute, two miles in
half an hour. I've always walked at this speed — ever since I
was in the Army. Timing is just a knack. I can tell how fast a
train is going by counting the telephone poles as they go by."

I asked how long he had been taking morning walks.

"I've been taking these walks for thirty years now," he
said. "I got in the habit of getting up and moving around
smart in the early mornings on the farm, and then when I
got into politics, I couldn't stop. I began to take these walks
when I was Judge of the Eastern District of Jackson County,
out home, knocking around Independence and Kansas City
mornings before breakfast. Then I walked all over Washington when I was in the Senate. You can't think clearly if you
don't exercise."

"Apparently you like to keep moving," I said.

"I like being on the road," Truman said. "Fact is, I like
roads. My father and I had the road overseer's job in Grandview, where our family farm is; he had it first and I had it
after he died, when I took over the farm. That was before

the first war. Back in those times, every man in Missouri had to give either two days' work or six dollars a year toward the roads; some of the overseers took the six dollars and put them in their pockets and let the roads go to pot. We took the work, my father and I did, and we had the best roads in Missouri, in and around Grandview. We didn't get any richer, but we had good roads. My father worked so hard on the roads it killed him.

"When I got to be Presiding Judge, out home [of the Jackson County Court, an archaically misnamed office, which is not judicial at all but executive, corresponding to the county commissioner's office in most places, and having charge of the county's business affairs; Truman was Presiding Judge from 1926 to 1934], I found out that there were some overseers claiming they were putting in thirty-four culverts under the roads at so much per culvert — nearly two thousand dollars apiece, as I remember. I found out they had no idea of installing the culverts; they were just going to pocket the money. It was going to be worth sixty thousand-odd dollars to them in one year to not build culverts. I fired all but fourteen overseers in the county and hired four supervisors, and I began to make them work. I was about as popular as a skunk in the parlor.

"In '28, I went out to build the county some new roads. I had two engineers, Colonel Edward M. Stayton — he's a retired general now — and N. T. Veach — he was and is a Republican. I could then, and I still can, get along with a decent Republican, though Mother never would let one, decent or otherwise, land on the front porch if she could help it — she was such a rabid Democrat. Anyway, I took these two engineers, and we drove over every inch of the three hundred and fifty miles of surfaced roads in Jackson County — only you couldn't call them surfaced roads, really: they were just roads with piecrust on them, water-bound macadam that would scale off in no time. The people voted me ten million dollars to build roads — the first bond issue was six and a half million, then in '31 they voted me three and a half more — and I gave them two hundred and eighteen miles of roads that they're still driving on, as good as the day they were built. They were as fine as the system in Westchester County, New York State."

"I gather you've travelled on roads quite a bit, too," I said.

"Roads are meant to be used," Truman said. "When I was fixing to give Jackson County a new courthouse, I wanted to see some big public buildings with my own eyes before I spent all the money the people voted me for it — nearly four and a half million — so I drove twenty-four thousand miles through Oklahoma and Arkansas, into Texas, to Shreveport, Louisiana, up around to Minnesota and St. Paul, to Denver, Milwaukee, Racine, Chicago, and Brooklyn, looking at the best courthouses and capitols and city halls. I even went and looked at a life-insurance building in Montreal. The man who drove me on that trip was a fellow named Fred Canfil."

I said I had met Canfil on a visit to Kansas City and had found him quite a character.

"Fred's *two* characters!" Truman said. "Fred's a little rough, but Fred's all right; he's as loyal as a bulldog. You know, I took him along to Potsdam with me, as a pro-tem member of the President's Secret Service detail. He was the most vigilant bodyguard a President ever had. While the conferences were going on, he would stand by a window with his arms folded and scowl out the window at everybody who passed in the street, as if he would eat them alive if they bothered the President of the United States. Fred's a federal marshal out home, so one day after a meeting I took him up to Stalin and I said, 'Marshal Stalin, I want you to meet Marshal Canfil.' Well, after *that,* the Russians treated Fred with some respect, I tell you. As I say, Fred and I drove around the country in '34 looking at buildings, and we drove far enough to have gone plumb around the world."

The kind of debris we had seen from the car on the way out occasionally cluttered the path on which we were walking. Here and there, we came to a piece of driftwood, or a ridge of tangled marsh grass and twigs, or, as at a point we now reached in our course, a cluster of branches from one of the tremendous willow trees that lined the walk. Crossing this barrier, the President lifted his knees sharply, like a drum major, and surefootedly made his way through without breaking his pace for an instant. I dropped behind.

When I had caught up, Truman went on, "Then, after the second war began in Europe, I drove another thirty thousand miles across this country, looking at the construction of Army camps and seeing all the waste they were building into them. Then I came back and set up the Truman Committee. If I hadn't taken that drive, I'd still be just Senator Truman instead of being in all this fix."

I told the President I had heard that he used to have a reputation for being a very fast driver.

"I like to move," he said, "but in all my driving I've never been arrested for speeding. I try to observe the laws of this country. Once, when I was in the Senate, I was driving my family from Independence to Washington, and as I was about to get into Hagerstown, Maryland, I went through a stop sign that I couldn't see because some damn fool had parked his car in front of it. The Madam was in the front with me, and Margaret was in the back with a lot of books we were bringing back East with us. All of a sudden a fellow came along, wasn't looking where he was going, and he swiped me as I came out of the intersection. He hit the left rear fender. It knocked the car cater-cornered. The side where the Madam was sitting hit a lamppost, and part of the post fell down on the roof of the car and gave her an awful jolt; her neck has never been quite right since then. The car was just able to limp along under its own power to a repair place, but it was a total wreck: there wasn't enough left of it to save it. We just took our books and things out and put them in a brand-new Pontiac I bought, and went on our way when we were ready. Thank heavens, the insurance company stood in back of the bill. Well, the other driver that hit me had been a local fellow — the authorities knew him — so they'd taken me to the police station and all of that, until they figured out I was a U.S. senator. I wasn't going to get out of it by telling them myself, but they found out, and then they fell all over themselves. They ended up with a formal ceremony giving me the keys to the city. Besides, they had learned that I wasn't at fault. The truth comes out about an innocent man sooner or later, but sometimes it's too late, especially if they've already hanged him."

The President, who was evidently beginning to be warmed up by his marching, took off his gloves and put them in his overcoat pocket. "In Washington, once," he said, "I went through a stop light right behind another fellow who'd gone through it, too. An officer stopped both of us. He asked me for my license. He looked at it, and he said, 'Are you the Senator Truman I've been reading about in the papers — the Truman Committee fellow?' I allowed I was. He said, 'You've been doing a good job in there, Senator, you go along now. Just let me get this other fellow out of your road till I give him a ticket, then you can roll along.' I said, 'No, sir, Officer, I'm a citizen like anyone else. You give me a ticket.' I made him give me a summons. But I guess he tore up his end of the thing — the stub. I sent a contribution to the Policemen's Fund for the customary amount. Never heard anything more from it. The truth of the matter is, I had no desire to hear anything! Come to think of it, though, I *did* hear something: I got a nice letter from the secretary of the Policemen's Fund, thanking me for the contribution."

The President walked on a few steps in silence. We were in broad daylight now. The low mist was burning off, and the sky was blue above us. Finally, apparently taking off from a reminder in his previous remarks, the President said, "I'm told that the Truman Committee saved the United States government fifteen billion dollars in waste, delay, and inefficiency. We weren't working for publicity on that job. We never gave anything to the papers until a case was closed, till everything was black-and-white and there wasn't a chance of maligning a citizen in public. All we wanted was to do a good job for our country. I think you'll still find a lot of politicians who feel the same way. You know, people cuss the politicians all the time, but how do you think this country would get along if it weren't for the honest politicians? *Some-body's* got to get in there and do the work! Do you know my definition of a politician? 'A politician is the ablest man in government, and after he dies they call him a statesman.' "

Again the President paused. Then he said, "There's no reason why a public servant should want anything for himself. You know, I've noticed that wherever you find a crooked politician, you'll find a crooked businessman behind him. Building the roads in Jackson County and putting up the county courthouse, I learned a thing or two about contracts and contractors; then in the Truman Committee I learned a lot more. Once in a while, you run across a contractor that likes to cut corners, and you usually discover that he's got a crooked, pipsqueak politician chasing errands for him. Why are some men so selfish? What do they think they get for themselves? Not happiness — not that. There was a banker out in Missouri I knew — he's dead now — who used to lend money to businesses that were on the way up, and he'd watch the companies, and if he saw one that was sound, he'd wangle this way and that way until he had control of the thing. He wound up with fifteen million dollars in his pocket, but he'd ruined fifteen lives doing it. Now, what good was that?

"And yet sometimes," Truman went on, "I think a liar is worse than a thief. I have in mind all the lying slander you see in public life in this country today, and in the newspapers. You remember what Shakespeare said: 'Who steals my purse steals trash, but he that filches from me my good name makes me poor indeed.'* I think a publisher, or any newspaperman, who doesn't have a sense of responsibility and prints a lot of lies and goes around slandering without any basis in fact — I think that sort of fellow actually can be called a traitor. Truth is one thing. A politician can stand a dig now and then if it's the truth. But smears are something else. These fellows talk about being un-American! To my

---

*Truman had taken the liberty of cutting these lines, which are from *Othello*, somewhat, to make a tighter epigram of them, but he had quoted correctly the words he kept. The whole passage reads:

> Who steals my purse steals trash; 'tis something, nothing;
> 'Twas mine, 'tis his, and has been slave to thousands;
> But he that filches from me my good name
> Robs me of that which not enriches him,
> And makes me poor indeed.

mind, there's nothing as un-American as a lying smear on a man's character. And some of these columnists! When you come down to it, there's just one thing I draw the line at, and that's any kind of attack on my family. I don't care what they say about me. I'm human. I can make mistakes. Any man can make mistakes, even if he's trying with all his heart and mind to do the best thing for his country. But a man's family ought to be sacred. There was one columnist who wrote some lie about my family when I was in the Senate, and instead of writing him a letter I called him on the phone, and I said, 'You so-and-so, if you say another word about my family, I'll come down to your office and shoot you.' He hasn't printed a whisper about them since. I'm saving up four or five good, hard punches on the nose, and when I'm out of this job, I'm going to run around and deliver them personally."

The President unbuttoned his coat and threw it open, without breaking his stride.

"Mr. President," I said, "you spoke of having had books in your car when you had that accident in Hagerstown. What sorts of books would they have been?"

"All kinds," he said. "Some legal, some just for pleasure. You see, I was born with flat eyeballs. I had to wear glasses the very first thing when I was a boy. I couldn't get out and play much ball, for fear of busting my glasses, and I was blind as a mole without them. That was when I got in the habit of reading so much. I've always been a heavy reader."

I said someone had told me that for many years he had carried some poetry in his wallet, and I asked him if he still did.

"Yes," the President said, "I still carry it."

He did not seem inclined to say anything more about the poetry in his wallet. Changing the subject, I said that in Kansas City I had met a Western District Court judge named Albert Ridge, who told me that during the days after the First World War, when he and other ex-artillerymen used to loiter in the Truman & Jacobson haberdashery store, at Seventeenth and Baltimore, Harry Truman, the captain of his old battery, had kept urging him to improve himself. One of

the things Truman had done, Ridge said, was give him a list
of ten books that any young fellow who wanted to get ahead
ought to read.

"That's right," the President said. "I used to drive the boys
who hung around the store pretty hard. Especially the Catholics. I used to make them go to Mass. I wasn't going to have
any Catholics lay their backsliding at the door of a Protes-
tant! No, really, I'm just joking. Those boys were all very
good about getting themselves to church. I'd forgotten about
that list for Al. It's true. He'd been a private in my battery,
and he came to me during that time after the war — he was
studying the law; he wanted to educate himself — and we
had a balcony up over the store, and I used to send him up
there to work on his books nights, when the other boys were
just horsing around, and once he asked me for a list of ten
important books to read, to help him get ahead. Al did improve himself, too: he passed his bar exams, made a fine
record as a lawyer, and now he's a federal circuit judge out
home. I can't remember now what the ten books were."

"Judge Ridge is hazy about them, too, now," I said. "He
does remember Plutarch's *Lives, Bunker Bean,* and a book
called *Missouri's Struggle for Statehood.*"

"Those sound right, for a starter," the President said.

"If you had to do it over again," I asked, "what ten books
would you recommend to an Al Ridge today?"

"Well, first of all, of course, you'd have the Bible. I'd pick
the King James Version, if Al would feel like struggling
through it — although the Revised Version's practically as
good, practically the same thing. Then you'd want some biographies of great men; everybody meets up with difficult
decisions, and it's good to know how some big men faced
things in the past. Personally, I've always been partial to a
book called *Great Men and Famous Women,* edited by C. F.
Horne. It was published in 1894, when I was ten years old.
Mother gave it to me for my twelfth birthday. There are lots
of lessons in that book. You'd want Plutarch's *Lives.* I've been
quoting Plutarch all *my* life. You'd want some Plato, especially the parts about the old fellow who took hemlock.

You'd have to read Shakespeare — four or five of his plays and all his sonnets. I'd include the complete poems of Robert Burns — there was a fine edition published a few years ago. Then you'd want some Byron, especially *Childe Harold.* Let's see — how many is that?"

We figured out that that was seven books.

"O.K. Then you'd want Creasy's *Fifteen Decisive Battles of the World,* so you could understand a little about military affairs. I'd include Benjamin Franklin's *Autobiography;* you'll find a good deal in there about how to make the best use of every minute of your day, and a lot of horse sense about people. And for a fellow like Al, who was interested in law, and, for that matter, for anyone who wanted to know the basis for the rights we enjoy under law, you'd have to include Blackstone's *Commentaries.* That's ten."

I asked the President if he still found time for such reading.

"Only when I'm off on a vacation," he said, "or sometimes out on the Chesapeake on the boat. Down at Key West last spring, we had a lot of fun analyzing poets. Bill Hassett and I spent a whole breakfast on 'The Walrus and the Carpenter.' "

"Is there anything you'd want to add to the list of ten books to prepare a man specifically for life in the Atomic Age?" I asked.

"Nothing but the lives of great men! There's nothing new in human nature; only our names for things change. Read the lives of the Roman emperors from Claudius to Constantine if you want some inside dope on the twentieth century. Read Hammurabi's code of laws. Did you know, by the bye, that those laws were engraved on a column of stone eight feet high? Hammurabi had laws covering murder, stealing, divorce, and protecting helpless people from being gypped and defrauded — all the same troubles we have with people nowadays. Men don't change."

We were approaching a place where the concrete path we had been following rejoined the roadway. The limousine and the agents' car were waiting at the junction of the path and the drive. The President said over his shoulder to Nicholson, "Well, Nick, I've got up quite a head of steam! How about you?"

"Me, too, Mr. President," Nicholson said.

"Let's call it a walk, Nick," Truman said.

Nicholson told me later that the limousine, which had been brought to this point along the roadway by one of the agents, had come one and eight-tenths miles from the place where we started walking. We boarded it now for the trip back into town. When Truman had settled himself in the car, he reached into a trouser pocket for a handkerchief and wiped away the tears that rolled from his eyes after he stepped from the cold outdoors into the heated car. Then he drew out his wallet, took a piece of letter paper out, unfolded the paper, and held it out to me.

"You were asking about the poetry I carry on my person," he said. "There it is. It's from 'Locksley Hall.' I've been carrying that ever since I graduated from high school. I've copied it and recopied it a dozen times."

I took the paper and read, in Harry Truman's bold, slightly slanting hand, in ink, these lines:

For I dipt into the future, far as human eye could see,
Saw the Vision of the world, and all the wonders that would be;

Saw the heavens fill with commerce, argosies of magic sails,
Pilots of the purple twilight, dropping down with costly bales;

Heard the heavens fill with shouting, and there rained a
*   ghastly dew*
From the nations' airy navies grappling in the central blue;

Far along the world-wide whisper of the south-wind rushing
*   warm,*
With the standards of the people plunging thro' the thunder-
*   storm;*

Till the war-drum throbb'd no longer, and the battle-flags were
*   furl'd*

In the Parliament of Man, the Federation of the World.

There the common sense of most shall hold a fretful realm in awe,
And the kindly earth shall slumber, lapt in universal law.

When I had finished reading, the President said, "Did you see that part in there giving a forecast on the airplane, and on air warfare? Don't forget that Tennyson wrote those lines over a hundred years ago. And notice also that part about universal law. We're going to have that someday, just as sure as we have air war now. That's what I'm working for. I guess that's what I've really been working for ever since I first put that poetry in my pocket. Do you realize that was half a century ago, less six months?" He looked thoughtfully out the limousine window. Suddenly, he exclaimed, "Look at there, Nick! There's a fellow in summer pants. He's got summer khaki pants on, and white socks."

"And a green sports shirt," said Nicholson.

"Yes, sir, he's got a green sports shirt on," the President said. "He must be pretty tough or foolish — one. I reckon he's lost track of the seasons, Nick."

"I think he has, Mr. President," Nicholson said.

On the way back into town, the limousine was slowed almost to a standstill at one place by a press of traffic. The President pulled himself forward on his seat and said, "I've noticed before, there's a bottleneck here for people coming in to work. We're going to have to do something about this place, Nick." Then he said to me, "Do you know, we're going to have a great problem in this country in a few years with traffic? At the rate we're building automobiles and people are buying them, this country's going to have some terrible congestion on its hands — unless it builds more roads and better roads. Roads and bridges. . . . Well, was that a good walk, Nick?"

"Yes, sir," Nicholson said. Then he added, smiling at me, "Frank, here [the driver], says if this fellow is anything like the other reporters as far as physical condition goes, he'll have to go and lie down from now until time for press conference."

The President looked at me and said, "Can't you take a little physical exertion?"

"Maybe it's not the exercise," Nicholson said. "Maybe it's the hour."

"All the same," the President said to me, "you'll find you'll feel better for having taken this walk. A man in my position has a public duty to keep himself in good condition. You can't be mentally fit unless you're physically fit. A walk like this keeps your circulation up to where you can think clearly. That old pump has to keep squirting the juice into your brain, you know."

Eventually, the limousine made its way into the White House grounds through a back entrance, and along a cement-paved driveway to the West Wing, where the President's offices are. When the car had stopped, the President said to me, "Want a swim?"

Mindful of the coldness outside, I was hesitant.

"Come on!" the President said. "You need a little conditioning."

The two agents had got out of the front seat, and Nicholson opened the door for the President, who pulled himself forward and stepped out. I followed. The President walked quickly up a path under a canvas marquee and onto a concrete porch outside his private office. The agents stayed by the limousine.

"Excuse me a minute," the President said, stopping by one of the French windows of his office. "I want to check up on the temperature." He leaned forward and looked closely at a thermometer suspended on a bracket in such a way as to be easily visible from both indoors and outdoors. "Thirty-one," he announced, straightening up.

We walked a few paces farther along the porch, past the Cabinet Room, on our left, to where the passageway turned right and became a colonnade alongside the low-lying structure that linked the West Wing with the main building. At the juncture in the ell, Truman said, "Let's just see what the pressure gauge is doing," and he stepped up to a barometer that hung in the sheltered corner. Again he leaned forward and looked closely.

"Pressure's up again," the President said with some satisfaction; then, straightening up, he turned and began walking slowly along the colonnade. "Thirty point twelve and still going up. Temperature steady. Northwest wind. We'll have good weather for three or four days. It's bound to be fair. You see, our weather forms up away to the northwest, over Bering Strait, then it moves across the country to the eastward; there's also another weather center, down over the Caribbean, and it works on the first one. So if you watch the weather map, you can tell pretty well what's coming along." He stopped in front of a door. "The Weather Bureau sends me a map every morning," he went on. "You'd better not bet on the weather against me! Jim and Nick and Gerry and the other Secret Service agents have tried it, to their regret. Now we've got a good, strong high-pressure area moving in on us, and with conditions the way they are, we can count on at least three days of fair weather. I won't promise that there won't be a single cloud in the sky, but it'll be generally nice. If you have anything important you want to do, any trips or such, you can count on going ahead."

The President turned, opened the door, urged me through it ahead of him, and then stepped inside himself. We were in a long, narrow room, containing a swimming pool. To our right was a door, evidently leading to dressing rooms, and through it now came a young man in khaki trousers and a white T shirt, whom the President introduced to me as Sergeant Gasber. (Master Sergeant Earl Gasber, I learned from him later, was an Army physical-therapy technician who had been keeping the President in training since May, 1949.)

"How're you feeling this morning, Mr. President?" Gasber asked.

"Never felt better in my life," the President said, with obvious conviction. "We've got a guest this morning, Sergeant. Do you think we can fix him up with some bathing trunks?"

"I think so, sir," Gasber said.

Telling Sergeant Gasber and me to come along and see

what we could find, the President led the way through the door into a corridor and turned in to a dressing room on the left. I could see that there was a small gymnasium at the end of the corridor, and that there were other dressing rooms opening off it. "Most of these suits are for the fat fellows on my staff," the President said, indicating a number of pairs of trunks on a row of hooks along the wall of the room, "but maybe we can find one that'll fit a skinny fellow like you. Try that one with the zebra stripes. That's a small pair, isn't it, Sergeant?"

"Yes, sir," Gasber said. "That pair ought to work."

The President went into one of the other dressing rooms, and the Sergeant went out to the pool. A couple of minutes later, I heard the clattering of some balance scales, and then the President's voice, in dejected tones: "That's terrible, Sergeant! A hundred seventy-eight and a half!"

"Oh-oh!" Gasber called back. "I'm sorry, sir. Those scales aren't accurate. I've been having a little trouble with General Vaughan and General Landry about their weight. I adjusted the scales so they'd be two pounds too heavy for General Vaughan, then I moved them down to one pound over-weight for General Landry. I forgot to turn them back, sir. That should read one seventy-seven and a half."

"That's all right, then," the President replied, relieved. "I was afraid I'd picked up two whole pounds overnight. I guess you gave the Generals a real fright, and that was worth it."

When I was ready, I went out to the pool. The Sergeant told me the water was heated to seventy-eight degrees for the President. The President called out that he was going into the gym to do a little exercise, and in a few moments we could hear the squeaks of a rowing machine. "He takes about fifty strokes," Gasber told me. "Then he does setups on a board that's on a forty-five-degree incline; he can touch his toes easy. Then I go in and give him some resisting exercises for his arms and back." While we were waiting, Gasber volunteered the information that the President is extremely punctilious about his appointments with him. "One day last summer," Gasber said, "we had an appointment for four-forty-five in the afternoon. I smoke and he doesn't, so I always go outdoors here to have a cigarette, so the smoke won't bother him when he comes in — I figure he gets enough smoke blowed in his face all day long. So that day I went out for a smoke about four-thirty. There was a Cabinet meeting going on in the Cabinet Room at the time, which I didn't know; I guess they could see me, but I couldn't see them. The first thing I knew, one of the doors to the Cabinet Room flew open and there stands the President of the United States. 'Sergeant,' he says, 'these fellows are keeping me overtime today. Looks as if I'm going to run a little late. You'd better go on home. I don't want to keep you late.' " The Sergeant also told me that the President took a lively interest in Gasber's specialty — kinesiology, the science of motion, particularly as it applies to the human muscular system. As for the President's own muscular tone, Gasber said, "Why, for a man pushing sixty-seven, it's remarkable! The way he bounces back from things! I only hope I'm in half as good a shape when I'm his age."

Soon Gasber went into the gym to give the President his resisting exercises, and I took a swim. While I was in the pool, Truman returned to his dressing room and got into an electric sweatbox. He called me into his room, after I had left the pool, to talk.

"The Sergeant keeps me in this thing for ten minutes," the President said. His head protruded from a hole in the top of the box; his glasses were off, and he was turbaned with a towel. "Ten minutes are just enough to lose one pound. Of course, I'll get it back during the day, though goodness knows where from — not from making a hog of myself, that's one thing certain. Doc Graham will be in after my swim and sun lamp. He looks me over every day, but I don't know why. He never finds anything. Do you know the Doc?"

I said that I had met General Graham, and that he had told me the President's health was sustained, even through his most trying days, by three health-giving qualities of temperament: cheerfulness, courage, and a mighty stubbornness.

The President said, with a smile, that he was as healthy as

a mule. "And a mule," he said, "has an abundance of all three of those things."

I said I understood that Graham came from Kansas City, and asked whether the President had known him out there.

"Never saw him before I went to Potsdam," he said. "I've known his father all my life. Old Dr. Graham is seventy-four now and he'll still get up at three in the morning to visit a sick person; he's one of the most sacrificing men I know. When I got to Potsdam, I heard the son was nearby. They told me he'd landed on Omaha Beach with a hospital unit, then he'd been with an airborne outfit in Holland, and got wounded, and then he was the head surgeon of a hospital at Stuttgart. So I asked to have him come up and see me at Potsdam. He came up, and I liked him, and I said, 'How'd you like to go to Washington to take care of somebody?' I thought he'd be pleased, but he said, 'No, thank you.' I asked, 'Why not?' He said he'd had about a dozen years of training in the best colleges and hospitals in the country, he'd taken the Hippocratic oath, he was dedicated to alleviating the suffering of the greatest possible number of people — why should he throw all that away on one human being? But, I said, what if that human being was the President of his country? He said he had a hospital full of men who'd shed blood for his country; he couldn't leave them. So I said, 'Do you realize who you're talking to?' Then he said, 'Yes, sir. I'll obey orders, sir.' So he stayed with the hospital until all his wounded men were discharged or moved home, and then he came to me. He's a bird!"

The President looked at a clock on the wall opposite him. "Doc ought to be here any minute now," he said. "One thing Doc Graham did for me: he got me interested in some of the finer points of botany. That's a hobby he has. You know, I used to have a terrible, unreasonable prejudice against orchids. It wasn't just because they're society flowers. I believed that they were parasites, and I hate parasites of any kind. But Doc Graham convinced me that they're saprophytes, so they don't live off their fellows. I got reconciled to them then. I even went to an orchid show here in town. . . .

Sergeant, I think you'd better let me out of here now. I feel a pound lighter."

I went back to the pool, and after the President had taken a shower, he came out, wearing a pair of navy-blue trunks and with his glasses on again. He said, "It's a shame this pool can't be put to greater use. You know, schoolchildren all over the country chipped in pennies so this pool could be built for F.D.R. He really needed it. It's just a luxury for me. I wish it could be put to some good use."

The President climbed down a chromium-plated ladder at one end of the pool and struck out for the opposite end with a highly personal stroke, a little more back than side stroke, designed, apparently, to balance progress through the water with the need to keep his glasses dry. "Maybe it's a good thing for Presidents to have a swimming pool, come to think of it," he said as he swam along. "Old J. Q. Adams, when he was President, used to go for early-morning walks, the way I do. He'd walk down by the Potomac and some mornings — of course, Washington was a small town in 1825 — some mornings he'd slip off his clothes and take a dip in the river. Well, there was a shrew of a newspaperwoman — Anne Royall was her name — and she'd been trying for a long time to interview old J. Q., and he wouldn't see her. So one day she tracked him on his early-morning walk, and when he took his dip, she sat herself down on his clothes. She wouldn't let him out of the river until he answered her questions. Anne Royall was quite a customer. She was later tried in a court here in Washington, and she caught a big fine as a common scold."

While the President swam on — he did about six lengths of the pool — I went in to dress. By the time I was dressed, the President was under a sun lamp in his dressing room and General Graham had arrived. I called out my thanks and took my leave. As I started away, the President's voice called after me, in a tone of kindly derision, "Get a good nap, now!"

3. PRESS CONFERENCE

Harry Truman liked to keep one jump ahead of the clock. His arriving four minutes late at his press conference on Thursday morning, November 30th, was therefore noticed and commented upon by some of the reporters who were waiting for him in Room 474 of the old State Department Building, across the street from the west office wing of the White House. This conference caused frightful headlines all over the world about the possible use of the atomic bomb in Korea or China, and it also provided a hair-raising example of how bad news can be manufactured. The calamity of this conference was largely of the reporters' making, though it must be said that the former captain of artillery, now Commander in Chief, was sometimes able to be carried away, on matters of very grave consequence, by considerations which *appeared* to be tactical; it sometimes seemed as if he thought of atomic weapons as just guns under his — or his field officers' — captaincy. Still hovering over him, of course, was the moral issue of his decision to use the atomic bomb at Hiroshima, about which no more needs to be said than is well known: Truman's decision was essentially a tactical one — namely, that bringing up that gun at that time would save footsoldiers' lives. But the newsmen at the conference that morning knew all this, and they also knew that Harry Truman was given to fast answers, and they used these bits of knowledge to squeeze a hot and dangerous story out of the President. It was unfortunate, all in all, that Truman couldn't have been delayed long enough to let him skip the whole thing.

At ten-thirty-four, when Truman did arrive at the ornate conference room, two hundred and eight reporters there — about as big a crowd as he had ever had for a press conference — stood up in honor of the President. Truman was wearing a dark-blue suit and a tie that had on it a figure of the legendary strong man Paul Bunyan carrying over his shoulder a great tree as easily as if it were a mere carbine; the President looked, as he somehow managed to look even in the most depressing periods, pleased with the world. As his personal staff took seats facing the reporters, he stepped to the microphone provided for him at front center and briskly greeted the reporters and asked them to sit down. He said he had a statement he wanted to read to them; there would be copies available when they got ready to leave; he would take it as slowly as he could. He began, then, to read a typewritten document.

The President's prepared statement represented the considered collaboration not just of some of the junior minds on his staff but also of the topmost officials of the State and Defense Departments. The statement had been proposed two days before, on Tuesday, November 28th, the day Chinese intervention in Korea had become undeniable fact. Tuesday afternoon, after meetings of the National Security Council and the Cabinet, successively, had taken place in the Cabinet Room of the White House, Dean Acheson, Averell Harriman, and some members of Truman's staff sat around trying to decide where they were supposed to go from where they were — wherever that was. One question they discussed was when and how President Truman could address the country on the new crisis with maximum gravity, dignity, and effect. One of the White House staff remarked that a carefully prepared statement, which the President could read at his press conference on Thursday, might help communicate to the public the seriousness of the situation. The others agreed. The Secretary of State said he would assign Ambassador at Large Philip C. Jessup, an expert on the Far East, to draft such a statement. The White House designated George McKee Elsey, a thirty-two-year-old administrative assistant to the President, to work with Jessup.

Jessup telephoned Elsey that evening and again the next morning to discuss the outlines of the statement. Neither man mentioned the atomic bomb. Early Wednesday afternoon, Jessup sent a draft, which contained no reference to the atomic bomb, to Elsey, who sent one copy to the President's Press Secretary, the late Charles G. Ross, and went over another with the President's special counsel, Charles S. Murphy, and two of Murphy's assistants, David Bell and David Lloyd. At four-thirty, Elsey and Lloyd went to an office in the old State Department Building and began to rewrite the statement. At six-fifteen, they took their draft, which did not mention the atomic bomb, to the White House and met with Jessup, Murphy, Bell, Assistant Secretary of Defense Marx Leva, and, later, Theodore Tannenwald, Harriman's counsel. Until ten-thirty, with time out for some supper in a cafeteria near the White House, the seven men went over the draft sentence by sentence. Various members of the group phoned their superiors for opinions on specific points. When they adjourned, Jessup took a copy of the revised draft for Acheson, Tannenwald took a copy for Harriman, and Leva took copies for Marshall, Bradley, and Lovett. At eight-thirty Thursday morning, Elsey and Murphy began to receive by phone suggestions for changes, all of which were incorporated in a final revision; no one at the highest level suggested mentioning the atomic bomb. At nine-forty-five, Ross took the final copy to the President, who read it for the first time and approved it as it was. Ross hurried it out for mimeographing, so that copies would be ready for the press conference at ten-thirty.

At the conference, the President began to read the statement: "Recent developments in Korea confront the world with a serious crisis. . . ." He tried to read slowly, but soon he was going along trippingly. The heart of the statement was a promise to meet the new situation in three ways: "We shall continue to work in the United Nations for concerted action to halt this aggression in Korea. We shall intensify our efforts to help other free nations strengthen their defenses in order to meet the threat of aggression elsewhere. We shall rapidly increase our own military strength." The statement was sober, dignified, and unlikely to do any particular harm. It contained no stirring rhetoric, such as Roosevelt or Churchill would have used in the circumstances. Truman, who was, after all, no one but himself, favored a blunt and straightforward prose, devoid of what he calls "five-dollar words." Unfortunately, the statement contained nothing that a hardboiled city-desk man would consider news, so when the President came to the end of his reading and told the reporters to ask question, they got ready to do some news manufacturing.

Half an hour before the conference, the President had convened his staff in the President's office in the White House for a meeting of the sort his staff calls pre-press. Here the President and his assistants had tried to anticipate all the questions that might be asked by reporters. They had discussed Korea, jobs, patronage, lame ducks, a conference Truman was scheduled to have the next day with Congressional leaders, forthcoming supplemental appropriations — just about everything *except* the atomic bomb. That was not mentioned once.

The first reporter to ask a question was Mrs. Sarah McClendon, who represented six newspapers in Texas and one in Ireland. "Mr. President," she asked, "do you think, in view of this situation, that we should delay any further general mobilization and control of materials and price controls and supports and —"

As he was to do fourteen more times in the next few minutes, the President broke in before the reporter had finished the question. "That matter," he said, "is being constantly considered. I do not intend to answer the question."

Anthony Leviero, of the *New York Times,* asked, "Mr. President, are you about to name a Supreme Commander for the—"

"I have been ready to name a Supreme Commander for a long time."

Leviero tried to round out his query. "You are waiting on European —"

"I am waiting on agreement with our European allies."

Raymond P. Brandt, of the *St. Louis Post Dispatch,* asked, "Mr. President, in what detail were you informed about these MacArthur moves?"

"Every detail," the President said.

Brandt asked, "Did you or the State Department raise the question of whether this offensive would affect the chances of a negotiated settlement with the Peiping government?"

"The whole matter was clearly discussed with General MacArthur every day."

Edward T. Folliard, of the *Washington Post,* began a question: "Mr. President, there has been some criticism of General MacArthur in the European press —"

"Some in the American press, too," the President interjected, "if I'm not mistaken."

"Particularly," Folliard added, trying to keep his question on the track, "in the British press —"

The President broke in again, observing, "They are always for a man when he is winning, but when he is in a little trouble, they all jump on him with what ought to be done, which they didn't tell him before. He has done a good job, and he is continuing to do a good job." Then Truman turned directly to Folliard and said, "Go ahead with your question, Eddie."

Everyone laughed. Then Folliard, taking an exaggeratedly deep breath, said, "The particular criticism is that he exceeded his authority and went beyond the point he was supposed to go."

Quickly the President said, "He did nothing of the kind."

There was a long pause. The reporters still had no news. The pause made it seem that they had been bewildered by the speed and aggressiveness of the President's replies, and, like a fighter taunting a tired opponent, the President asked the whole room, "Well, what's the matter with you?"

At this, three or four reporters jumped up, and the President recognized Laurence H. Burd, of the *Chicago Tribune,* who asked, "Mr. President, a few months ago this government declined the offer of Chinese Nationalist troops. Has that been up for reconsideration, in view —"

The President, interrupting again, said, "The offer of Nationalist Chinese troops was refused for the reason that we didn't — we hoped not to be involved in a world war. That situation still continues."

"Along the same line, then," Burd went on, "our Formosa policy of neutralization —"

"Still continues."

There were questions from other reporters about the

Chinese Communist delegation to the United Nations, about further mobilization, and about supplementary appropriations to pay for the fighting. Then Mrs. Elizabeth May Craig, who for many years had attended Presidential press conferences as correspondent for papers in Portland, Kennebec, and Waterville, Maine, asked, "Mr. President, what Congressional leaders will you see?"

"The usual ones," the President said.

Mrs. Craig asked, "Will that mean Republicans — include Republicans —"

"They will come in the White House; it's the usual conference that I have, with the usual agenda."

Mrs. Craig pressed her point: "Will it include Republicans?"

"It always does. Of course it will." The President addressed Mrs. Craig with the air of an exasperated teacher addressing a slow pupil. "Don't you remember, May?" he asked, and the reporters laughed. But Truman was serious. "Remember back," he said. "There have been nine or ten of these conferences. If you will look back and edit them, you will find that your question will be answered."

Mrs. Craig bobbed her head and said, "My editor tells me not to take anything for granted."

Again the reporters laughed, and the President, laughing with them, said, "That's too bad." Then, suddenly, his face was very serious again. "Of course," he said, "that is one of the things that's the matter with the country. It just exactly states — you have answered a national question when you said that. Confidence in your government is the first thing to keep it running as it should."

Underneath the laughter, an atmosphere of contest — an almost certain corollary at press conferences of the reporters' wanting to know everything and the interviewee's unwillingness to tell everything — had been firmly established. At this point, the old hands were ready to move in and dig out some news.

Jack Doherty, of the *New York Daily News*, asked, "Mr. President, will the United Nations troops be allowed to bomb across the Manchurian border?"

"I can't answer that question this morning."

Diosdado M. Yap, of the *Manila Chronical*, asked, "Mr. President, in increasing our military strength, do you consider using Japanese manpower?"

"Using what?"

"The Japanese manpower," Yap said, "in increasing our military strength — speaking of the United Nations —"

"We will cross that bridge when we come to it," Truman said.

Leviero asked, "Mr. President, will attacks in Manchuria depend on action in the United Nations?"

"Yes, entirely."

"In other words," Leviero continued, "if the United Nations resolution should authorize General MacArthur to go further than he has, he will —"

The President broke in to say, "We" — evidently meaning the government — "will take whatever steps are necessary to meet the military situation, just as we always have."

Doherty then asked, "Will that include the atomic bomb?"

This was a moment when the habitual speed and bluntness of Harry Truman's responses — together with the testy artillery captain's bravado which sometimes tripped off his tongue when he spoke as Commander in Chief — served the reporters well and the President ill. "That includes," he quickly said, "every weapon that we have."

Paul R. Leach, of the *Chicago Daily News*, asked, "Mr. President, you said, 'every weapon that we have.' Does that mean that there is active consideration of the use of the atomic bomb?"

As he frequently would do in the rapid interchange of press conferences, the President in his answer repeated words his questioner had used. "There always has been active consideration of its use," he said. He added at once, "I don't want to see it used. It is a terrible weapon, and it should not be [used] on innocent men, women, and children who have nothing whatever to do with this military aggression. That happens when it is used."

There, as far as the President was concerned, the matter rested. There was no particular story in that sequence of statements, and, next, Charles Parmer, of radio station WMBG, in Richmond, asked a question that changed the subject: "Mr. President, Senator Byrd says not a single dollar for Yugoslavia, and he backed it up this morning with the Southern bloc. Have you any comment?"

There was laughter again. The President said he had no comment. Then he changed his mind and said, "We would expect that from Senator Byrd."

At this point, Merriman Smith, representing the United Press, stood up and asked a question that pulled the story out. He said, "Mr. President, I wonder if we could retrace that reference to the atom bomb? Did we understand you clearly that the use of the bomb is under active consideration?"

"Always has been, Smitty," he said. "It is one of our weapons." This time, the President did not repeat the Leach phrase "active consideration" but did use again an important word he had used in answering Leach — "always."

Now Robert G. Nixon, of International News Service, asked, "Does that mean, Mr. President, use against military objectives or civilian —"

The President broke in to say, "It's a matter that the military people will have to decide, Bobby. I'm not a military authority that passes on those things."

Leviero suggested, "Mr. President, perhaps it would be better if we are allowed to quote your remarks on that directly."

At that time reporters were not allowed to put anything the President said in his press conferences in direct quotations, but only to report the gist of what he said, unless he specifically authorized them to use his actual words. Possibly sensing in some dim way that Leviero had been trying, by his question, to tell him something — to tell him, in fact, that the reporters had woven a dangerous web — the President hesitated. "I don't think — I don't think that is necessary, Tony."

Frank Bourgholtzer, of the National Broadcasting Company, said, "Mr. President, you said this depends on United Nations action. Does that mean that we wouldn't use the atomic bomb except on a United Nations authorization?"

"No, it doesn't mean that at all," Truman said. "The action against Communist China depends on the action of the United Nations. The military commander in the field will have charge of the use of the weapons, as he always has."

The reporters had their story. Questioning went on, but the big story was sewed up. The President, who throughout was so busy meeting each question as it came that he neither followed the tendency of the questions collectively nor understood the way the patchwork was being put together, nevertheless seemed to sense that he had somehow been pushed. He began to answer questions rather abruptly, and at last, in reply to one from Mrs. Craig as to whether the Korean conflict was "going beyond police action at this time" — in other words, whether we were openly going to war with China — he lost patience. "I can't answer that question, May," he said. "That is what we are examining. We have exerted every effort possible to prevent a third World War. Every maneuver that has been made since June 25th has had in mind not to create a situation which would cause another terrible war. We are still trying to prevent that war from happening, and I hope we may be able to prevent it." With increasing heat, he said, "All these attacks and speculations and lies that have been told on the members of this government have not helped that situation one little bit. There's a big one of the front page of the paper this morning, about Acheson having interfered with the command in the Far East." (He was referring to a demand by three Republican senators that Acheson stop sniping at MacArthur.) "There isn't one word of truth in that, and never has been. Acheson has attended strictly to his business as Secretary of State, and he has done a good job." By now in quite a temper, the President said, "I am getting tired of all this foolishness." Then, suddenly, he recovered his good humor and, with a broad smile, declared, "I'm going to bust loose on you one of these days."

That threat brought a loud laugh from the room. After three more questions — unimportant ones — Merriman Smith, the senior news agency man among the White House correspondents, said, "Thank you, Mr. President," where-upon all the news-agency and many of the afternoon-newspaper reporters in the room rushed for the door.

At ten-forty-seven, the U.P. wire carried the following bulletin:

WA10A Washington Nov. 30 — (UP) — President Truman said today that the United States has under consideration use of the atomic bomb in connection with the war in Korea.

One minute later, the A.P. moved its bulletin:

A127WX Washington Nov. 30 — (AP) — President Truman said today active consideration is being given to use of the atomic bomb against the Chinese Communists if that step is necessary.

Not until five messages and seventeen sentences later, in its "bulletin matter," did the A.P. explain that the President's remarks on the atomic bomb had not been included in his prepared statement but had been made in response to reporters' questions. Charles Ross, distressed by the implication in the bulletins coming over the ticker in his office that *new* consideration of the use of the atomic bomb had been undertaken as a result of the Chinese intervention, called the White House correspondents together and explained that this was not true.

The A.P.'s message A133WX, a few minutes later, said, in part:

He said . . . the decision of whether to drop atomic bombs was one for the commander in the field.

At once, the New York office of the A.P. sent a directive to its Washington bureau suggesting that in the "first lead" — the first rounded story on the conference — the MacArthur reference should go to the top. The Washington bureau had already framed, and was beginning to move, message A147WX:

First lead Truman Korea
Washington, Nov. 30 — (AP) — President Truman said today use of the atomic bomb in Korea has always been under

consideration — and whether it is used is up to American military leaders in the field. . . .

By this time, an inexorable process — the exploitation of a good story — was well begun. At eleven-fifty-five, the A.P. sent out its "noon advisory":

> *A159 Washington is rounding up congressional comment on President Truman's atom bomb remarks and will move it shortly.*
>
> *Reaction from abroad is expected.*

Ross was now quite upset. Afternoon newspapers were beginning to appear with scare headlines. Various government officials were calling in to find out what the story was all about. The Voice of America people phoned to ask what they were supposed to say to the world about *this* one. Just before lunchtime, Ross called in James S. Lay, Jr., executive secretary of the National Security Council; his own assistant, Eben Ayers; and George Elsey, to help put the matter straight. They established that the Atomic Energy Act of 1946, known as the McMahon Act, is explicit about who can order use of the bomb. "The President from time to time may direct the Commission (1) to deliver such quantities of fissionable materials or weapons to the armed forces for such use as he deems necessary in the interest of national defense . . ." Ross, Ayers, and Elsey then collaborated with Edward Barrett, Assistant Secretary of State for Public Affairs, on a statement that made two things clear: that there had been no *new* consideration of using the bomb, and that the President, who is the only one who can authorize the use, had not done so. Ross gave the statement to the press at about one-forty-five. (Five days later, Charles Ross died at his desk of a coronary occlusion.)

Before the clarification moved out on the news-agency wires, the damage had been done. Every New York afternoon paper was carrying immense front-page headlines saying that Truman might use the A-bomb — as if it were to happen at any moment. Afternoon papers all across the country played the story hard. Even after the clarification,

Congressional comments went out on agency wires. Senators Maybank, Flanders, O'Mahoney, Russell, McClellan, and others contributed their august confusions to the already mixed-up story. Senator Brewster was quoted, perhaps inaccurately, as saying, "We ought to use the A-bomb against these troop concentrations and ammunition dumps. I think it would save a thousand of our troops in the next two weeks." According to the A.P., Senator George said, "If we use the bomb, it means war."

The foreign reaction, which the A.P. so confidently expected in its "noon advisory," developed. There were alarming headlines in Paris. However, the M.R.P. newspaper *Aube* was reassuring: "UNITED STATES KEEPS SANGFROID." (The next night, Premier Pleven said, in an address to the French Assembly, "The erroneous version of a reference made by President Truman to the atomic weapon caused a legitimate and understandable emotion in Europe.") Big headlines in Finland gave the impression that MacArthur had already received the go-ahead. In Vienna, the story had the lead spot in all the morning papers except the Soviet Army sheet, *Osterreichische Zeitung. Volksstimme*, the Communist paper in Vienna, threw in an ingenious invention of its own, declaring that Truman's statement proved that the United States planned to intensify pressure for a Western European army. All the papers in Rome carried sensational headlines. *Il Momento* reported that the Tokyo bomber command was ready to take off with the bomb one hour after Washington gave the order. The Socialist *Avanti* had this headline: "WASHINGTON WILL DISREGARD UNITED NATIONS." The sensible Swedes featured the second, clarifying statement; their newspaper stories made it clear that Truman's statement had been in reply to questions and had been taken out of context. In Poland, the *Kurier Codzienny* headed its story "ATOMIC BOMB PLANS OF TRUMAN, ACHESON & CO." In Moscow, Tass put out its own version of the first bulletins: "President Truman has given it to be understood that the ruling circles of the United States are considering the possibility of using the atomic bomb against the Chinese People's Republic if necessary." The *Times of*

India ran an editorial under the heading "NO NO NO." The *Indian News Chronicle* spoke of "the immense risk of earning the passionate hatred of the Asian peoples."

In London, at about five o'clock Thursday afternoon, when the first misleading news-agency flashes reached the ticker against the wall of the library in the House of Commons, Parliament was in the midst of a two-day debate on foreign policy, during the course of which Eden, Churchill, and others pressed Attlee to fly to America and talk with Truman. All too quickly, a whisper ran along the benches that Truman had said MacArthur could use the atomic bomb any time he wanted to. Within a few minutes, someone was circulating a letter addressed to the Prime Minister, declaring that if Attlee endorsed the President's statement, it would not be possible for the signers to go on supporting the Government. The paper was passed among the Members as debate continued, and more than a hundred of them, including Alice Bacon, chairman of the Labour Party, signed it. One of the Prime Minister's secretaries whispered to him what the gist of the bulletins was, and at once Attlee said, "Then I shall have to go to Washington to see the President." He called an emergency Cabinet meeting, and at six-forty-five it took place in his rooms in the House of Commons. The meeting lasted only eight minutes; Attlee told the Ministers of his plan to fly to Washington, and they unanimously approved. Messages went off to Washington through both British and American channels. Concluding the foreign-policy debate that evening, Attlee said, "His Majesty's Government consider that a decision of such grave import could not be taken on behalf of the United Nations without the fullest prior consultation with those member states who are at present participating in the international police action in Korea." Then he announced his intention to visit Truman, and was cheered for it. In Paris, the next day, speaking of Attlee's trip, *Franc-Tireur* said, "Thus a false, bad news story has produced the best of true stories." That, however, was about all the good that came of it.

4. A WEIGHING OF
WORDS

At a few minutes before eight o'clock on the evening of Thursday, December 14, President Truman entered the Cabinet Room, in the West Wing of the White House, where he had arranged to meet, on the hour, with the Secretary of State and a number of his advisers and document-drafters for a final going over of a radio speech he was to deliver the following evening. He regarded this speech as the most important one of his career up to that time. The Chinese Communists, who had intervened in Korea not long before, had split the United Nations forces and seemed to be routing them, and Truman had decided to declare a state of national emergency. The preparation of the speech by the President and his staff had taken nearly two weeks — a fortnight that had been particularly tense and trying for him. During that period, the Chinese intrusion into Korea had forced him to make several tremendous decisions; a visit by Clement Attlee had taken a lot of his time and energy; his old friend and Press Secretary, Charles G. Ross, had died at his desk of a heart attack; and his intemperate letter to the music critic of the *Washington Post*, Paul Hume, who had given a recital by Margaret Truman an unfavorable review, had been unexpectedly, widely, and embarrassingly published. The President was now ready to "freeze" the speech; that is to say, he was calling a halt to major revisions and henceforth would undertake only minor corrections to achieve accuracy of detail and the desired nuances of tone. The President would have a night and a day to go over and over the speech, honing its rough spots and practicing his elocution of it.

There were only two junior staff men in the Cabinet Room when the President arrived; most of the drafters, who had been working on the speech all day, had hurried out to a cafeteria at seven-thirty to get some supper. "I see I'm early, as usual," the President said to the two men who were on hand. "How are you gentlemen this evening?" After receiving their mumbled answers, the President sat down, not in the chair he customarily occupied as presiding officer of the Cabinet, at the middle of the long table, but at the end toward his office, in the position normally taken at Cabinet meetings by the Secretary of Commerce, Charles Sawyer—a place where Truman sometimes would sit to conduct small, informal meetings. The President tested the chair he had taken, by squirming and by pressing his back against its back. "Most comfortable chair I've had at this end of the table," he said. "This isn't Charlie Sawyer's chair; somebody has switched chairs here. Charlie's chair is bigger than this—has a high back. I don't feel good in it. This is a lot better." He looked at the mantel clock at the opposite end of the room, under a portrait of Woodrow Wilson; the clock, whose chime, if it had one, had evidently been silenced, now declared by hand that the hour of eight had been reached and passed by half a minute. "That clock!" the President said. "I was sworn in under that clock on the evening of April 12th, 1945. It said nine past seven when I started in to swear the oath — I remember, I looked at it. And I remember the faces all around me: everyone was crying and carrying on. None of us could believe that F.D.R. was gone. It was nine past seven."

Seven men — the rest of the squad of speech-drafters and advisers — now entered the room. "Come on in, gentlemen," the President said. "We're all ready to go. You're late." (It was eight-three by the mantel clock.) He greeted various men by name. When all were seated, and when Charles S. Murphy, his Special Counsel and boss of the drafters, had handed out copies of the near-final version of the speech, Truman said, "Let's wait a minute or two for Dean [Acheson]. He'll be here soon, I'm sure. Well, how are you all? Tired, I'll wager. Our household is all in a turmoil. Margaret is just back from a recital in Knoxville, and she had to go up to New York tonight to discuss a television broadcast. Then she and the Madam are planning to leave for the holidays in Independence tomorrow. It's come up quickly, and I don't know just what I'm going to do about getting them accommodations."

The Secretary of State now arrived. "There you are, Dean!" the President exclaimed. Acheson threw his overcoat and hat on an empty chair against the wall, then took the seat on the President's left. "I'm sorry to call you in on this, Dean," the President said. "It makes another long day for you, I know."

"What about *your* day?" the Secretary asked.

"Oh, I'm used to this," Truman said. "I don't feel as if I have any life of my own any more." Then, grinning, he added, "Speaking of my private life, this afternoon a bunch of broadcasting fellows [the Broadcasters Advisory Council of the National Association of Broadcasters] were in to see me, and I told them, 'The President of the United States is two people—he's the President and he's a human being.' I told them, 'The President has to spend about half his time keeping the human being in line, and, at that, he doesn't do a very good job of it.' "

All the men around the table laughed, and since this was the first time any of them had heard the President josh himself about the Hume letter — for he seemed to be doing that — their laughter was fortified by relief.

"On the subject of long days," Acheson said, "I have an anecdote for you. Last Sunday, General Marshall left my office to go home — for the weekend, you might say — at three o'clock in the afternoon, but a new situation arose, and at three-forty we had to call him up and ask him to come back. As he was about to go out of the door of his house to return, Mrs. Marshall said to him, 'Do drop in some Sunday when you can stay longer.' "

The President laughed and then said, "Some people think the men in the government like their jobs. These people never think that government men are willing to work their hearts out because they believe in what they're doing. . . . Well, I guess we'd better get down to work. Murph, have you a legible copy of this thing for Dean?" Murphy, who was sitting two seats to Truman's right, with an empty chair between them, handed the President a copy of the speech and the President passed it on to the Secretary of State. "After I get through with you fellows here," Truman went on, "I'm going to take this speech home and study it out some more, both tonight after you go to bed and tomorrow morning before you get up. Would you like me to read the thing page by page, and go over each page as we move along, or shall we read the whole thing through and then go back over it?"

The Secretary of State said, "Wouldn't it be well to read it through once?"

"I kind of favor page by page," the President said. "After all, I have a pretty good idea what's in here. I've put a lot into this thing. Most of it's mine. Besides, I've talked it over with Murph and the others several times. Looka here." He pointed to a notation at the top of the first page of the manuscript. "This is the tenth draft. Well, anybody have any objections to page by page? . . . O.K., let's go!" The President began to read from the manuscript in front of him, in the measured, classroom cadences of his public addresses: " 'My fellow-Americans: I want to talk to you tonight about what our country is up against, and what we are going to do about it. Our homes, our nation, all the things we believe in are in great danger. . . .' "

When the President had finished reading the first page, which reviewed events in Korea since June, he said, "That strikes me as a pretty good page. Anybody have any argument with that page? . . . No arguments? Say, something's wrong here! This can't be *that* good. Well, I'll go on to page 2." The next page concluded the summary of events and presented a four-part program of action for the United States: continuing adherence to the principles of the United Nations, continuing coöperation with other free nations, strengthening the military forces of this country and its allies, and expanding and steadying the economy of the United States.

As the President concluded the page, the Secretary of State said, "I have two substantive points on that page."

"What are they, Dean?" Truman asked.

"First, where you say, 'By this act [the Communists] have shown that they are willing to risk world war to get what they want,' I don't like that word 'risk.' I don't think we should leave any doubt in anyone's mind that we will never start a world war — that if it starts, it will have to be the other fellow who starts it. Perhaps we could say something like 'have shown that they are willing to bring the world to the brink of war.' "

David Lloyd, one of the President's young speech-drafters,. sitting three seats to Truman's left, said, "Mr. President, can you say 'bring' and 'brink' in quick succession?"

Marshall Shulman, a speech-drafter for Acheson who had been helping Murphy's team with this manuscript, and who was seated between the Secretary of State and Lloyd, said, "What about 'push'? '. . . are willing to *push* the world to the brink . . .' "

"Say, I think you've got something there," the President said to Shulman. "That's just what the Russians are doing—pushing everybody. Let's see how that went, now." Truman began to write, dictating to himself as he went, " '. . . to—push—the—world—to—the—brink . . .' "

"My second point," Acheson said when the President looked up, "is in connection with this sentence: 'We will continue to work — and where necessary to fight — for the principles of the United Nations — the principles of freedom and justice.' That is true enough. But I think we ought to be very careful, once again, to make it clear that it is the other fellow who is inclined to start fights — not we. Could we say, 'We will continue to work for — and if necessary to defend with arms — the principles of the United Nations'?"

"That's good, Dean," the President said.

Lloyd said, "It ought to be 'where necessary,' rather than 'if necessary.' We are already fighting for those principles in one locality."

Acheson said, "Which would you say, Mr. President — 'if' or 'where'?"

"I reckon 'if' comes to me more easily," the President said. " 'If necessary.' Yes. Now, let me write that down." Again the President dictated and wrote the amending words. When he had finished the sentence, he looked at it again, reviewing its punctuation, which would matter not in the spoken but in the printed version of his speech. He said, "Awful lot of dashes in there. I don't think we need that second dash, after 'defend with arms,' do we?" He looked up, and then he seemed to notice for the first time that the seat to his right had — perhaps accidentally — been left empty; it was the position Charlie Ross had often occupied at speech-freezing sessions. The President looked around the table and said bleakly, "Who's going to take care of grammar and punctuation now?" (Ross, who had always been the arbiter of syntax, inflection, spelling, and punctuation on these occasions, and who had left in one of the drawers of the desk at which he died a set of notes entitled "The Truman School of English Composition," had often, during speech-freezings, teased his former high-school classmate, the President, about such things as his stubborn insistence on regarding the diphthongs "ie" and "ei" as identical twins.) The President put his pencil down on the manuscript and said quietly, "You remember how Charlie used to pester us all the time to have studio pictures taken of ourselves? 'For the record,' he used to say. Just today, the Madam and I received a wonderful picture of Charlie that he'd had taken not long ago at Bachrach's. It's an excellent picture of Charlie. We just got it today."

"You need the dash," Murphy said, in his North Carolina drawl, gently pulling the President back to work. "The phrase opened with a dash and must close with one. A phrase has to be enclosed by similar marks."

The President said, "I don't pretend to know about these things — Charlie always took care of the grammar for me — but it seems to me you've got a pile of dashes in that sentence. Could you open and close your phrase with plain old commas, Murph?"

"Yes, sir," Murphy said, "you could do that."

The President crossed out the dashes and marked in commas. Then, abruptly brisk, he said, "All right! We've made some progress. Page 3!" Then, slowly and gravely, as if facing scores of millions of citizens, he intoned the next page of the manuscript. In this part of the speech, he began an elaboration of the four-part program he had outlined on the previous page.

When Truman had finished reading the page, the Secretary of State said, "That first sentence, Mr. President: 'Now I want to talk to you about each of these things.' Couldn't you say 'talk *with* you'?"

"Strikes me I'm just talking *to* the people, Dean," the President said.

" 'With' seems to me a little easier, more informal," Acheson said. " 'To' sounds as if you were laying down the law a little bit."

"Some people think I do lay down the law, Dean," the President said in a slightly glum but ironic tone. Then he suddenly seemed a little angry. "*Some*body has to lay down the law around here *some* of the time," he said. "Some people confuse liberty and license; they think that this country owes them nothing but privileges, and that nobody ought ever to lay down the law to them about their moral responsibilities. Let's just say 'to.' "

Leon H. Keyserling, chairman of the President's Council of Economic Advisers, on Murphy's right, said, "In the passage here where we're saying we will take all honorable steps to avoid war by negotiation, this sentence — 'There is no conflict between the legitimate interests of the free world and the Soviet Union that cannot be settled by peaceful means' — to make it grammatical, you have to add 'and those of' before 'the Soviet Union.' "

"O.K., Leon, I'll take your word for it," the President said pleasantly, adding the phrase.

Shulman said, "After the sentence 'We are ready, as we have always been, to take part in efforts to reach a peaceful solution of the conflict in Korea,' wouldn't it be good to add a new sentence, like this: 'Our representatives at Lake Success are taking part in just such efforts today'?"

The President liked the suggestion and made the addition.

"Then, if you do that," Murphy said, "why not move up to this place, right after the sentence you have just added, the sentence from the next page — 'We do not yet know whether the Chinese Communists are willing to enter into honest negotiations to settle the conflict in Korea'? That fits like a key in a lock, because then you'd go on as it stands: 'If negotiations are possible . . .' "

Theodore Tannenwald, Averell Harriman's counsel, sitting at the far end of the line on the President's left, said, "Doesn't that last sentence have to read, then, 'If *such* negotiations are possible'?"

"Ah, there speaks a barrister!" the Secretary of State exclaimed. " 'If such negotiations' is passable, but wouldn't 'If the aforesaid negotiations' be preferable? Or, still better, 'If negotiations on the part of the party of the first part'? Ah, the lawyer's tongue!"

After the laughter that followed the Secretary's sally had died down, Tannenwald withdrew his suggestion, with a shrug. The sentence order on page 3 was settled as Shulman and Murphy had suggested, and the President went on to the next page: " '. . . Our forces are in Korea to uphold the United Nations. We may have been driven back on one battlefield, but we will not give up the great purpose for which we are fighting. General Collins, Chief of Staff of the Army, who returned a few days ago from Korea, reported that our military forces are well able to inflict heavy losses on the Communists if they renew their attack. Our troops are well able to take care of themselves. . . .' " The President read on to the bottom of the page; then, at once, he jumped back to the earlier passage. " 'Our troops are well able to take care of themselves,' " he repeated. "I am very sorry to say that that sentence will have to come out of there." The sentence had been added to the speech that afternoon by Murphy's team. "I can't give any such assurance. I'm seven thousand miles from the battlefield, and I can't say for sure. In one way, that sentence is true—nobody can fight like an American. But, you see, we just learned in messages from Tokyo this very afternoon that the right flank of our line on the west coast is vulnerable. There has been a lot of new infiltration down around our right flank, and if the Chinese Communists put a substantial number of men in there — they could throw nearly a hundred thousand men at us in that little area — they might be able to give us trouble. That's why we're moving our men around from the east coast — to get in there and protect that right flank. Some of them are already at Pusan and they can move up into the line pretty fast now. If we can fill them in and secure the right flank, as I believe we can, we may be able to receive any new attack in such a way as to get rid of a lot of Communists, if they come in there blowing their bugles in any large numbers. They may receive a very salutary lesson. I think if we can pull back a little, to where their supply lines are stretched out, we may hold them a good long time and win out in the end. I've thought so all this week, while everybody has been hollering about a Dunkirk. I'm not giving up, you must understand that. But at this moment I can't honestly give the impression that our soldiers are going to stay right where they are. I don't know that for a fact at this time."

David Bell, another of the President's young drafters, who was seated at the end of the line on the President's right, said, "The purpose of that passage, Mr. President, was to reassure the mothers and wives and families of our G.I.s over there in Korea — to let them know that our boys are not going to be left out on a limb, and also to make them feel that their men have been doing a good job."

"Oh, there's no use to doubt that," the President said. "Our soldiers have pulled back under pressure in very good order — not once, they did it twice. This last withdrawal, from Changjin Reservoir down to Hamhung, was one of the greatest fighting retreats that ever was. Those Marines have old Xenophon beat a mile. There's only one man — no, two — that I've ever read about who could do as well, and I mean Stonewall Jackson and Robert E. Lee."

George Elsey, sitting on Bell's left, said, "If you take out the sentence you read, Mr. President, don't you also have to take out the previous one, about what General Collins reported?"

"Why take that out when it's true?" the President said.

"Doesn't that Collins sentence leave things hanging in mid-air?" Elsey asked.

"I don't think so," the President said. "It says we can inflict heavy losses on the aggressor. I think that ought to be said. The whole purpose of our foreign policy at this stage is to show an aggressor that he can't get away with it cheaply. It's going to hurt him. Isn't that right, Dean?"

"Precisely," Acheson said.

"I don't mean to be finicky, Elsey," the President said, "but you know, I believe that tomorrow night I'll have the biggest audience I've ever had, and I've had some pretty big ones. I don't think there's ever been a more important declaration of national policy — I *know* there's never been since I got to be President — than this one. It's terribly important for me to make this statement clear and forceful. We have to weigh every word and every idea in it. I know that you fellows have worked exceptionally hard on this one for me. We've got some things out in the open with this speech; we've got some decisions made. It's funny how a pending speech will clear the air on policies. We've worked hard, but we've got to work some more. After I get through here, I'm going to take this home and scrutinize every word in it."

Mention of late hours brought a prompt suggestion from Murphy. "I propose," he said, "that we hold approval of this passage in abeyance, and perhaps some of us can come up with something in the morning."

The President agreed and went on to read the fifth page. About two-thirds of the way down, he came to the sentence "Unity with our allies is the foundation of our effort." He broke off, and declared, "That cannot be said with too much emphasis. We and our friends have *got* to stay together if we're going to keep this old world steady. Right here in this country, they've divided us with their campaign of lies and slander. I think this last election and some of the dirty things that went on did pull us apart, and it's going to take a lot to get us back together. But we'll get together — I know that. When your shoe pinches, your toes are bound to be close together. The same with our allies abroad. One thing sure: the Russians would like nothing better than to split our friends away from us. We can't give *that* to them on a platter. We've got to stick together."

Tannenwald said, "Why don't you emphasize the point even further, and say, 'Unity with our allies *must be* the foundation of our effort'?"

The President nodded and started to write down "must."

"No," Lloyd said. " 'Is' is stronger. 'Must be' is something you have to achieve. 'Is' is something you already have."

"I believe you lost another word, up there at the end," the President said in a kindly way to Tannenwald. "This is a tough bunch. Matt Connelly and Bill Hassett used to sit in here and try all through a speech to pry one word into the thing, and they hardly ever succeeded. Did they, Murph?"

"No, sir," Murphy said.

The President crossed out "must."

David Stowe, sitting to Lloyd's left, said, "There's one sentence in here that bothers me: 'We will continue to provide assistance to European countries, and to other free countries in other parts of the world whose defense is important to our defense.' Do we mean to say that? Do we mean to limit our aid to those countries whose defense is militarily important to ours? Do we mean to help Spain and Argentina, because they happen to be strategically placed, and not India and Peru, because they're less so? I didn't think that was the idea. I thought the idea was that we're all in this together — that the solidity of the free world is itself a defense for all."

"Well taken," Acheson said. "Why not say 'because'? '. . . because their defense is also important to our defense'? That shifts the emphasis."

"Why *not* say that?" the President agreed. "That's just the way it is. We're going to help all the other free countries *because* the common defense of all of them is vital to our defense. How did that go exactly, Dean?"

This time, the Secretary of State dictated and the President wrote.

"What about the last sentence on the page?" asked Robert C. Turner, a professor in the School of Business of Indiana University, who had been brought in temporarily as an economics consultant, and who was sitting between Stowe and Tannenwald. " 'Working together, we can present a common front for the peaceful settlement of differences with the forces of Communist imperialism.' Is that English — and is it logic?"

"What about that?" the President said. "That *is* gobble-dygook."

There was considerable discussion of that sentence, and of the ones between which it was supposed to fit sequentially, until, at last, the President said, "We can straighten out this part later. Mercy, look at how that clock is going around! I'll mark that sentence and try to fix it up. I'm going to carry this home and work on it till all hours of the night. Then I'll be up long before any of you and go over it again. I've cut out my walk and swim and all of that tomorrow morning, so I can work on this speech. I guess some of you'll think, the way I'm bragging on myself, that I'm asking for a medal. Once I gave John Snyder a medal that consisted of a tin whistle — But that's neither here nor there."

On page 6, which the President now read, there was a passage that troubled the Secretary of State. It was one that specified the number of months it would take to increase the strength of the armed forces of the country to three and a half million. "It's a question of security," Acheson said. "I have in mind that you are making things too easy for the intelligence services of a country I need not name. All they have to do, if this goes through, is tune in their radios to the President of the United States and then write down in their little black books: 'The United States will have three and a half million under arms at the end of —— months.' "

"This has been checked out with the Defense Department," Murphy said. "Both General Marshall and General Bradley read this passage this afternoon and made no objection. We're aware of the security problem, but we're also aware of the traditional obligation to tell our people how the strength of their nation stands."

"Couldn't you broaden the time factor?" Acheson asked. "Couldn't you say that 'we will increase the number of men and women on active duty to nearly three and a half million with the utmost expedition'?"

The President's speech-drafters guffawed.

"Dean," the President said, "I'm afraid you're being shot at. These buzzards won't stand for any fancy language."

"In any case," said Keyserling dryly, "the figure of — months may be unrealistic. The goal may be reached sooner, or maybe later. The result depends upon many complex factors in our financial, production, and manpower programs."

"I'm inclined to agree," the President said. "We had a most informative meeting of the National Security Council this afternoon, during which it was made clear that you just can't say we're going to have so-and-so million men under arms in such-and-such months, and get them by merely saying it. We could call up enough men tomorrow to make a total of three and a half million, just by calling out the National Guard, but the point is that before you take each man, you have to have uniforms, housing, arms, a place for training — any number of things — to be ready for him. I don't know whether your minds will carry you back to 1941 and 1942. Do you remember that first time, when the extension of the draft only just barely got thorugh — by one vote, it was? The result was that right after that F.D.R. and the War Department got fearful that Congress might reverse itself and they pushed things much too fast" — the President made a pushing gesture, over the table, with both hands — "so that they were taking men in faster than they had camps to put them into. We don't want to repeat mistakes we've made before. We've got to proceed in an orderly manner and get things done just as fast as possible — but no faster."

The President cut out the reference to a specific number of months. In the course of further discussion of manpower, he spoke of the likelihood of calling up the Reserves. There was a visible stiffening on the part of several of the younger staff men.

"Some of these boys aren't going to be around here for the next speech," Stowe said ominously.

Even those who had become tense laughed, and then the President said, "You've got something there, Dave. But I guess it's no laughing matter to some at this table. Still, if we didn't laugh at our troubles some of the while, we'd have a hell of a time."

The President read page 7. Turner then said, "Here's a sentence that reads, 'We have ordered a very rapid speedup in the production of military equipment.' You can't order production, Mr. President. You can order procurement, you can direct that orders go out to industry for goods and supplies, but only industry can produce the goods — so long as we have a free-enterprise system."

"Isn't that a matter of semantics?" Acheson asked. "Isn't that just splitting hairs a bit?"

There was some discussion of the point; then Keyserling said, "I believe this is, as the Secretary suggests, really just a semantic quibble. I think 'order' is all right."

"I don't care what word you economists use, just so we get the military equipment," the President said. "I have to think back again and again to the period of 1941 and 1942, when we had the same problem. Back then, I was put in the position [as Chairman of the Senate War Investigating Committee, the so-called Truman Committee] of needler to the plants that were lagging. We had a terrible time then getting people to realize that the good of their country had to come ahead of their own selfish interests, and I suppose this time, whether you say 'order' or say 'please,' we'll have the same trouble getting people to stop thinking about their own stomachs and wallets."

Part of the discussion of the word "order" had revolved around the pace of the projected speedup, and Bell now said, "You'll have an opportunity, Mr. President, to go into this matter of the speedup a little more thoroughly in your State of the Union Message to Congress."

"Misery sakes!" the President exclaimed, in sudden despair. "That's coming along soon, isn't it?" As if involuntarily, he looked at the clock at the opposite end of the room. "I don't know how the devil I'm going to get my State of the Union Message done, with all the things I have to do in the next few weeks," he said, and he put his elbows on the table, clasped his hands, and, putting his head down, leaned his forehead on the ends of his thumbs. His thumbnails pressed into his flesh. "I guess I'll just have to forget that there's any such thing as Christmas and New Year's and family this winter," he said.

Acheson said something to cheer the President up, and then the President, with the new moons of his thumbnail prints still showing on his forehead, went on to read the eighth page. When he had finished, Keyserling said, "In the sentence 'We must have more productive capacity,' we'll have to find some other word than 'capacity.' That has a special, technical meaning in industry that is too restrictive for what you intend there. 'Power' or 'strength' or 'might' would do."

" 'Power,' " the President said, and wrote the word.

Bell said, "Here, where we say, 'Workers will have to put in more hours,' did you know, Mr. President, that there is a persistent rumor around Washington that government workers are going to be boosted to a forty-eight-hour week?"

"That rumor doesn't scare me," the President said, " 'cause I'm already on a seventy-hour week."

"That's true!" Acheson said. "Such an order could be used to cut down the hours of work of some of us. . . . Look here, this strikes me as a clumsy sentence: 'We must produce more and more of the things we need most — the vital metals and fuels, the specialized tools and equipment, and also certain farm products.' We ought to be either more or less specific: *What* metals? *What* farm products?"

After some talk about this, Acheson said, "Well, I see we won't get anywhere by trying to be more specific, so couldn't we simply say, 'We must have more and more of all forms of the vital produce of farm and factory'?"

"What are you grinning about up there, Dave?" the President asked Bell.

"Sir," Bell said, "I just didn't think that sounded like the way you would put it."

Everyone laughed except the Secretary of State, and as the President's laughter subsided, he cried out, "Oh, Dean! Dean! Dean!"

Finally, the sentence was made to read (to the openly displayed but now discreetly silent dissatisfaction of the Secretary of State), "We must produce more — more steel, more copper, more aluminum, more electric power, more cotton, more of many other things."

When page 9 had been read, Murphy said, "In this passage that we wrote in today on taxes, we have simply assumed, from conversations we have heard around here, that we're justified in saying that you want 'to put the increased cost of defense as nearly as possible on a pay-as-you-go basis.' If that assumption is incorrect —"

"It's perfectly correct," the President said. "I gave the Secretary of the Treasury and the Bureau of the Budget directions some time ago to find ways and means of doing just that. I repeated the directions emphatically only yesterday. The passage is correct as it stands."

Keyserling said, "I think this is a negative sentence: 'If we don't hold prices down, inflation will undermine public confidence, weaken our whole economy, and make us more vulnerable to aggression.' That depends on fear for its effect. I think we ought to turn the sentence around and say something positive, like 'The only way to make ourselves invulnerable to aggression is to keep our economy robust.' "

" 'Robust'!" exclaimed Lloyd derisively. "What about 'buxom'?"

Again there was laughter, and then the President said, "You see what you get around here, Leon."

Keyserling, however, had been so intent on his idea that he hadn't quite taken in either the tone or the substance of Lloyd's counter-suggestion, and now, with unrelenting seriousness, he said, "What I suggested was a reversal in sense: 'The only way to make ourselves invulnerable to aggression is to keep our economy —' What was that word you suggested, Lloyd?"

"I withdraw 'buxom,' " Lloyd said, playing it just as straight as Keyserling, "and suggest we try 'strong.' "

" 'Strong,' " Keyserling said, evidently relieved to have his idea rounded out.

The President solved the problem by cutting the sentence

out altogether. "Good!" he then exclaimed. "Anything more on that page? . . . Nothing? Page 10." He read on.

When Truman had read page 10, Murphy said, "On the question of wage and price controls being applied progressively by the Economic Stabilization Agency, rather than all at once, I just want to report to you our conviction that there will be criticism from some quarters — sincere and severe criticism — because you're not moving as fast as some people would like to have you move."

"Thank you for pointing that out, Murph," the President said. "But we'll have criticism no matter what we do. That's what the President of the United States has to expect, Murph. Criticism is something he gets every day, just like breakfast. If we clamped controls on all across the board, we'd be criticized — and maybe by some of the same people — for moving *too* fast. You know that we've studied this out as carefully as we could, and concluded that without proper field staffs and without proper enforcement machinery the thing would just be a farce. Instead of helping the housewife, we'd be driving her into buying meat, for instance, on the black market. Why, at its height the O.P.A. had sixty thousand people all over the country making it stick. We can't just rush into these things blindfolded. I think we're going to move just as fast as we can back up our moves."

Murphy had a further question on the next page, the eleventh: "Just to make sure we're accurate, is Charles E. Wilson resigning as *president* of G.E. to come down here, or has he been chairman of the board?"

"Wilson is president of General Electric," the President said at once. "The chairman of the board is a fellow named Reed — Philip D. Reed."

"Thank you, sir," Murphy said. "Just wanted to check."

After the President had read page 12, Acheson, in a good humor again, said, "Listen to this sentence: 'But the job of building a strong America cannot be done in Washington.' I'm afraid a great chorus would arise over that sentence, 'And how!'"

"'. . . cannot be done *just* in Washington,'" Elsey said.

"There's a four-letter word with some value to it," the Secretary of State said. "I welcome that small word to our midst."

There were no changes on page 13. When the President had read page 14, Turner said, "In these sentences — 'Many of you who are young people will have to spend time in the armed forces of your country. It will be time well spent, for nothing you do in later life will be of greater service to your homes, your communities, or your friends' — take out 'It will be time well spent'? It will *not* be time well spent. No amount of saying that it will be time well spent will make it so. The next clause — 'nothing you do in later life will be of greater service,' and so on — is absolutely true. Delete 'It will be time well spent'?"

Without comment, the President drew a line through the sentence. Then he read the peroration of his speech; his voice was grave and he seemed to be quite moved. " 'As I speak to you tonight, aggression has won a temporary victory in Korea. We should not try to hide or explain away that fact. By the same token, we should draw renewed courage and faith from the response of the free world to that aggression. In Korea, for the first time in history, a world organization has undertaken to protect freedom, under law, by meeting international aggression by force. What the free nations have done in Korea is right, and men all over the world know that it is right. Whatever temporary setbacks there may be, the right will prevail in the end. Because of all these things I have been talking about with you, I will issue a proclamation tomorrow morning declaring that a national emergency exists. This will call upon every citizen to put aside his personal interests for the good of our country. All of our energies must be devoted to the tasks ahead of us. The American people have always met danger with courage and determination. I am confident we will do so now, and, with God's help, we shall keep our freedom.' "

The President looked up and said defiantly, "That's a good page. Anyone have a quarrel with that page?"

"I cannot quarrel with that page, Mr. President," Acheson said. "I have only one small point. 'As I speak to you tonight, aggression has won a temporary victory in Korea.' 'Victory' may be too strong; we don't know. The event is in the balance."

"What about 'military advantage'?" Shulman suggested.

"All right," the President said, "I'll buy 'military advantage.'" He wrote the words in, then glanced at the clock. "Look what time it is!" he said. It was ten-thirty-eight.

While the President had been making the last change, Elsey had stood up and walked over to a corner of the room, where he picked up an enormous gavel, with a handle nearly four feet long and a head at least a foot long. This had come to the White House as one of the thousands of presents sent Truman by citizens of the Republic. Elsey now put the gavel on the table in front of the President and said, "If you adjourn us with this, I think even the ones who are asleep will hear you."

"That *is* a gavel," the President exclaimed, picking the big mallet up. "I'd forgotten that thing was in here." As he examined it, he said, "This country's gavel-crazy. It must mean we love order, or something like that." There was a small metal plate on the head of the gavel, and the President, squinting close to it, read the name of the Chattanooga farm-equipment man who had sent the present, and an inscription: "Whatsoever a man soweth, that shall he also reap."

"How true!" Acheson said. "Especially in these dark days, how true!"

"That certainly is a gavel," the President said.

"That's not a gavel," Lloyd said. "That's a maul."

"It *is* practically a maul," the President said. "Say! You could use that on a plug and feather. [A stonecutter's tool.] It would be real handy for a plug and feather." He put the gavel down and said, "I want to say that I appreciate the effort all of you have put into this speech. I know how hard you've worked over it. Here we are on the tenth version of it. I thank you very much. Right now, it looks to me like a good speech, one of the best we ever did, but I want to take it home now and hash it over some and see if I can make it better. Dean, what a hell of a two weeks I've had!"

"These have been hard days for you," the Secretary said, shaking his head.

"Tell these fellows what you were saying this afternoon about the Presidency, Dean."

"I simply remarked at the National Security Council meeting," Acheson said, still speaking to the President, "that, first of all, you have to be a glorified Grover Whalen; you have to receive delegations of Indian chiefs and high-school essay winners and officers of the American Society of Bigger and Better Goat Farmers presenting you with their prize goat. Second, you have to keep on good terms with Congress — and who knows better than I what that means? Third, you have to deal with the press. Fourth — a small matter — you have to run the country's economy and war effort, enough work in itself for twenty Chief Executives!"

"And don't forget, he is also Commander-in-Chief of the armed forces," Truman said, making a characteristic switch to the third-person-singular pronoun.

"And you're Commander-in-Chief," Acheson said. "Otherwise, you're an idle man."

"It *is* a tremendous job, Dean," the President said. "A really huge job. One to make a person stop and think. And yet they will say that all a man wants is to keep the seat of his pants in the President's chair. Really, all a man wants is to do the right thing for his country. Any man faced with this job, no matter what he's like, no matter how much or how little he's capable of to begin with — any man will be lifted up by the dignity and responsibility of this job to a place where he can meet it. I guess there are other men who could do this job better than I can, Dean, but — "

"What did the cook say to the admiral, Mr. President?" Murphy asked.

"That's what these fellows always ask me when they want to tell me I'm all wet," the President said to Acheson. "It comes from a story Admiral Nimitz told me once. It seems it was a certain admiral's birthday, and his crew threw a party for him. When the cake came on, the admiral tasted it and then called for his cook, who was a great, big, husky fellow, and the admiral said, "Cook, this is a fine cake. It's one of the best cakes I ever ate. I never ate a cake as light as this.' And he went on and on about the cake, about its color, its icing, the way it chewed, and all of that. The cook shifted from foot to foot while the admiral sang the praises of the cake. After about five minutes of this, the cook straightened himself up and said, 'Admiral, you sho' do talk silly!' So, whenever these fellows want to tell me I'm talking silly, they ask me what the cook said to the admiral. Anyhow Dean, I've been elected to this big job, and the country elected me, so I'll just have to do as well as I know how."

At that, the President stood up abruptly, with his draft of the speech in his hand, and said, "Which reminds me: I've got chores to do." He started for the door. "I'll run along to my study in Blair House. You know, there's no difference between my office here and the one over at home, except this one's round and that one's square. The work's the same shape in both places. Well, see you boys in church or some-place. Good night, gentlemen."

5. GHOSTS IN THE WHITE HOUSE

From time to time, President Truman, like an anxious homeowner whose place was being done over, would take a close look at the repairs being made within the central, residential part of the White House. One Saturday morning, he took me along on one of his tours. He was also accompanied on that inspection by a retired major general, Glen E. Edgerton, the Executive Director of the Commission on Renovation of the Executive Mansion, and William D. Hassett, the President's seventy-year-old Correspondence Secretary, who venerated anything with a bit of history in it almost as much as the President did. Harry Truman, who had always been outspokenly proud of his profession, politics, had often told his friends that if he had been forced, in his younger days, to undertake a second-choice career, he would have had a hard time deciding whether to be a farmer, an architect, or a historian. He inherited his love of the soil. Architecture had begun to appeal to him forty years before, when he had become a devoted apprentice of the Masonic order, which uses the forms, the techniques, and the tools of the building craft as symbols of a perfect ethical system; he was now Past Grand Master of the Missouri Grand Lodge of Ancient, Free and Accepted Masons, and, besides being the thirty-third President of the United States, was the first President to have been elevated to the thirty-third degree of Masonry while in office. Masonry made architecture one of his hobbies; responsibility for the construction of various public buildings, notably the Jackson County Courthouse in Kansas City, had made it one of his studies. His devotion to history resulted from his having been born, as he had told me on our morning walk, with "flat eyeballs" a structural astigmatism so severe that he had had to begin wearing glasses in his sixth year. He had become a precocious bookworm, and had concentrated from the first on histories and biographies that his mother put in his way. During recent months, his reconnaissances of the White House had given him periodic opportunities to indulge two of his three enthusiasms to his heart's content.

Our party gathered in the President's office, in the West Wing of the White House. Starting there, and continuing as we walked slowly from the West Wing, along a colonnade of the low-lying structure that contained the President's swimming pool, toward the main building, Truman and General Edgerton reviewed for my benefit the reasons the repairs had been necessary, and what had been done up to that time. Late in 1947, the President said, he and his family had begun to be worried by the fact that the second-story floor perceptibly sagged, especially when there were large receptions. Then, one day, two or three floor beams gave way under Margaret's piano, in her suite on that story. The President, with his thorough knowledge of the craft of building, began to detect certain other structural faults in the White House, and in February, 1948, he asked a committee — including Richard E. Dougherty, then President of the American Society of Civil Engineers; Winchester Englebert Reynolds, Federal Commissioner of the Public Buildings Service; Lorenzo S. Winslow, the official White House architect; Douglas W. Orr, then President of the American Institute of Architects; and Howell G. Crimm, Chief White House Usher — to take a careful look at the old building. What this committee discovered by the next October was enough to make the Truman family decamp quickly to Blair House, across Pennsylvania Avenue and in the next block to the west. The committee formally reported that the structure of the building had been riddled and unbuttoned. For nearly a century and a half, various Presidents had been enthusiastically "improving" the White House with progressively modern conveniences; all their work had been done piecemeal, with complete abandon. Doors had been cut through walls wherever they seemed to be needed, without regard for what the walls were supporting; chases had been scooped out of the walls for wiring and pipes; holes had been bored in floor beams, studs, struts, and columns for bell cords, buzzer wires, cables, pipes, and telephone lines; loads not foreseen by the original builders, such as bathtubs and tiled bathrooms, had been built in at random; worst of all, a heavy steel-and-tile roof had been imposed, a quarter of a century before, on fragile interior walls and piers. No coordinated records had been left of these termitic operations, and nobody had ever taken the trouble to review the entire structure. And all the while, the White House was resting on footings only eight feet deep in a stratum of soft clay, more than twenty feet thick, above a solid gravel bed; the whole beautiful edifice was settling and sliding into the ancient swamp called Foggy Bottom.

On the basis of the committee's discoveries, the Commissioner of the Public Buildings Service prepared an estimate of the cost of repairs and asked Congress for an appropriation to cover them. A nationwide tumult went up over the request: many distressed citizens got the impression that Harry Truman, after banging around in the White House for only three years, had brought the building to this terrible state of deterioration all by himself, and had hung a balcony on it to boot. Congress, at the President's suggestion, created the Commission on Renovation of the Executive Mansion, consisting of two senators, two representatives, and Messrs. Dougherty, Winslow, and Orr. These gentlemen, who went to work in June 1949, soon found themselves debating whether to raze the old pile entirely and erect a new building in its place or to gut the existing shell and give it new insides. For sentiment's sake, they decided on the latter course; they then got an appropriation of five million four hundred thousand dollars from Congress, hired General Edgerton to direct the job, advertised for bids from contractors, selected the John McShain Company, of Philadelphia, and caused the work to be started at the end of 1949. A little more than a year later, when our routine inspection took place, the repairs were better than halfway along. It then seemed possible that the White House would be ready for occupancy in October, 1951.

Our walk from the West Wing and the recital of this background by the President and Edgerton were interrupted while Truman stopped, as he had once before with me, and looked at the thermometer and barometer at the beginning of the colonnade; he gave us a short parenthetical discourse on another of his hobbies, the weather, ending with a forecast for the District of Columbia and vicinity for the next couple of days; outlook excellent. The President and Edgerton then resumed their review of the restoration. Toward the end of their account, we stood for a short time in a sheltered, sunny corner near the far end of the colonnade, shut away from the main building by a high plank wall which, besides cutting off the end of the colonnade, ran on south through a barren rose garden and down into the White House grounds. This fence and the pool building screened the West Wing from the area around the main building where, on weekdays, workmen had free scope. Now General Edgerton pulled out a ringful of keys, chose one, and opened a small door in the fence. The President led us through it and across a flagged area, to a door at the west end of the main building. We were entering, he told me, the ground floor; that is to say, the floor under the main story.

We found ourselves in an eerie space. Hemmed in by thick, ancient masonry walls, which were patinated with old plasters and paints of many faded shades, we stood nevertheless on a raw concrete floor, and we looked up and saw over our heads another bare concrete slab, supported by rows of naked concrete columns. There were as yet no partitions. Directly before us, along what would evidently become a hallway, were suspended from above, at about chest height, some very big galvanized-metal hot-air ducts. The scene was anachronistic; it was as if someone had decided to set up a modern office inside a deserted castle.

"Those aren't permanent, are they?" the President asked Edgerton, pointing at the ducts.

"No, sir," Edgerton said. "Those are just to give some diffusion of central heat in these areas during the cold weather."

"Good," the President said. "Now, let's see where we are. That's the housekeeper's office" — he pointed toward the empty southwest corner, on our right — "and next you have the doctor's office and clinic. And that," he said, moving along a central corridor and still indicating the pillar-tenanted hollow to our right, "is a little room where the ladies can leave their wraps in case of a reception or party; it's called the Museum, for some reason. Then back over here to the left you have the kitchens. You see, the family dining room is directly above them, and the state dining room is opposite that, upstairs. Over here, we have some pantries. I reckon that's where they stored Jackson's cheese till they were ready to eat it."

I asked the President about Jackson's cheese.

"When President Jackson was about to retire, in 1837," Truman said, "some of his admirers up in New York State — I reckon they were from Herkimer County; that's where the best New York cheese comes from — decided they wanted to show their love for old Jackson by giving him the biggest cheese in the world. I believe a fellow named Meachem was the one who got the thing up. Well, sir, they pressed a cheese that finally weighed fourteen hundred pounds, most as tall as a man and big around as a silo. They brought the cheese down here in a wagon. They stopped along the way to exhibit it in New York, Philadelphia, and Baltimore, and it was getting riper all the time. They finally got it in here, and they cut it on the day of Jackson's last reception — that must have been toward the end of February 1837. A crowd stood around that thing, picking and chopping away at it, and they say that when the company got done eating and stealing cheese, there was only one small piece, about big enough to go with a piece of pie, left for the President himself. The whole White House smelled cheesy. The crowd had tromped and traipsed cheese on all the carpets, they'd wiped cheese onto the curtains, and they'd sat it into the sofas and chairs. It cost the taxpayers twenty-seven thousand dollars to do the place over when Van Buren moved in."

We walked along the central alleyway of pillars, beside the air ducts, and the President pointed through a small coppice of posts and piers to an open space on the right, and said,

"Here's the first of the oval rooms. They've got them stacked one on top of the other, one on each floor. This one is where the Presidents received foreigners — diplomats, kings, and suchlike — who came over here. This is where the Presidents would pick up credentials from new ambassadors that had just arrived. I don't like these oval rooms."

I asked the President why not.

"My office in the West Wing is oval," he said. "I like a square office."

General Edgerton led us to the edge of a hole in the floor slab, which, he explained, was the mouth of a stair well. Down through the well we could see two basement levels. One of the greatest gains of the renovation, Edgerton told me, would be two floors of basement, where there had been none at all before.

"Now there'll be room to store things," the President said. "I hate to think of all the valuable relics that have been thrown out of the White House, or sold away, just because there wasn't room for them. Why, when Chester Arthur moved into the White House, in 1881, he took out twenty-four wagonloads of things from the attic, and he had a rummage sale on the lawn. There'd been some of Jackson's furniture up there, and they say that one of the prizes Chet Arthur got rid of that day was a pair of Lincoln's pants. That whole treasure only brought in three thousand dollars. It would be nice if we could get some of those things back again."

"I can think of some items that were moved out for reasons other than the pressure of space and the want of basements," Hassett said. "I have it on reliable authority that the sideboard for stimulants — in other words, the bar — which had been stoutly provisioned for eight years by Ulysses S. Grant, was thrown out by his successor, Rutherford B. Hayes, in 1877. Hayes was a strict teetotaller and a shining light in the gents' auxiliary of the W.C.T.U., and his good wife was called by the topers of that day Lemonade Lucy. The sideboard, I understand, wound up as a bar in Hancock's Saloon, down Pennsylvania Avenue. Hancock's was worthy of such an embellishment; it was an elegant saloon,

where, I've heard, Daniel Webster had some years previously got tanked up for his thundering reply to Hayne on
the supremacy of the Union. Even I, young as I am, can
remember when Hancock's served the best chicken Maryland and hoecake in the whole District of Columbia."

"It was a shame to lose those things out of here," the President said, shaking his head.

I asked whether the intention was to restore the interior
more or less as it had been before the building was dis-
mantled.

"Oh, yes indeed!" the President said emphatically. "It's all
going to be exactly the way it was before. For instance, down
here on this floor there were a whole lot of groined arches
that, with all this steel and concrete, wouldn't support a
thing; but they're going right back in. When the place is finished, you won't know that you aren't in the selfsame building as before — except the floor won't tremble and shake
under your feet when you walk."

The President led the way toward the far end of the building. "Let's see, then," he said. "Down here at the east end of
the ground floor, we have the room for the china collection.
We'll move the collection back in. It has pieces that were
brought into the White House all along the line. Old
Monroe was against foreign entanglements, but he wasn't
against his wife's bringing in some fancy chinaware from
Europe. It has a border with a peculiar shade of orange to it,
as I remember. Jackson had a French dinner set in blue and
gold with an eagle in the pattern. We'll move all that back in
here." The President now pointed to the southeast corner.
"There you have something they called the Social Room,
which was really the ushers' room, and around here on the
opposite side there's a room that F.D.R. made into a library."

"Speaking of libraries," Hassett said as we began to walk
back toward the center of the building, "the record of the
White House, from the bibliophile's point of view, has been
shameful. Why, there wasn't a single book in the place in
1850, when the Fillmores became the tenants. Mrs. Fillmore's method of installing a library was to purchase authors by the yard, on the shelf. Of course, she had good

pickings, on a yardage basis. Dickens and Thackeray were flourishing just then."

Near what had been the pantry, there was a crude wooden stairway, leading both upstairs and down. Edgerton told me that it was for the workmen, and was crammed into the space that had been, and would again become, the elevator shaft.

I asked how long the White House had had an elevator.

"T.R. put it in," the President said.

"The old cage is at the Smithsonian Institution," Hassett said. "We sent it over there not because it was intrinsically curious but just because of the aura it seemed to have. Try to assess the notables who were raised on high by that box, from Theodore's time through Franklin's!"

"I wanted to get that old bird cage back in here," the President said, "but they told me you couldn't get modern elevator works in with it."

"Incidentally, Mr. President," Hassett said, "Alexander Wetmore, at the Smithsonian, wonders how long the museum will be able to keep the elevator. He has a frightful problem of selection over there. I think that possibly the atmosphere of levitated personalities is beginning to wear off the thing. What is your pleasure?"

"Maybe he can keep it a little longer," Truman said rather wistfully.

The President started up the workmen's stairs. When we had all four climbed to the next story, he said, "Now we're on the main floor, where the big state rooms are." His constant use of the present tense as he described the features of the White House made the tour seem a kind of fantasy, a game of imagining pompous halls populated by the ghosts of Presidents, visiting kings, ambassadors, levee guests, hangers-on, and ushers. The air smelled mostly of damp concrete, but it was not hard to believe that the President could stretch a point and detect, even now, a whiff of Herkimer cheese here and there, and it was possible to imagine, watching his bemused expression, that in the echoes of our voices through the empty spaces he heard the sighs, and the shuffling of the reluctantly departing feet, of generations of disappointed office-seekers. Yet what we saw was dull and drab. We were standing, once again, on a crude concrete slab among bare concrete columns, and the only difference between the state floor and the ground floor was that here the ceiling was nearly twice as high. "We're in the family dining room now," the President said, and cocked his head a little, as if listening for the clatter of imported plates and for hints of the gossip of his predecessors. Then all at once he was down to earth. He pointed toward the northwest corner of the ceiling and said, "That's where Margaret's piano came through."

We crossed a hypothetical hallway. "And here's the state dining room," the President said. "This'll hold a hundred guests."

Beside us, on the west wall of the building, which had been stripped to bare masonry, we could see where a fireplace had been, and where a flue had geed off above it. "You know, General," the President said, pointing at the soot-blackened scoring, "when they stripped that wall down, I finally found out why that ornery fireplace in here used to smoke so much. I never could do a thing with it. Whatever I tried, the smoke still poured out into the room, enough to make your eyes smart. Look up there! You can see where the flue is crooked, and its gets smaller and tighter above the place where the throat goes into the flue. That's no way to build a chimney."

"You're right, Mr. President," Edgerton said, in the dry tones of a technical man. "There's a delicate relationship between throat and flue, and if that relationship is disturbed, the development of eddies and counterdrafts is to be expected."

"You have to taper a throat just so," the President said, "and beyond it, the flue has to be even in size and regular. I hope this one's going to be cleared up, so when we lay a fire in here, we won't have all that smoke and confusion."

"It will be," Edgerton promised.

"Do you see, up there, all the cracks and spalls in the stonework?" the President asked me, pointing to the masonry high up the wall. "The day after the English set fire to the White House, in 1814, it rained, and the cold rain on the hot masonry is what caused all that."

Then the President stepped out rather briskly through the central hall area, to the eastward. "Along here," he said, "you have the parlors. First the Red Room, then the Blue Room — there's your oval again — then the Green Room. On the end, there, is the East Room. It's the biggest in the place; it's forty by eighty-five, I would estimate. That's where the big state receptions are held. You know, the White House was started in 1792, and the first ones to move in were John Adams and his wife, in 1800, and when they moved in, only six rooms in the whole building were ready to be lived in. This East Room was just a stone shell, so Abigail Adams used to string up her wash to dry in here. Imagine it! Later on, when the room was all dolled up, Jackson bought twenty spittoons to go in here. They cost twelve-fifty apiece."

The President led the party back to the center of the hallway, and, turning toward the north — the Pennsylvania Avenue side — he said, "This is the entrance hall. Here we have one of the few differences from before. Instead of tucking the stairs around the corner, out of sight, we're going to take and start them up from this outer foyer, to make a real state staircase out of them, for big functions. By the way, General," he said, with a new light in his eyes, "I want to discuss this state stairway with you a little. I want to change it around some."

"Don't switch things on me now, Mr. President," Edgerton pleaded.

"I want to change it around so it doesn't bend back on itself. The way you fellows have it now" — the President stepped forward into the big empty space of the past and future entrance hall to demonstrate, with parallel strokes of his arms, the directional problems of the so far imaginary staircase — "the way you fellows have it now, you have the staircase starting up this way, straight away from the front of the building, then it turns around a hundred and eighty degrees and goes back up the rest of the way to the upper landing, where it turns all the way back again. The bad thing about your scheme is that when you count in a marble railing and banister, your first rise will cut off the view of state processions for the crowd standing out here in the hallway. What I want is to have you go in sideways with your first flight, then have a landing, turn ninety degrees left, and go on up and around. Then we can all see the state procession even if we stand way back here." The President moved to the eastward, deep into the hall space, to attain the view he had mentioned of the chimerical procession. He seemed to stretch up on his toes a little and to crane for a sight of famous people. "You see?" he asked Edgerton.

Edgerton pursed his lips. "The architect," he began slowly, "was afraid that what you suggest would give us some structural problems. For instance, right here on the turn, we badly need this column —"

The President interrupted. "The trouble with creative professional men —" he said. Then, realizing that he might be offending Edgerton, he broke off, patted the General on the back of the arm, and, smiling, said, "Excuse me, General, I mean all professional men *except* engineers. The trouble with professional men, especially architects, is that they have too many inhibitions. They can always think of a reason why you can't do this and you can't do that. I know an architect down in Shreveport, Louisiana, who doesn't have any inhibitions. He'll *always* find a way. Edward F. Neild. He helped me build our courthouse out in Jackson County. There wasn't a problem he couldn't lick." The President's face took on a mischievous look. "Come to think of it, General," he said, "I do remember one time when a couple of engineers showed some inhibitions. This was when we were giving Jackson County a new road system, back in 1930. There was a stretch of road I wanted to put through straight. These engineers — they were wonderful engineers, you understand; they just had this one bee in their bonnet — they had all kinds of reasons, like this column of yours, why that stretch had to jog this way and go along awhile and jog back again. So one day I said, 'Come on,' and we got in a car and drove out to the place where the stretch of road was going to be built, and I got out of the car, and I walked it off, straight

as if I was plowing a furrow, and I told them, 'Put it there.'
Which they did. People are still driving on that road, and I'll
bet my hat they're glad they don't have to jog this way and
that way every time they do it."

Edgerton took this rallying goodhumoredly, but didn't
commit himself on the state stairway.

Our party now went to the workmen's stairway in the elevator shaft and climbed to the next story — the second floor.
Here the cement underfoot was damp with moisture that
had been dripping from a recently set slab overhead. Starting again with the northwest corner, the President said,
"And here are Margie's rooms. She uses the bigger one for
her parlor and the smaller one, in the corner, for her bedroom. It looks ample if you think of the footage, doesn't it?
But when you put these rooms into a building of this scale,
they look small. You'd be surprised how many people come
in here and say, 'Look at these dinky rooms!' "

Pointing out rectangular openings in the floor and ceiling
slabs against the west wall, Edgerton reminded the President
that a new service elevator would further encroach on Miss
Truman's space.

"That's all right," the President said. "Then, across here,"
he continued, moving toward the southwest corner, "we
have the Madam's rooms. Next in line there's a room and
bath for me."

I asked when the first modern bathrooms had been installed in the White House.

"Jefferson designed the original outhouses," the President
answered. "I don't know exactly when they put in proper
bathrooms, but I do know that Millard Fillmore was the first
one to bring in a bathtub, in 1850."

"Mr. President," Hassett said, "I'm afraid you've been
guilty, as I myself have been for many years, of perpetuating
a hoax. I've always said, too, that Fillmore introduced the
tub to these premises. I've been rereading some things by
H. L. Mencken lately, and I ran across his famous bathtub
hoax, of 1917, in which he told a wonderfully detailed cock-
and-bull story about the invention of the bathtub in 1842, by
an Adam Thompson. The thing is still being taken hook,

line, and sinker; serious histories cite its bogus facts. Mencken concocted therein this fib about Fillmore. I regret to state there's nothing to it, and I'm as guilty of gullibility as you are."

The President seemed reluctant to let go of his belief. "But," he said, "what about that account I've read of Fillmore's stopping off in Cincinnati and trying out a tub for the first time and —"

"That's all in Mencken," Hassett said.

"But I've seen a paper the American Medical Association drew up claiming that the vapors from the tub were dangerous for the President's health."

"I'm afraid Mencken invented that, too," Hassett said.

"I *do* know," the President said, falling back but still firing, "that the first pipes to bring water in were installed by Jackson, in 1833. Up to that time, the water had come from a spring in Franklin Park, in open wooden troughs." He shook his head. "I could swear those A.M.A. fellows didn't think it was a hoax about the tub."

"I feel robbed of a fact, too," Hassett said sympathetically.

"Then we have my oval study," the President said as we walked along the southern side of the building. "Come here a minute," he said, beckoning me to the central window. At first, I thought he wanted me to see the view, which was a breathtaking one — down over the White House grounds, across the Ellipse, the Mall, and the Tidal Basin, to the Jefferson Memorial, with the Potomac, the hills of Arlington, and the dry blue sky beyond. When I exclaimed at what I saw, the President said, "Yes, that old Frenchman did a pretty good job." The "old Frenchman" was Pierre Charles L'Enfant, who laid out the city. "What I wanted you to see was my balcony," he said then. I realized that I was looking out onto the famous structure, skirting the inner side of the columns of the South Portico, that had caused a national furor in 1948, when Truman ordered its construction.

The President was smiling. "I never could understand why there was so much fuss about my balcony," he said. "Think of all the changes there have been in the White House that

GHOSTS IN THE WHITE HOUSE 101

nobody ever howled about! Jefferson designed both the porticoes, and both of them were out of proportion. Monroe put the south one on, and Jackson put the north one on. Teddy Roosevelt built the West Wing and Hoover built the East Wing. Coolidge put on a top floor and a different shape of roof. Do you know why I put the balcony there in the first place?"

I said I had always supposed it was for sitting on in summertime.

"Not at all," the President said. "A man with my kind of work doesn't have time for sitting on verandas and porches. I put that on there for architectural reasons. It was for looks. It was to make the building look right. There were two reasons for it. First of all, the way they kept the southern sun out of the Blue Room downstairs was to put a clumsy big awning out in the portico, reaching clear out to those columns just under the windows of my study. After a while, every year, it would get to be an eyesore, flapping in the wind and getting filthy. No matter how you try, you can't keep canvas white outdoors in a big modern city. There's too much soot. Now, with the balcony, they can just recess rolling wood-slat shades in the underside of it, and you can let them down any time you want. The other reason was more important: for proportion. You needed something to break the skinny perpendicular lines of those portico columns out there. Jefferson was long on ingenuity, but he was short on proportions. In fact, General," the President said, turning to Edgerton, "while you're making all these repairs, there's one thing I wish you'd do for me. I wish you'd get a bulldozer and knock off the front two pillars of the other portico, on the north side. Did you ever look at the front of this house from Pennsylvania Avenue? Why, that front porch is just about twice the size it ought to be."

Edgerton, who had fidgeted at first, evidently fearing that another difficult subject like the state stairway was coming up, now saw that the President was joking, and he laughed heartily.

The party moved along toward the east. "This is the

Monroe Room," the President said of the next space.

"Some people call Margaret's parlor the Monroe Room," Edgerton said.

"That's right," the President said. "There's an honest difference of opinion. The reason they call this room the Monroe Room is that it had some furniture in it that Mrs. Monroe bought for the White House when it was rebuilt, after the fire of 1814. I think old Monroe actually slept in Margaret's parlor. That's why you have that argument."

The floor slab at the east end of this story was nearly two feet higher than the rest of the floor. Edgerton explained to me that this was because the great East Room, below, required a ceiling of extra height to make its proportions pleasing.

"You going to manage this incline here without stairs, General?" the President asked.

"Yes," Edgerton said, "we're going to get away with a ramp, and the slope will be fairly gentle, at that."

"Good!" the President said. "That's the Lincoln Room in the corner. You know, I found some chairs for this room that were in the White House in Lincoln's time. I'd observed the chairs in a painting over in the lobby of the West Wing — it's called *The Peacemakers,* and it's by Healy. It shows Lincoln with Grant and Sherman and Admiral Porter just before the end of the Civil War. And then after that I saw some chairs over in the Treasury Building that looked familiar to me. We compared them closely and found they were the exact same chairs. So I said they ought to come back in here where they belonged."

The President, standing at the foot of the ramp-to-be, looked across the raised platform. "This whole end of this floor used to be the executive office, right up to 1902," he said. "That year, Teddy Roosevelt built the office wing at the west end. You know, T. R. had an executive staff of nine men, and he thought he was crowded. Today, the President has something over seven hundred people in his offices. We've had to take over the old State Building, and you still have to use a shoehorn to get them all in. Can you imagine conducting the entire business of an administration in this space?"

We went next to the top floor. As we started up the crude stairway in the elevator shaft, Edgerton called to the President, who was again leading the way, "Low bridge! Watch your clearance there, Mr. President!"

A scaffold had been set across the well. The President dodged nimbly under it and climbed to the top. The rest of us followed him. We stood again on damp concrete. Above us were bare steel roof trusses supporting hollow terra-cotta tiles, from the top of which the surfacing of the roof had been removed.

"Are you going to get me a new roof, General?" the President asked.

"Well," Edgerton said, "the trusses, beams, and columns will be mostly the same, but we're going to strip that tiling out and replace it with more up-to-date covering and surfacing. We can meet the cost of that and stay within our appropriation."

"Good! Good!" the President said. "Coolidge put that roof on here," he said to me. "He put this whole penthouse, they call it, up here, by pushing the roof up and squeezing some rooms under it. You might say this was the only time in his life that Cal raised the roof. This new roof he put on weighed one hundred and eighty tons, and Cal supported the whole thing on interior walls that were just sitting on the floors underneath. My heart trembles when I think of the disasters we might have had — big receptions we used to hold, of fourteen hundred and sixteen hundred people, downstairs, none of them knowing that a hundred and eighty tons might drop on their heads at any moment. T. R. and Cal certainly did a rotten job of renovations in 1902 and 1927. But we're going to do it right this time, aren't we, General?"

"I must say they did some surprising things, Mr. President," Edgerton said. "See here." He moved to the north side and pointed up to an exposed truss. "When we cleared the walls under this jack truss, we found a column supporting the east end, but look here — they just *forgot* to put a column under this end. This end was just sitting on bricks, lath, and plaster. It was quite an operation to get our new column in there without disturbing anything."

"All I can say is God must have been looking out for us," the President said.

We walked to the east, while the President explained that this floor had been used for guest rooms, servants' rooms, work rooms, and a sunroom. We turned, and came to a raised platform jutting out from the center of the south side. The President said, "General, I guess you're going to have to build steps up to the sunroom, here, aren't you?"

"Yes, sir," Edgerton said. "You have to deal with a change of elevation of more than three feet there."

"The Madam thought it would be that way," Truman said. "That's what she told me. I guess she was right."

Opposite the potential sunroom, on the north side, were a number of rooms that were not going to be changed at all; their original floors and walls were untouched. As we looked into them, the President told me that they were linen and pressing room and clothes closets. "There's the room where they store the Madam's clothes, and there's the place they keep mine," he said, pointing into two of the rooms.

As we walked back out of the unchanged area, Edgerton said, "You'll notice, Mr. President, that Coolidge put a hip roof up here. We've found that we can eliminate the hips without disturbing the profile of the building at all, so we're going to be able to give you considerably more space up here."

"Good!" the President said. "Well, if we've seen the insides, I propose we adjourn to the outsides."

We descended the workmen's stairway to the first floor and went out through a temporary wooden front door onto the North Portico and then walked down to the driveway. Edgerton showed me the tops of the new concrete footings under the exterior walls. "They go down twenty-two feet, to the solid gravel bed," he said. "She won't settle now! It was quite a job getting those foundations in under there. We would dig a pit, four feet square and twenty-odd feet deep, down to the gravel under a section of wall; then we'd pour it full of concrete; when that had set, we'd dig another pit, next to it; and so on, all the way around. We had to sink a hundred and twenty-six pits altogether."

The President, who was familiar with all this, was not listening. "Say," he said, pointing off to the left, "I sure wish we could get rid of that East Wing. It's out of harmony with all the rest, the way it stands up there. You want a low-lying structure like the West Wing, for balance. The east side is where they used to have the stables and barns. The Presidents kept cows until 1866. Andrew Johnson got rid of them. Hoover sold the last horse. And as for this portico of old Jefferson's — look at that thing, gentlemen! I ask you! I'd like to rip off the whole front half of that portico."

"Well, Mr. President," Hassett said with heavy irony, "after your third and fourth terms — no, even later than that, after you have been declared dictator with full and clear title — you can simply decree, 'In the name of my unlimited authority, the North Portico of the White House shall henceforth and forever be half as big as it is now.'"

"Ho! Ho! Ho!" the President said, caricaturing round laughter. "You're so-o-o *funny*, Mr. Hassett. You're such a *humorous* man, Mr. Hassett."

As we began to walk along the driveway toward the West Wing, we passed a Secret Service agent who was standing guard at the front of the building.

"Good morning, Jim," the President said.

"The building looks better, Mr. President," the agent said.

"Got a property here I'm trying to sell, Jim," the President said. "These folks here" — indicating Edgerton, Hassett, and me — "thought they were interested, but they want something with a little more elbow room to it. Can't find any takers, Jim. Guess I'll have to come down in my price."

The agent laughed. "That's good, sir," he said.

"If you think this portico is bad," Hassett said to the President as we walked on, "you should see the design Jefferson submitted in the competion for the whole building! He copied it practically stone for stone from Palladio's Villa Rotonda, near Vicenza. It had a huge dome with a weather vane on top of it."

"Yes," the President said. "I guess we're lucky they chose old Hoban's design." James Hoban was the architect who designed the White House.

"Hoban wasn't so original either," Hassett said.

"You mean because this building looks a little like that Irish building — Leinster House, isn't it, in Dublin?"

"No, sir," Hassett said. "Hoban was more shameless than that. They've established that he cribbed his design straight from some plans by James Gibbs, the disciple of Sir Christopher Wren, and designer of St. Martin-in-the-Fields, in London. Hoban just copied off the whole shebang from *A Book of Architecture*, which was a collection of Gibbs' designs. I've seen the Gibbs and Hoban designs for the front façade side by side. I'm afraid our man was a rank plagiarist."

"Mr. President," Edgerton said, "did I ever show you my photograph of Hoban's ghost?"

"No, you didn't."

"Oh, you should see that."

"Well, what are we waiting for? Let's go!"

"It's down in my office. Do you mind walking around there?"

"Let's go."

We walked to the south side of the White House, where a number of barracklike contractors' offices, tool houses, and workmen's shacks stood. On the way, Edgerton discussed several pending White House problems with the President — for instance, the dimensions and the nature of the water pipes coming to the building from the city mains. On that and every other point Edgerton raised, the President had a definite opinion.

When we came opposite the South Portico, the President halted us, and said to me, "Now look at that balcony and judge for youself. It fits in just over that line of window pediments, and it breaks the long line of the portico columns, just as I said. The proper proportions for classic columns, length to diameter, is nine to one. Jefferson stretched these way out to fifteen to one! They were unsightly!"

We walked on, and soon came to a shack that bore a sign reading, "Office — Commission on Renovation of the Executive Mansion." Edgerton unlocked the door and made way for the President to lead us inside.

The office contained two desks. While the engineer hunted among his files for the photograph he had spoken about, the President looked brightly around. "Here's McKellar!" he said, noticing a photograph of the Senator from Tennessee hanging on the wall. "He's the Chairman of our Commission." The President peered at an inscription on the picture frame. "Why, looka here!" he said. " 'This pine frame was made from a roof timber installed in the White House circa 1815 and removed in 1927.' Isn't that interesting? That's one of the good, sound timbers Cal took out in '27, drat him."

"Here it is!" Edgerton exclaimed, coming up with a photograph. He showed it to the President. It was a picture, about nine inches by twelve, taken during an early stage of the work now in progress: the bare, shored-up walls of the White House stood up all around, and within them was the nearly finished excavation, deep down, for the two new basements. The picture was evidently a time exposure. In the distance, near a bulldozer, some men stood. One of them was transparent. He had presumably walked away during the exposure.

"It's Hoban, come back to see what we were doing to his building," Edgerton said.

"It's Hoban, all right," the President said. "Has he given you any trouble?"

"None at all, none at all," Edgerton said.

"You've got a nice place here," the President said, looking around again. "What's this?" He moved over to some framed verses on one wall. "To Glen Edgerton," he read out loud. " 'The Low Green Tent,' by Reuben L. Anderson, your five-foot eighteen-inch friend."

"He's nearly two feet taller than I am, so he calls himself my five-foot eighteen-inch friend," Edgerton said.

"Well, let's take a look at this," the President said, and he read, with a Hiawathan lilt:

*"Every man's a would-be sportsman, in the dreams of his in-
    tent,*
*A potential out-of-doors man when his thoughts are pleasure
    bent —*

"It swings along O.K. —

"But he mostly puts the idea off, for things that must be done,
And he doesn't get his outing till his outing days are gone.
So in hurry, scurry, worry, work, his living days are spent,
And he does his final camping in a low green tent.

"Hurry, scurry, worry, work! That's the way it is." The President sighed.

"That fellow's my plumbing contractor on this job,"
Edgerton said.

"Is that a fact?" the President said, with obvious interest.
"You know, most people think that men who work with their
hands never have a thing in their heads, but as a matter of
fact that's where some of your really deep thinkers are.
There's many a time a steelworker or a carpenter will work
with his hands and create something fine with his mind at
the same time. There was a blacksmith up in New England
before the Civil War; he used to decline Latin verbs while he
worked. He'd prop a volume of Horace or Lucullus up by
his bellows, and he'd learn it by heart. He was one of the
best-educated men in the country."

"Sure," Hassett said. "That was Elihu Burritt. You know,
Mr. President, he was one of the early proponents of a world
government, such as we have — or hope to have — in the
U.N. He used to write and make speeches in favor of a
congress and court of nations. They called him the Learned
Blacksmith."

"That's the fellow!" the President said. "Say, General," he
then said, "do you have some of the things they took out of
the White House down here? I'd like to see some of that
again."

"Sure enough," Edgerton said, and led us into an adjoin-
ing room, which looked like a cross between a museum and
a junk shop. He showed us a number of curiosities: an old

brick with a dog's footprint in it, a pike blade that had been buried under the North Portico, a sturdy pair of workmen's shoes some proud mason had many decades ago bricked into the home of the Presidents. Against one wall was a sort of notice board, which had samples of relics attached to it by hooks and wires, souvenirs to be given to citizens who applied for them. There were pieces of wood of various sizes that could be carved into letter openers, walking sticks, and other useful objects (as some of the samples had been); bricks with brass plaques proclaiming them to be from the White House; scraps of décor made into paperweights; and so on. Edgerton told me that such material would be disposed of to interested applicants, under a special Act of Congress, "in consistence with its symbolical value and not for commercial consideration."

The President spotted on the notice board some photographs of fireplaces. "Aren't they going to put those back in?" he asked.

"No, sir," Edgerton said. "Some of the main hearths and mantels are going back in, but these you see — perhaps six or seven — are going to be replaced."

"And you're going to unload those on the public?"

"That's the present plan, sir."

"How about giving me one for Christmas next year?"

"The legislation makes it clear that the President of the United States can have anything he wants from among the surplus material," Edgerton said.

"Oh, pshaw!" the President said. "I was just teasing. I don't want anything for myself. I was just thinking that I'd like to get one of those fireplaces for the library we're building out in Independence for the Department of the Interior. I just hate to see these things scattered around carelessly. There's so much history in that old place."

6. FORTY-EIGHT HOURS

On January 9th and 10th, 1951, in order to watch President Truman making his diurnal way through the thickets of power—the rank, trackless, strangely beautiful tangles of dreadful responsibilities and pompous trivialities through which he was obliged to move — I followed closely two days of his official life. On the first morning, Tuesday, January 9th, Truman awoke in his upstairs bedroom in Blair House at five-thirty, assaulted not by an alarm clock but by a habit of early rising that dates back to the ten years of his young manhood he spent on a farm. He arose, shaved ambidextrously, bathed, dressed, and descended to his study. There, for two hours and a half, he worked on the tremendously important Economic Message to the Congress that he was to send to the Capitol on the following Friday morning; this was a document containing the administration's estimates and plans, which could guard or break the economic health of the country, and it was full of verifiable data and untested theories and ideas on taxation, inflation, price controls, and wage controls — for all of which, in execution and in the long run, only the President himself could answer to the citizenry. The President's effort that morning was mainly to simplify the language of the message. (Whenever he could, he spent an hour in his study, reading the papers, perusing documents, and writing letters, and then went for a walk and a swim in the White House pool; this morning the demands of the Economic Message forced him to give up his exercise.)

At eight-thirty, the President sat down at breakfast alone, as Mrs. Truman and Margaret had not yet returned from a holiday in Independence; they were both due that day in New York, where Margaret has an apartment. At a few minutes before nine o'clock, the President was taken by car to a private entrance to his office, in the West Wing of the White House. For an hour, he dictated personal letters to his shy, quiet private secretary, Rose Conway; he also read various documents that were put before him, and decided, and noted on them, the courses of action to be taken, if action was required. One of the papers was his schedule for the day, with a typed line or two briefing him on each appointment.

At exactly ten, the President got up from his desk and went to the door separating his office from its anteroom, the office of his Appointments Secretary, Matthew J. Connelly, and told those members of his staff who were waiting there for his summons to their daily conference with him that he was ready for them. They went into his office. Present were the President's three Executive Secretaries (one for appointments, one for correspondence, and one for the press), the Assistant to the President, the President's Special Counsel, three of his Administrative Assistants, his three Aides (military, air, and naval), and his Executive Clerk. The President handed out the papers he had for some of his staff members, and then called on each of them to bring up his business. The subject matter of the staff conference was as varied as the Presidency itself, and disposing of it consumed thirty-six minutes. During the conference, the Executive Clerk put on the President's desk a pile of documents that needed his signature — a pile which the Clerk would supplement during the day, and to which Truman would turn from time to time all day long, in moments snatched between appointments, until he had signed his name, altogether, more than four hundred times.

When the President had dismissed his staff, he received James S. Lay, Jr., Executive Secretary of the National Security Council. This Council was an inner cabinet, whose function, according to its directive from Congress, was to "advise the President with respect to the integration of domestic, foreign, and military policies relating to the national security." It consisted of the President, the Vice President, the Secretaries of State, Defense and the Treasury, the Chairman of the National Security Resources Board, the Director of the Central Intelligence Agency, and others designated by the President. Lay, who headed the Council's staff, saw the

President every morning. On this morning, as on every other, Lay spent fifteen minutes briefing him on developments in this country and all over the world that affected, or might affect, the security of the United States. Much of the knowledge on which the President was obliged to base tremendous policy decisions came to him by ear; during such lectures, he could not let his attention stray for a second.

The President was due to meet at ten-forty-five, for a kind of pep session, with the Committee on Mobilization Policy of the National Security Resources Board, an advisory group composed of three leaders each from the fields of business, labor, and farming, and three representing the public as a whole. Chairman W. Stuart Symington of the N.S.R.B. had requested the meeting not to transact any business but to clarify the status of the Committee. Charles E. Wilson's Office of Defense Mobilization had been set up a few days before, and neither Symington nor the members of this policy committee knew whether their advice would still be wanted or needed. The President's talk with Lay began to run over, and the White House Receptionist, a huge, easygoing Southerner named William Simmons, who held the same position under Roosevelt and who, it is safe to say, had shaken the hands and could call out on sight the names of more famous people than any other American then alive, led the Committee members from the lobby of the West Wing into the long, narrow Cabinet Room, which abuts the President's office. The President entered the Cabinet Room by his private door at ten-forty-nine, and Chairman W. Stuart Symington took him around the room to shake hands with everybody. Someone asked Truman if he would mind sitting at one end of the long Cabinet table, to pose with the Committee for three press photographers who had just been admitted. He sat down and called cheerily to the others to gather around. "Here, pull the chair up!" he said. "Now! One on the other side. Who'll sit here on my right? Mr. Symbol!" (This nickname for Symington had apparently come to him on the spot; nobody around the White House had heard him use it before.) "Now, let's see — on my left I'd better have — our only lady! Come on, Anna!" He beckoned to

Mrs. Anna M. Rosenberg, the then new Assistant Secretary of Defense, who from the start had been one of the three members representing the public on the Committee. The photographing took so long that by the time the President had moved to his regular seat, at the center of the Cabinet table, with his back to the row of French doors along the outer wall, and the others had settled themselves in their chairs, ready for business, the President was twelve minutes behind schedule. The session had been allotted only fifteen minutes all told.

Someone complimented the President on his State of the Union Message, which he had delivered before the Eighty-second Congress the previous afternoon.

"I'll tell you something," Truman said. "That's the first time since I've been President that I've lost sleep over a speech. For two or three nights there, I stayed awake over that one, and I'm not a man who loses sleep — never have been. It was just that I felt this was the most important declaration I'd ever been called upon to make. I felt it was terribly important to make the speech objective."

"It *was* objective," someone said.

"I tried to make it objective," Truman said. "It's not easy for me to be objective, you know. I'm a partisan fellow." Then, informally getting down to work, he said to the gathering, "This crowd's nothing new to me. I see a lot of faces around this table that I worked with when I was in the Senate, and especially during the war. I'm pleased to see all of you again. The reason we got together here today was that I wanted you to know that I'm glad to have the kind of advice you people can give. I want you to deal frankly with me. Talk things over, reach your conclusions, and make your suggestions to me just as frankly and bluntly as you want." With an explosive grimace of exuberance, the President added, "Maybe I'll even comply with some of them!" Everyone laughed. "Seriously," he went on, "I'm very much interested in your work. I just hope that all you busy people can take enough time to get the job done the way it has to be done. Stu, you take over now."

Symington began a little speech he had evidently worked

out in advance. "Because of the reorganization of the government to meet the world situation," he said, "this group wanted to know whether to go ahead or not, and —"

"It certainly should!" the President broke in, with extreme earnestness.

Symington went on, "This is the only true advisory body we have that is free from politics and that draws its opinions from all levels and all occupations in the country. These distinguished people come here on a voluntary basis. They're giving their time generously and freely. All they ask in return is that their advice be carefully listened to. If they have suggestions, criticisms, or complaints, they want to be able to come straight to you, to the top executive power —"

"That's what I want, Stu," the President said.

"They will hold two meetings a month," Symington continued. "They want the President to be at one of those meetings."

"I'll be there," Truman promised.

Now ex-Senator Frank P. Graham, another of the members representing the public, spoke, more to Symington than to the President. "The sort of advice we unanimously agreed at the last meeting to hand along was typical of the kind we think can be useful."

"That's correct," Symington said. "I see the President regularly every Wednesday, so even though the President wasn't with us, I was able to pass our opinion on to him quickly and directly."

Looking around, Truman said abruptly, "I want you all to know that I need your help."

Anna Rosenberg spoke up. "Can I say something? Since I've been working down here in Washington, I can see things more clearly than I used to. Everybody down here is so tied up with operations — with getting things done — that they can't afford the luxury of stopping to think, and of trying to find out what people across the country are feeling about things. There's just too much to do. Out at the Pentagon, we start work at eight o'clock in the morning and we don't stop till midnight. I've always been a pretty hard worker, but I've never worked like this before. When I go to

New York for the weekend, people ask me, because I've been in the Pentagon, 'What's going on?,' 'What about Korea?,' 'What's the war situation?' I find I don't know as much as they do from reading the papers. I've been too busy. That's why I'm glad I told General Marshall that I'd take the job with him only on condition that I could stay on with this body. Right at this very moment, the Armed Forces Policy Council is meeting out at the Pentagon, and nobody out there *dares* miss that, but I insisted on coming here, because I think nothing is so important as this, Mr. President. Here you have people from all over the country who *know* what their people are thinking. This Committee can stand off and assess the situation, because it's not immersed in operations."

"I'm sure that's so, Anna," Truman said.

"Mr. President," Symington put in, "I want to make sure you met our newest member, Mr. [Herschel D.] Newsom, the Master of the National Grange. As you know, he's taking Mr. Goss's place." Albert S. Goss, Newsom's predecessor as Master of the Grange, had died of a heart attack after speaking at the *New York Herald Tribune* Forum on October 25th.

The President said to Newsom, "I know you'll fill Mr. Goss's shoes all right, Mr. Newsom, from what I've heard about you." Then he said, to the Commitee at large, "Along the lines of what Mrs. Rosenberg was saying, I think it's true: sometimes you can be too busy to think. You take my case. I was up till midnight last night on the Economic Message that has to go down to the Congress on Friday. Then I got up at five-thirty this morning and worked on it till eight-thirty. I had to take a forty-one-page, single-spaced document and try to get the gobbledygook out of it, so it would make sense to people who aren't economists — and yet still be true. We're just finishing the Budget Message; that goes down on Monday. So the next thing I have to face is an off-the-record budget seminar on Saturday morning. I have to get up in front of every blame expert in town over in the old State auditorium Saturday morning and tell them what our budget is all about. I have to know just about every figure in the whole budget, and it's going to be a printed document this thick." The President calipered an imaginary budget with his right thumb and forefinger, and found it about three inches thick. "After that, we have to spell out our program in detail to the Congress. That means at least ten special messages. So you can see that your President doesn't have much to do! That's why you people can be so useful."

"Mr. President," said William Green, president of the American Federation of Labor, "each and every one of us here gains a new sense of our obligation to meet together and discuss the nation's problems and to coöperate as fully as possible. Our only question is: How can we serve our people? This group represents all segments of our national life — labor, industry, farmers, private citizens. All have one mood and one common desire: to give the best we have to give. I feel sure that after this encouragement from you, we'll be able to do a better job."

"I know that's so," Truman said.

"Mr. President," said James G. Patton, president of the National Farmers Educational and Coöperative Union, "I noticed in your State of the Union Message you said that all non-military expenditures would have to be cut back in favor of defense expenditures. We hope you realize that there are many apparently civilian expenditures, especially in the fields of agriculture and conservation, that it will be important to continue for the mobilization effort. We certainly learned that in the last war."

"Oh, I agree, Mr. Patton," Truman said. "I think you'll find that our budget takes that point into consideration."

Philip Murray, president of the Congress of Industrial Organizations, said, "Mr. President, do you think you can get support for the type of tax program you advocated in your message?"

"I think so," Truman said. "I hope so. The two tax bills we got through the last Congress were unprecedented in our history. By following along closely with the Senate Finance and the House Ways and Means Committees, I think we'll get what the country wants. What we're going to ask for is fantastic in figures. It will hurt everybody, rich and poor. Over the long haul, though, I think it will stabilize our monetary system and help to hold down this inflationary spiral we're in. Then, when we come out of this thing, we'll be a sound and solvent nation."

Marion B. Folsom, chairman of the Commitee for Economic Development and treasurer of the Eastman Kodak Company, said, "Mr. President, I can say that by and large the business community was delighted to hear you speak of doing this thing on a pay-as-you-go basis. Otherwise, there would be nothing to do but let inflation take up the slack."

"Yes," the President said, "and you're sitting on hot lead when you do that. When the proper time comes, Mr. Murray, we'll ask for a tax increase to try to pay for our mobilization as we go along. All the economists seem to be agreed that's the soundest thing to do, and that's what we'll try to do."

Otto A. Seyferth, a steel man who is president of the United States Chamber of Commerce, said, "All of us were gratified to see the way you put your plea for unity yesterday. And I think you'll find there is unity at this stage."

"There is," the President said, "but there's not enough unity, considering the seriousness of the situation. I believe there's greater unity than there was a short while ago. Back in October and November, during the election campaigns, we had a bad situation. We had a personality campaign going on. We've got to argue the issues rather than personalities. If we can get some moral responsibility into this thing, we won't have any trouble at all."

"In discussing the issues," Graham said, "I hope the emphasis can be put on truth."

"You know that, don't you, Doctor?" the President said. "You got skinned in your primary by lies!"

Graham said, "Is there some way to get through to the peoples of the world — not behind the Iron Curtain; that has to come later, I suppose — to get over to the non-Communist world that we stand for equality and justice? We get all this propaganda from the Left, abroad, about America being the aggressor and the imperialist. We're not! Everyone who knows the truth knows we're not. When we went out to Indonesia [on a Good Offices Committee for the United Nations], we couldn't get anywhere at first, because the Indonesians were convinced that America was looking for an empire. But when we proved to them that we weren't 'agents of Wall Street' and 'economic imperialists' and all of that, they got into a mood to discuss things with us. The Communists beat the airwaves night and day with lies. Can't we stress the truth about ourselves? The truth is in things like the Point Four program."

The President said, "I'm of the opinion that we'll carry the votes of the world all right if we do what you've been saying, Doctor. If we preach the truth as loudly as they preach their lies, we'll be all right. Well," he said, standing up, "I've got to get back to my schedule!" Bidding, the Committee goodbye collectively, he left by his private door.

It was eleven-eight. Though the President had shaved a few minutes off the quarter hour he had allowed himself to talk with the Symington Committee, he was running late, and when he returned to his office, he found a new complication: Dean Acheson was waiting for him, with a foreign-policy question that could not be put off. The Secretary of State took only eleven minutes to outline the problem and get an answer from the President, but by the time Acheson left, the next appointee, who had been told to be on hand promptly at eleven, had been waiting nineteen minutes. The heel-cooler was Representative Harry P. O'Neill, of Pennsylvania, who had three Scranton businessmen in tow. The note on the President's schedule pad, under the names of O'Neill and his entourage, read, "Congressman O'Neill asked for this a week ago, stating they wished to discuss question of getting a war plant located at Scranton, Penna." The President received the O'Neill party with great enthusiasm and with a distinct recollection of having met one of O'Neill's companions, a man named Rogers, on the campaign train in 1948, and of having said to Rogers then, "If I only get one vote, and that's yours, I'm still going to make a fight for this thing." He also recalled having stopped over in Scranton on his way to the Chicago convention earlier that year, to speak to the Irish-American Society. As for the defense plant, he told them that that was something they would have to take up with Charles E. Wilson, the director of the Office of Defense Mobilization. He said jokingly that the President of the United States isn't allowed to make any *important* decisions. The group left in good cheer.

At eleven-thirty-three, eighteen minutes late, the President received Congressman Frank L. Chelf, of Kentucky. The Congressman asked after the President's family. The President said they were fine, and added, with evident emotion, that he was particularly pleased that Margaret was getting such good crowds for her concerts. Chelf, who is something of a Southern gallant, was moved to remark that the President is a perfect father — "a regular Lord Chesterfield," he said. He then summarized a bill he had introduced into the Eighty-second Congress, H.R. 38, which had to do with the reapportionment of seats in the House of Representatives in line with the 1950 census; the President listened, and said he would study the effort Chelf was making to pick up marginal seats for certain predominantly Democratic states, in order to offset Republican California's great gain.

At eleven-forty-six, the President started on foot from his office, with his Press Secretary and his three Aides, for the auditorium on the fourth floor of the old State Department Building, where he had been due at eleven-thirty, to present five Congressional Medals of Honor to the next of kin of dead or missing soldiers. The day was bitterly cold, and in Connelly's office, outside the President's Oval Office, someone said, "Don't you want to wear an overcoat, Mr. President?"

"It's only across the roadway," Truman said. "I'm in good condition; I couldn't catch cold if I tried."

On the way across the street, the President's Military and Air Force Aides, Harry H. Vaughan and Robert B. Landry, who were flanking him, teased him, and Truman talked fiercely back, in flamboyant, chuckling counterattack. In the corridors of the old State Building, and all the way up to the fourth floor in a slow elevator, the two uniformed jesters carried on their hurried, earthy work and gave the heavily burdened Chief of State, their friend, four minutes of Old Times. Then, suddenly, in a little room off the auditorium, the party walked into an opposite atmosphere. There waited, solemn and proud, the bereaved next of kin of the five men whose memories were to be honored. At once, as if he had put off a Shriner's fez and put on the cap of Commander-in-Chief, and in changing hats had changed hearts, too, Truman silently shook hands with the five, and by a soft look in his enormously magnified eyes seemed to show that he shared their pain and pride. The relatives were then led into the auditorium. The President, spotting a carafe and a glass on a wide window sill in the small room, hurried to it, poured himself a glass of water, gulped it down, and then followed, sad-eyed, after the heroes' kin. Inside the auditorium, a battery of moving-picture cameras had been set up, and beside them a crowd of still photographers stood in an aggressive block. On the left side of the room, as the President entered, other relatives of the medal winners, including one young wounded soldier on a hospital wheel bed, were already gathered. The President stood behind a desk at the front of the room; the next of kin were seated in a row on his left; behind him were arrayed, at ease, his Aides and the Secretary of the Army, Frank Pace, Jr.; and to his right stood his Assistant Military Aide, Colonel C. J. Mara, with the citations in his hands and the medals lined up in front of him on the edge of the desk.

The first to be called forward was Mrs. Mildred D. Dean, the wife of Major General William F. Dean, who commanded the 24th Infantry Division in the early phases of the Korean campaign, and who was listed as missing in action near Taejon. While Mara read General Dean's citation, the President stood with his hands clasped in front of him, kneading them together. When Mara had finished reading, he handed Dean's medal to the President, and Truman gave it to Mrs. Dean, mumbling, so that those present could barely hear him above the snapping of flashlight cameras, "I can't say this gives me pleasure, Mrs. Dean, because I know you'd a lot rather have General Dean back here than to have this medal. But he did a fine job, and he deserves this great honor."

After the second presentation, the President made another appropriate remark. The third recipient was Mrs.

Madie S. Watkins, widow of Master Sergeant Travis E. Watkins, of Gladewater, Texas, killed near Yongsan. Mrs. Watkins, a very pretty girl of twenty-two, was obviously having difficulty keeping her face fixed in a proud smile, and while Mara was reading in her dead husband's citation (". . . he rose from the foxhole to engage them with rifle fire. Although immediately hit by a burst from an enemy machine gun, he continued to fire until he had killed the grenade throwers. . . . Despite being paralyzed from the waist down, he refused all food, saving it for his comrades . . .") her shoulders began to shake spasmodically. Mara read, "Refusing evacuation, he remained in his position and cheerfully wished them luck. . . ." Mrs. Watkins broke into tears. The citation finished, the President handed Mrs. Watkins her husband's medal, took her hand, and, visibly affected himself, said, "I know this is hard for you, young lady, but never forget this as long as you live: this medal is the highest honor your country could give to a soldier. Never forget that." Next came an elderly mother, who cried, too, and whom Mrs. Watkins, with her emotions finally under control, comforted when she returned to her seat. Last was a father, who stood through the affair with a rigid face.

Still very much moved, the President looked up at the crowd in the room and spoke a few quiet words, not widely reported on, that gave the ceremony a significance broader than the honoring of five soldiers, words deliberately tossed into the so-called Great Debate which the Korean War had stirred up — whether this country should send ground troops overseas or rely for security on geography, aircraft carriers, and long-range bombers. "I want to take this occasion," the President said, "to pay tribute to the infantry. You'll notice that all five of these Medals of Honor were awarded to ground soldiers. I don't think we ought to forget that they are the ones we depend on to hold the airfields and ports that our planes and ships operate from. They're the ones who fight from the holes in the ground and ridges and machine-gun nests. They're not the glamour boys of the services, but *they are the ones who win the wars*" — he bore down heavily on these words — "and they are the ones who make it possible for us to have freedom in this great nation of ours."

The ceremony was over, but that authority that is higher than the Presidency — the Public Eye — now took over; photographers, of both still and moving pictures, began commanding the Commander-in-Chief and his bereaved company where to stand and how to look. For almost as long as the ceremony itself had lasted, the cameras worked to catch an impression of what had happened, although the sharp emotions of the award ceremony were now already either dead or false. The President tried, especially when the newsreel cameras began to turn, to put the next of kin at ease, muttering to them that they should keep moving their faces around, look animated, like him — *he* was getting to be quite an actor, he told them. Once, in an effort to help both the cameramen and the despairing relatives get the thing over with, the President suggested that the next of kin stretch out their hands, so that he could clasp them together in his; the result was a strange and stiff tableau, which the cameramen politely recorded. Then, looking straight into the Public Eye, the President spoke up again. "Today," he said, "I've given Congressional Medals of Honor only to men who didn't come back. This is the first time I've ever done that even though I've awarded more Medals of Honor than all the other Presidents put together — but the reason I've given so many is just because of these terrible times that permit these medals to be earned and deserved." At last, at about twelve-twenty, the cameramen were satisfied. The President then went around and shook hands with every relative in the auditorium. It was nearly twelve-thirty when he hurried back across the street to his office.

In the meantime, back in the West Wing, Matt Connelly, the President's Appointments Secretary, had been rearranging things. Connelly was the Cerberus of the President's personal hell. Cerberuslike, he had three heads, which he used all at once: one for planning Truman's schedule up to three weeks ahead; one for greeting visitors and getting them through appointments on the current schedule; and one for dealing, tactfully, firmly, and finally, with those who would not get in to see the President but who, for various reasons had to, be allowed close to the presence of power — i.e., as far as the anteroom. All three of these heads, it happened, were deceptively enveloped in a single, well-formed skull. Since Connelly controlled to a great extent, the access to the highest center of authority in the government, he himself had immense indirect power, which he wielded with craft, caution, loyalty, and also — because he had been close to Truman ever since 1941, when he became an investigator for the Truman Committee — with a shrewd understanding of the wishes of the Boss, as he and everyone else on the staff called the President. As a kind of insurance in his perilously powerful condition, Connelly had, literally behind him, at the only desk besides his own in the anteroom, the assistance of Miss Roberta Barrows, who had sat at the same desk during Roosevelt's time, and who had the requisite tact and wisdom for one at the portals of authority. Not only did she see no evil, hear no evil, and speak no evil, but also, and just as valuably, she saw no good, heard no good, and spoke no good; she simply took phone calls and kept everyone who rang through aware of the impressive humility of the Presidency of the United States, which had (she made the caller feel) time and courtesy to spare for every citizen, no matter how lowly or importunate. She also kept a record of all appointments. During the medal ceremony, Connelly, seeing that the President was running late, had Miss Barrows put through a call to Frederick J. Lawton, Director of the Bureau of the Budget, who had a half-hour appointment for noon, and ask him to come in at two-forty-five instead. The first afternoon appointment had been scheduled for three-fifteen. Connelly tries to keep a dead spot in the early afternoon, to give the President a chance to get ahead with some of his desk work, which must otherwise be done at night or before breakfast. Today he had to put Lawton in the dead spot.

The President returned to his desk, picked up his phone at twelve-twenty-eight, and, without the help of a secretary, put through a call to Senator Allen J. Ellender, of Louisiana, at the Senator's apartment. The conversation went like this:

TRUMAN: "I heard you were sick in bed, and I just wanted to tell you to hurry up and get well, and I wanted to thank you for that goose you sent me the other day."

ELLENDER: "Did you eat it?"

TRUMAN: "Certainly did. Best goose I ever ate."

ELLENDER: "That was a banded goose. I'll bet you didn't know you were eating a banded goose."

TRUMAN: "No, I didn't know that."

ELLENDER: "And I'll bet you couldn't guess in a thousand times where that goose came from."

TRUMAN: "That looked to me like a wild goose. I suppose it must have been banded in Canada. Those fellows migrate down here from Canada."

ELLENDER: "You're wrong! That goose came from your home state. It was banded in Missouri on November 27th, and I shot it in the marshes in Louisiana on December 27th. That goose was one of your old Senate constituents."

TRUMAN (delighted): "Can you beat that! If I'd known that, it would have tasted a lot better when I ate it!"

ELLENDER: "They have a new way of snaring geese out in Missouri. They lay out a little path of corn on the ground leading right into the snare, and the goose is so dumb he just puts his head down and eats his way into captivity."

TRUMAN: "Sounds like the way a woman traps a man — in more states than Missouri — doesn't it? [In a kindly tone.] You get yourself back on your feet soon — hear?"

Ellender thanked the President for his solicitude, and the two men hung up.

The President signed his name a few times, and then Connelly opened the door and showed in Truman's twelve-thirty appointment. This was General George C. Marshall, the Secretary of Defense, for one of the President's "fixed appointments," which come at the same hours each week. His fixed appointments, besides his meetings with his staff and with Lay every weekday morning, included, at that time, sessions with the Democratic leaders of Congress, and later the Secretary of State, on Mondays; the Secretary of Defense, and then the Cabinet, on Tuesdays; the Chairman of the

N.S.R.B., and the Chairman of the Democratic National Committee, on Wednesdays; the press, the Secretary of State again, and the National Security Council, on Thursdays; and the Cabinet again, on Fridays. This time, because Marshall wanted to discuss Army manpower, he brought in with him Anna Rosenberg, his Assistant Secretary charged with that problem, who was seeing the President for the second time in one day but might not see him again for a month; and David Stowe, one of the President's Administrative Assistants, whom the President, at a staff conference some time before, had assigned as a watchdog over all manpower questions. Marshall reviewed the Defense Department's complicated plans for drafting men, which he and Mrs. Rosenberg were going to have to present to Congress in a few days. The President (with the citations for dead and missing soldiers not long out of hearing) was obliged, in the course of the following half hour, to make several decisions that would affect hundreds of thousands of young men and their families. For example, a decision he was asked to make, and did make, was this: a plan had been advocated to draft not only healthy eighteen-year-olds into the Armed Services but also (in order to distribute the burdens of defense fairly) young 4-Fs — men excused because of infirmities — into some kind of government service; should this plan be proposed to Congress now, because of its manifest fairness, or should it be put off, because adequate preparations could not be made to induct a large number of 4-Fs before the summer? The President, while he approved the principle of spreading the load, finally decided not to propose the plan until its details had been more carefully worked out.

At one o'clock, the President went to Blair House for lunch. Afterward, he lay down and slept for half an hour. He was back in his office at two-forty-five, and started right in signing his name again.

By that time, two men had been waiting in the anteroom for some minutes: Lawton, whose morning appointment had been postponed, and William D. Hassett, the President's Correspondence Secretary, who, hoping the dead spot in the daily schedule had not been usurped, wanted to slip in and give the President something he had for him. Hassett had taken three dog-eared books of Truman's piano music — volumes of Beethoven sonatas, Mozart sonatas, and Mozart duets — and had had the Library of Congress trim the frayed pages, reinforce the torn ones, and rebind the books in hard covers. While waiting for the President to return from Blair House, Hassett had riffled through the books, making sure that in repairing them the Library of Congress had not obliterated any of the President's pencilled notes to himself. At the beginning of Beethoven's "Moonlight Sonata," for instance, which is scored in four sharps, he found a rather petulant reminder in Truman's hand: "*C♯ Minor!*" There was also, on the second page of the same piece, where an F-double-sharp made its second, and therefore unmarked, appearance in one measure, a big, hortatory "*X*" beside it; and there were as well some quite angry, incoherent pencil marks between clefs of the Allegretto, which is scored in five flats. Hassett satisfied himself that the Library had practiced its usual discretion. Connelly came in just before two-forty-five, and when Hassett saw him, he said, "Pshaw! I was hoping to get in with these before *you* got back."

"Not today, Bill," Connelly said firmly. "We got behind this morning."

Hassett, and the bound volumes of music, retired for another, better day.

Connelly showed Lawton in to the President. There followed the fifteenth, and last, meeting between the director of the Budget and the President on the Budget Message, which was to be sent to Congress on the following Monday. As each section of the federal budget had been blocked out, Lawton had taken it to the President and discussed it with him; the President kept the typed drafts of all the sections in shiny brown cardboard folders, in the lower righthand drawer of his desk, and occasionally, between appointments, he would take out one section or another and go over it. By now, he had memorized nine-tenths of the summary figures and had a fair idea of the rest. The budget had reached the page-proof stage, and this afternoon Lawton went over corrections and additions with the President. During the conference, a question came up on which the President wanted the opinion of his friend Secretary of the Treasury John W. Snyder, so, at three-two, he picked up the telephone and, again without benefit of secretary, put a call through. A little later, the President asked Lawton to spend some time with him on Friday afternoon, to help him prepare for the budget seminar Saturday morning. Lawton, who understands the pressure of time on the President, left at three-twelve. The President signed his name some more.

Connelly slipped George McK. Elsey, one of the President's Administrative Assistants, in at three-fifteen. Elsey, who had studied at Princeton and Harvard to be a historian, had, among many other duties, the job of helping the President keep his papers in order. He talked with Truman now for seven minutes on a matter involving the President's personal file.

At three-twenty-two, Elsey stepped out and Connelly swung the President's door wide open for Senator James E. Murray, of Montana; Congressman Michael J. Mansfield, of the same state; and Senator Murray's son and assistant, Charles A. Murray. Senator Murray pointed out to the President that, according to the 1950 census, Montana was losing population, and that this was because both the mines and the farms of the state had been progressively mechanized; that the state was building new plants for aluminum, chrome, and manganese; and that Montana therefore needed new power facilities, over and above those of the Fort Peck and Hungry Horse Dams. The President said he would take the matter under advisement and discuss it with the Interior Department.

The Senator from Montana and his companions were replaced, at three-thirty-two, by Senator Brien McMahon, of Connecticut, chairman of the Joint Committee on Atomic Energy, who, after touching briefly on some atomic matters, asked the President whether there had been any decision on a request — previously discussed with Truman by Chester Bowles, when Bowles was Governor of Connecticut — for authorization to locate a big new steel mill at the Connecticut port of New London. The President told McMahon that the matter had been cleared by the proper agencies and that the first steps could be taken in getting the plant set up.

At three-fifty, the President received William Hillman, a magazine writer and editor, who was laying the groundwork for a biography of Truman he wanted to write.

At four-six, the President went into the Cabinet Room and called a meeting of the Cabinet to order. Truman's Cabinet meetings were for the most part informational sessions, at which general problems were discussed but big decisions were seldom made. Cabinet members dared not throw on the table, for mauling by their colleagues, projects that were dear to their Departments. They took up such matters in private with the President. Truman usually went around the table for opinions on matters that were important to him. This day he also read his latest draft of the Economic Message and asked the Secretaries, one by one, to comment. The meeting adjourned at five-thirty.

At five-fifty, after signing his name nearly a hundred times, and after reading some documents, the President packed a stack of papers five inches thick into a briefcase and was driven to Blair House. There he put in more than an hour's work in his study on the papers, interrupting himself only to call Mrs. Truman and Margaret at the New York apartment at exactly six o'clock. At seven-thirty-five, he left by car for the home of James M. Barnes, a former congressman and Administrative Assistant to Roosevelt, to attend a small birthday dinner for Speaker of the House Sam Rayburn. There were about twenty guests, mostly senators and congressmen. After dinner, the President played the piano for the company; later, he cut into a game of poker. He went home shortly after midnight, got into bed, and for more than an hour studied the federal budget.

After four and a half hours' sleep, the President awoke, dressed, and went to work again on his Economic Message, forgoing his exercise for the second morning in a row. He breakfasted alone, went to his office at nine, dictated letters and worked on papers, and admitted his staff promptly at ten. During this morning's staff meeting, he made some points about the Economic Message to his Special Counsel,

Charles S. Murphy, the head of the President's team of document-drafters, and gave Murphy his marked-up copy. After the meeting, Murphy retired for the day with his team to rework the entire message.

Congressman Overton Brooks, of Louisiana, who had an appointment for eleven-thirty, had appeared at ten-thirty. (An extraordinarily large number of people show up at the wrong hour for their appointments with the President, and as many come late, and therefore miss seeing him, as come early.) The President dismissed his staff at ten-thirty-five and since he wasn't to see Lay, of the National Security Council, until ten-forty-five, Connelly slipped Brooks in. Brooks discussed what had been marked on the President's appointment pad as "Louisiana matters;" i.e., politics.

After Lay's briefing, which followed, the President received, in succession, two hollow-eyed lame-duck Democratic congressmen, defeated men hoping for preferment in the Party. As head of the Party, the President could not afford to spurn Party men who had been beaten in elections; there was always the future to be thought of. Each of the two men left the President's office looking somewhat less hangdog than when he came in, for Truman, who had been a lame duck in a small way himself once (in 1924, when defeated for reelection as Judge of the Eastern District of the County Court of Jackson County, Missouri), was able to show, by his own example, that perseverance can pay off. One of the lame ducks, displaying a lack of tact that might have accounted in part for his having been defeated, said he had heard some rumors that the President was not feeling well — whispers that various events, such as some speeches by Senator Robert A. Taft on foreign policy, had reduced the President to a low state of mind and health. To this, Truman replied exuberantly, "I never felt better in my life. I can take these Republicans on, one by one, with one hand tied behind my back. Don't worry about me!"

At eleven-forty-five, after some paperwork during the blank quarter hour for which Brooks' appointment had been scheduled, the President received Robert Butler, his Ambassador to Cuba. Butler had called up from Havana eight days before, asking to see the President. On January 2nd, the President of Cuba, Dr. Carlos Prio Socarras, had made a statement binding his country with astoundingly unqualified allegiance to the United States. Butler wanted to make sure that the President knew about, and understood the entire significance of, this unusual obeisance. To his surprise, the Ambassador found that Truman had read President Prio's statement in full and was well aware of its implications.

At precisely noon (for, so far this day, everything had gone like clockwork), Simmons, the Receptionist, showed into Connelly's office, and Connelly conducted into the President's office, a party of about thirty distinguished men and women who were to witness the presentation to the President of the Woodrow Wilson Foundation Award. This award, for outstanding efforts for peace, had not previously been given to a President of the United States. The party, whose members now trooped by the President, shaking his hand, was headed by Dr. Harry D. Gideonse, president of Brooklyn College, who was to present the award, and Mrs. Eleanor Wilson McAdoo, Wilson's daughter. (During the Brooks gap, Connelly had brought in to the President a letter from Mrs. Woodrow Wilson saying that ill health would keep her away from the ceremonies but paying Truman — both as President and as recipient of an award in her husband's memory — her respects.) After all the guests had shaken hands with the President, they formed a stiff line around the wall of his Oval Office. Some of the President's staff came in.

An awkward pause followed, while moving-picture cameras and recording equipment were set up. Dr. Gideonse laid on the front of Truman's desk a huge, flat jeweller's case he had been carrying, and opened it, to show the President the bronze plaque, a foot in diameter, that was to materialize the award. On one side of the plaque, Gideonse showed the President a symbolical bas-relief by the Yugoslav sculptor Mestrovic; then Gideonse turned it over and showed the President an inscription, which noted that the award was being given to Harry S. Truman, "who, through his devoted support of the United Nations, and his courageous reaction to armed aggression on June 25, 1950, has sought to strengthen the United Nations in its defense of democracy against tyranny." The President bent over the desk and admired the plaque for some time, then called Mrs. McAdoo over to discuss it with her. Then he tested its weight and remarked on its heaviness. Then, because the sound technicians were still fussing over their equipment, he picked the plaque up and walked over to a group of ladies in the line of guests and held it out in front of them, showing them first one side and then the other, and the ladies exclaimed over it with exaggerated surprise and delight. "Ooh!" cried one lady above the ohs and ahs. "That thing's heavy! Don't drop it on your foot!" The President, who had been warned by Gideonse against that very accident, showed that he had a good grip on the huge medallion, and shook it, to demonstrate that in his arms, conditioned on a rowing machine and by setting-up exercises, the plaque seemed as light as a dinner plate.

At last the cameras were ready. The President went back to his desk and put the plaque down on it, and he, Mrs. McAdoo, and Gideonse assumed ceremonial postures: the latter two faced their Chief of State, in formal attitudes, as if they had just walked up to him on a grave errand and had not been chatting and chuckling familiarly with him for several minutes. Gideonse, who was trembling, held up a written speech and began to read it. The President stood, as he had during the reading of the citations for the Medals of Honor the day before, clasping and unclasping his hands in front of him. He wore an expression of keen and humble interest, but he could not help glancing quizzically from time to time at the shaking pages Gideonse held. During Gideonse's speech, Joseph Short, the President's Press Secretary, walked around behind the President's desk and slipped into Truman's hand a folded piece of paper; the President unfolded it, glanced at it, nodded gratefully to Short, and folded it up again. Gideonse read on for nearly ten minutes. When he was finished, he picked up the plaque and handed it to the President. The President put it right back where it had been, opened the piece of paper Short had given him, and read a statement of about two hundred and fifty words that had obviously been prepared for him by a speech-writer. When he came to the words "The seeds Wilson planted are now bearing fruit," he lifted his head and smiled at Wilson's daughter. He ended with a statement, whose graceful turn of modesty was somewhat vitiated by the palpable fact that he had not phrased it himself, to the effect that he accepted the award not in his own name but in that of the American people. "It is *their* award," he read carefully. "It is *they* who have made this decision — that while peace is precious to us, freedom and justice are more precious."

The President dropped the hand that held the paper, looked around, and seemed to realize that the statement he had just read was not adequate to his part of the occasion. He then turned to Gideonse and Mrs. McAdoo and said slowly, "I myself as an individual feel entirely unworthy of the honor you have conferred upon me." He paused, then, still groping, added, "As President of the United States, I highly appreciate the honor that has been conferred upon me by the Woodrow Wilson Foundation." He paused again, then suddenly broke his formal stance, smiled with an easy candor, and became himself. "I was in a field on July 2nd, in the year 1912, driving a binder and binding wheat," he said, "and there was a little telegraph station about a quarter of a mile from one corner of that field, which, being a hundred and sixty acres, was a mile around — no, more than that: it was half a mile long on each side, so it was two miles around it altogether — and when I had driven around it every time, I would tie the horses and run over to the telegraph station to see how the convention in Baltimore was coming along. That was the convention that nominated Mr. Wilson for the Presidency. And from that minute on I was a fan of Woodrow Wilson, who I think is one of the five or six great Presidents that this country has produced. And to receive an honor like this from a foundation dedicated to him is about the highest honor that any man can achieve. And I thank you very much for giving it to me."

An oval of applause broke out, and the President seemed to see that he had finally acquitted himself well enough. At once, the imperative cameramen moved forward and began to tell the President to look like an honored man: Closer to Gideonse and McAdoo! . . . Lift the plaque higher! . . . Head up, please, Mr. President! . . . Hold that! . . . Look this way! . . . Look that way! . . . Just one more!

When the photographing was over, knots formed, and the crowd broke up slowly. Several of the guests approached the President with cordial messages from mutual friends, and others offered him some thoughts on how to run the country. The President listened attentively to all, smiled, agreed, thanked, and seemed in no hurry (though in fact he must have known, so time-conscious is he, that he was already late for his next appointment). Finally, Connelly came in, and, with the effrontery and the gallantry of a Lord Nelson sweeping the sea of French and Spanish ships of the line, quickly threw everyone out.

There followed a half-hour fixed appointment with W. Stuart Symington, of the N.S.R.B., who discussed with the President the relative importance of various minerals and metals to the national security, talking particularly about the steps necessary to guarantee the continued importation of certain raw minerals from abroad. Symington also briefed the President on several matters that were to come up before a meeting of the National Security Council that afternoon. (The N.S.C., previously a fixed appointment for Thursdays, was that afternoon moved up one day, and from then on remained a Wednesday appointment.)

The President went to Blair House at one o'clock for lunch and a nap. He arrived back at his office a few minutes before three, and worked on papers. At three o'clock, his Executive Clerk, William J. Hopkins, brought in a fresh pile of documents to be signed, and for nearly fifteen minutes the President wrote his name, over and over.

Shortly after three, Republican Senator Wayne L. Morse, of Oregon, arrived in the anteroom, expecting to see the President at three-fifteen. Connelly pointed out to Morse that his appointment was not until Friday afternoon, but, since he was a United States senator, Connelly told him to hang around; he said he would squeeze him in soon.

At three-fifteen, the President received the Secretary of
the Interior, Oscar L. Chapman, who had requested an appointment a week before. Chapman outlined plans for new
legislation on submerged coastal lands — the socalled tide-
lands — in the light of Supreme Court decisions on the matter. The President, whom Chapman found amazingly well
informed on the subject, suggested a few changes in Chapman's proposed laws, and the Secretary said he would incor-
porate them into the drafts. Chapman then talked over with
the President the status and scope of the Echo Park power
development on the Colorado River. And, finally, he outlined some new Indian legislation his Department wanted to
get through Congress. Chapman talked overtime, and at
three-thirty-seven it was necessary for Connelly to open the
door and nod to the President across Chapman's back. Truman stood up and tactfully adjourned Chapman at the end
of his next paragraph.

The National Security Council was waiting for the President in the Cabinet Room. (Murphy's team, which had been
working on the Economic Message there, had been shifted,
in order to make room for the Security Council, into another large conference room, called the Fish Room because
of a small, bubbling aquarium in one corner of it.) The Security Council discussed with the President some top-secret
matters.

The Security Council adjourned at four-nine. Lawton, the
Budget Director, had come into Connelly's office at three-
fifty-five, asking to see the President on an urgent point
regarding the budget, and the President had a fixed appointment with William M. Boyle, Jr., the chairman of the
Democratic National Committee, at four o'clock. Out of
inter-party courtesy, however, both Boyle and Lawton now
deferred to the premature Republican senator from
Oregon. The President listened to a report from Morse on
the findings of a Senate subcommittee on Alaska, which
were soon to be made public; an outline of a difference
Morse had with the Civil Aeronautics Board in connection
with airlines to Alaska; certain suggestions by Morse for Republican appointments to defense posts; and a protest

against the overlooking of Oregon as a site for regional offices of federal defense agencies. The President took notes on all of Morse's points and promised decisions on them.

At four-twenty-five, Morse gave way to Boyle, who had been busy in recent days on Capitol Hill and now had for the President's private ear a compendium of political recommendations from Democratic senators and congressmen. The President also talked over with Boyle some general Democratic Party policies.

At five-two, Boyle retired and Lawton came in. Lawton's business, one final set of changes in the Budget Message, took only nine minutes.

Next, Hopkins brought in a fresh fall of the never-ending downpour of documents to be signed, and the President worked on them, and on other papers, until five-twenty-three, when he stuffed his briefcase full of unfinished work — including an entirely new draft of the Economic Message, which Murphy's team had sent in. He put on his hat and coat, stepped out to the anteroom to say good evening to Connelly and Miss Barrows, and went to Blair House. There he settled down at once to work on the new draft of the Economic Message. At five-forty-five, he called Snyder, to ask him to have supper with him and talk over the new version of the message. At exactly six, he called Mrs. Truman and Margaret in New York. Snyder showed up a few minutes before seven. The President and his old friend had two Old-Fashioneds each, had their supper, and then discussed the Economic Message until nine o'clock, when Snyder left. At nine-five, the President telephoned Clark M. Clifford, his former Special Counsel and message-drafter, who had retired to practice law, and talked over some aspects of the message with him. Then the President called the Secret Service, to arrange to have his walk and swim the next morning. After that, he sat in his study and worked over the message until a few minutes before twelve. He went to bed at midnight and put himself to sleep by rereading a couple of sections of the budget.

7. POSTSCRIPT

Partly because of the sharp duality in Truman that I have mentioned in the foreword, his evident feeling that he was distinctly Harry Truman *and* the President of the United States, I wanted to fill out the pictures given in this series with one more glimpse of him on the private side: a quiet evening in Blair House with the President in the company of none but Mrs. Truman, Margaret, and perhaps one close friend, like John Vinson. Twice dates were set for such an evening; twice they were cancelled, and twice I suspected that Bess Truman had put her foot down.

On the last Monday morning in February I received, for a third time, a terse message: Be at the Blair House at 8 p.m. on Wednesday, February 28.

This time there was no cancellation. I arrived punctually, rang, and was ushered straight through to the rear of the house into what seemed to be the dining room; it contained a large oval table covered by a green cloth. There were several men in the room. The President was not among them. No sign of Bess or Margaret. This was not what I had had in mind. A poker game? I knew that the President frequently joined a few friends in what he called "a study in probabilities," and that his poker, like his politics, had a component of compassion in it: two or three chips were withdrawn from each pot and were put in a pile called "the cat," and when any player went broke he could "pull the cat's tail" for a free stake to keep him in the game. That would suit me. But no, this table was far too big for poker.

Charles Murphy, the President's Counsel, came across the room, greeted me, and told me that I had been invited, on this evening, with a few others, to give the President some advice. The discussion was to be off the record; I should take no notes. (The issue, so much in the air during the months of the Watergate hearings in 1973, of the accuracy of men's memories of distant events certainly hangs over this account of mine of an evening more than two decades ago, of which I have no written record. I can only say, first, that this was the only meeting of the kind I ever attended, and second, that one passage in the discussion — the point of this recollection — so moved me that I have never been able to forget it. Of course I cannot remember the exact words that were used, but I do remember vividly certain of the President's gestures and certain images he threw up before our eyes.)

Soon the invited guests were all present: J. Howard Mc-Grath, the Attorney General; Senators Clinton Anderson, Mike Monroney, Thomas C. Hennings, Jr., and John J. Sparkman; Congressman Brent Spence; Philip B. Perlman, the Solicitor General; William M. Boyle, Jr., the Chairman of the Democratic National Committee; Clark Clifford, the President's previous Counsel; Murphy, and I. We seated ourselves around the table. I sat at one end of the oval; there was an empty seat at the middle of one side, to my right.

Mr. Truman entered, took the waiting chair, and said, without a sentence of introductory small talk, that he wanted our thoughts on a matter that had been troubling him for quite a while: What antidote should the President use against the poison of Senator Joseph McCarthy?

Mr. Truman delivered a pithy and bitter summary of Mc-Carthy's methods — his hectoring and innuendo, his horrors and his dirty tricks, his unsubstantiated accusations, his Big Lie, his bully's delight in the ruin of innocents, and, more specifically, his slander of what he kept calling "the Democrat Party" and his indiscriminate charges of Communism and homosexuality in the State Department. All this was tearing the government apart and undermining the moral fiber of the nation. What could the President do?

At some point in the discussion that followed, one of those present proposed that McCarthyism might be done in, once and for all, by a stroke of McCarthyism. I am quite sure I remember which one offered, and which others seconded, this proposal, but because of its nature and because I might be mistaken, I think I should keep my attributions to myself;

but it is important to say that the suggestion did not come from the Justice Department.

Concretely, the first man said, through one means and another a thick and devastating dossier had been assembled over a number of years, detailing, complete with dates, the hotel rooms in which Joseph McCarthy had stayed and the names of the Senator's bedmates in all those rooms. The list was practically guaranteed to blow Senator McCarthy's whole show sky high.

Truman listened to this presentation and to some supporting statements.

Then the flat of his hand came sharply down on the table. His third-person self spoke in outrage; the President wanted no more such talk.

Three pungent comments of Harry Truman's on the proposal that had just been made have stuck in my mind ever since. This was their gist:

You must not ask the President of the United States to get down in the gutter with a guttersnipe.

Nobody, not even the President of the United States, can approach too close to a skunk, in skunk territory, and expect to get anything out of it except a bad smell.

If you think somebody is telling a big lie about you, the only way to answer is with the whole truth. . . .

I cannot remember much about the rest of the evening, which was, for me, anti-climactic. The President certainly did not get any advice that was to be of much use to him in the coming months, and in the end it was McCarthy's own character, rather than anything Truman or anyone else did, that brought the Senator crashing down. The evening at that oval table was my last encounter with Harry Truman in office, and I was left at the end of my work with him with this burning memory — unable to write about it — of his indignation, both at the vicious methods of McCarthy and at the idea that some of his trusted friends would wish to splatter mud on the man who lived in him, the President of the United States.

GERALD R. FORD

FOREWORD

At his swearing-in as President, in the East Room of the White House shortly after noon on August 9, 1974, Gerald Ford said, "I believe that truth is the glue that holds government together, not only our government but civilization itself. . . . In all my public and private acts as your President, I expect to follow my instincts of openness and candor with full confidence that honesty is always the best policy in the end. My fellow Americans, our long national nightmare is over. Our Constitution works; our great Republic is a government of laws and not of men. . . ." And introducing his first Press Secretary, Jerald terHorst, to the White House reporters less than an hour later, the new President repeated his promise: "We will have an open, we will have a candid administration. . . ."

After what had seemed the interminable agony of Richard Nixon's dissembling and withholding and tampering with the truth, Ford's declaration of intent to offer the nation an open administration was received with universal relief and hope. The very next day, the *New York Times*'s Assistant Sunday Editor, Jack Rosenthal, a former Washington reporter, called his old friend terHorst to test this intent. He pointed out that Mr. Ford, the first unelected President of the United States, not having endured the gruelling exposure of an electoral campaign, was little known to the public, and he asked terHorst to see whether the President would allow a writer extensive access to him over a period of days, for the gathering of material for a large portrait. TerHorst, while encouraging Rosenthal, asked for a bit of time for the new administration to settle into stride.

The administration's shakedown — and the national euphoria — lasted exactly a month. On September 8 came the Nixon pardon. It had been arranged in secret, with no consultation outside the White House, and with no preparation of the public mind, and the American people's elated sense of new beginnings came tumbling down — and, with it, some part of their confidence in Mr. Ford's "instincts of openness and candor." And on that day Jerald terHorst resigned in protest.

Shortly afterward, Rosenthal renewed his inquiry with the new Press Secretary, Ronald Nessen. It was December before the two men met. Having consulted with the President, Nessen then agreed in principle to the *Times*'s proposal; he stipulated, however, that once the *Times* had assigned a writer, the President would have to meet him for "a sizing-up session" before the granting of final approval and before agreement on exact ground rules for the project.

On February 7, 1975, having been nominated for the assignment by the *Times,* I met with Mr. Ford and asked if I might follow him closely through a working week, and he replied at once that I might. When he asked what sorts of meetings I would like to sit in on, I said, "All of them. Everything." He saw no difficulty in that, he said; then he did quickly specify one exclusion: "my daily meetings with Henry."

We agreed that it would be best to make an arbitrary choice of a week at random, and to take our chances on whatever might happen during it, rather than to try a pick a week in which "special" occurrences might be foreseen; the events of the week would not in any case be news but only the backdrop against which the President's ways of being and doing would be displayed. Neither the President nor his Press Secretary asked to review any part of what I might. write.

The week of my visit, in the event, was the one beginning Monday, March 10, 1975. It was a week during which the principal focus of interest was on southeast Asia: the insurgent forces in Cambodia were closing in on Phnom Penh, and the North Vietnamese and Vietcong had just launched what was to prove to be the last offensive of the Vietnam war. Dr. Kissinger was away in the Middle East, and I saw less of Mrs. Ford during the week than I had hoped, because she was in bed with an episode of the neck pain from which she had periodically suffered in recent years; otherwise, the week could probably have been described as more or less typical for the President.

In order to have an exact record of the President's words, I taped two conversations with him, at breakfast on Thursday morning and after dinner on Friday evening in the residential part of the White House; I relied on my own notes to record all the other events of the week. I was fearful that my mere presence might distort the discussions in the Oval Office, just as a known electronic bug might; but after the first day or so I felt I had been absorbed into the furniture. Sometimes the President would explain my presence to strangers. More often I think I was taken for a staffer whose job it apparently was to keep scribbling madly in an effort to record all Oval Office translations, now that the infamous tapes were no longer being made.

I plunged into the Ford week with no such preparation as I had had for the sessions with Truman. I knew little more about Gerald Ford than did the rest of the public, and the days of the week became segments of a long worm of discovery. Under the gun of a newspaper deadline, I wrote my account flat out, on the mental run. Now, at this distance, some more leisurely walking thoughts about President Ford's Presidency, against the background of President Truman's, have had time to amble forth.

Both these men were successor Presidents, up from the Vice Presidency; each was an inheritor, each more or less comfortable with the psychic estate that was left to him. But how different the legacies — Franklin Roosevelt's and Richard Nixon's! Gerald Ford hoped from the first to restore public confidence in the Presidency after the Nixon debacle, but he evidently lacked the imagination to realize how deeply his pardon of Nixon would stain him with the color of the legacy. Part of what I saw of him, seven months after his succession and half a year after the pardon, was right in the Nixon groove, and obviously quite at home in it. He seemed to revel, for example, in all the appalling trivia — Barbra Streisand, Bob Hope, Bella Abzug's hat; and Miss

America and the Cotton Maid, who seemed to be given almost equal time, if not equal value, with Cambodia and Vietnam.

But Ford was quite unlike Nixon, just as Truman had been most unlike Roosevelt. There could be no doubt of Ford's man-to-man decency. He had an inner stability his predecessor lacked. Nixon's Quakerism was made of papier-maché; Ford at least tried to practice his Christianity, within his lights. Unlike Nixon, he had a cheerful and agreeable nature. But thinking of Truman's cocky decency, which seemed in the end more important than his limitations, whereas Ford's stumbling lingers in our minds, what were the differences — and did the working out of the differences offer any insights into the long flow of the Presidency of the United States?

There was a sharpness about Harry Truman's decency; it had a moral edge, well stropped on his hard tongue. Gerald Ford's was more accomodating; his speech of accession promised an era of "communication, conciliation, compromise, and cooperation" with a Congress dominated by the opposing party. (Compare Truman's testy "that do-nothing Eightieth Congress.") "I would rather wait and get your recommendations," he would say to a staffer. Again: "I would be very hesitant to say . . ." Again: "Why don't you think it through and come up with a plan?" Harry Truman's failings, by contrast, were aggressive ones — snap judgments and hasty and over-positive replies. By the fifth day of my week with President Ford I was moved to write: "He yielded, but only to a certain point; beyond that point he tranquillized." His was a "glacial caution." Calm and healthy and relaxed as Ford appeared to be, one got the impression in the end that his was a passive Presidency. It was almost as if he were letting decisions happen to him.

An essential element of an active Presidency is a strong sense, on the part of the incumbent, of history. To know what he thinks, and to act on the thought, a President must have a firm share in the communal memory. Truman had cultivated that in himself. The reach of Gerald Ford's historic memory was short indeed; back beyond the year 1949, when he entered Congress, it seemed to fall into a black hole. It has been thought that a major drawback of the first years of Jimmy Carter's Presidency was his unfamiliarity with Presidential-Congressional give-and-take, but the Presidency may also suffer when an incumbent remembers of history *nothing but* the refinement of those transactions. The limited historic data bank in President Ford's memory made him think of each day's dealings with The Hill as almost the whole of "how it works," and when on a given day he lost a round he seemed totally unperturbed, "as if nothing really had been lost — suggesting that nothing would have been gained, either, if he had won." Such a degree of cool sophistication in what is itself a historic process, though only a part of the whole, could bring one dangerously close to not caring what history would think of the whole. Indifference is surely at the core of passivity. By such a measure, Carter's Presidency appears to have been relatively active; Truman's certainly was.

Truman's reading of history gave him a sense of the identification of the Presidency with the electorate. When Truman used the pronoun "we" in press conferences — "We will take whatever steps are necessary" — he did not seem to be using the royal we, nor quite to be referring to the two people he hosted in his own clothes, himself and Mr. President; rather, he seemed to mean the entire government by, for, and of all the people of the United States. Ford inherited Nixon's awful imperial "I" (which seems to have clung also, alas, to Carter). Ford had no *Doppelgänger* in him, no "other" Presidential persona to share the housing of the body with the self; he was thoroughly integrated, he was at ease with his single self, *he* was the President. But that ease, floating in a vacuum of history, led to what struck me so forcibly by the Friday of the week with him: his alienation from the vast run of the citizenry.

I believe that Gerald Ford really wanted to be open with me, as with the public in general. His one restriction, however, denying me (and the public) access to all foreign policy discussion, betrayed the entire intention. In this too, he was obviously passive, for the obsession with secrecy, explicitly with respect to Cambodia, the official lying to cover up actions there, the contempt for history's proofs that the only strong foreign policy is one based on public understanding — these had been the massive and disastrous foibles of Henry Kissinger; Ford allowed them. And lost all chance, in the end, that his own "instincts of openness and candor" would win out.

8. MONDAY

A Stubborn Calm at the Center

Donald Rumsfeld, with a sheaf of papers under his arm, opened the staff door to the Oval Office and nodded over his shoulder to me to follow him, and we walked in. The President, seated behind his desk, greeted us; first names came easily to him, and because he and I had met before, he used mine.

It was 8:33. Monday morning. A rainy day.

Rumsfeld pulled a chair up to a corner of the desk and put the papers down. I sat against the curving east wall of the room, in a straight cane-backed chair. The President, holding a pipe to his mouth with his left hand, tipped a butane lighter into it and puffed up a cloud.

The Assistant to the President began talking and passing papers across the desk. A Navy steward in a red coat served coffee. I was too discomposed at first to be able to follow what was being said. I was conscious of the arching energy, on a table just to my left, of Frederic Remington's sculpture *Bronco Buster,* a cowboy bending to the rise of a violent caracole, the dark bronze horse under him seeming to explode with ferocity and joy. Not quite so sharply to my left was the utterly still figure beyond the desk, dark-suited, contained, reading some document his aide had handed him, pale drifting smoke the only motion there.

The President had given me permission to take a kind of voyage with him — to watch him closely through a working week. I had a unique opportunity, and at that moment its prospect staggered me. By the time the week was over, I would have been given access to a President of the United States of a sort no journalist had ever had. It was already clear that Mr. Ford was going to be even more accessible than was Harry Truman when, a quarter of a century ago, he allowed me a somewhat similar privilege. I would in fact

be doing something that less than a handful of Mr. Ford's
own staff of 533 had done: I would be with him, most of the
time, hour in and hour out, through the whole week's range
of his backbreaking routine.

I sat there trying to get my bearings. Charles Willson
Peale's foxy and sexy old Ben Franklin was squinting discon-
certingly at me from across the room through mod-looking
spectacles. Over the mantel one of Peale's seven Washing-
tons, this portrait full-length, the face austere and disap-
proving, looked past me and straight at his distant successor,
as if wondering, wondering. I was curious about the days
ahead. I wanted to know what I suppose every citizen
wanted to know. Our country had been through agonies of
failed leadership. Were we in the hands of steady men now?
What was the quality of this quiet person murmuring to his
aide? What was his style, and what secrets, if any, did it en-
code — or was all of him right out there on the surface?
How did he make decisions? Was he bright enough? How
stubborn was he? Was he at all flexible? Was the office
changing him? Had he been able to lift his vision from the
boundaries of the Fifth Congressional District of Michigan
to the full sweep from Maine to Hawaii where the electorate
lived that had had no chance to choose him?

The figure behind the desk was drenched in the dazzling
artificial light of this room. A dark pin-stripe suit, the lapels
just the right width for that year; a tie slashed with bold di-
agonal stripes. I searched the face, now tilting up from reading. There was a slight tuck on the lower right cheek, not
matched on the left. Higher on the left cheek were three
barely visible bumps, suddenly folded now into the creases
of a smile. Which faded quickly. At the foot of the long slope
of the bald forehead there were stark, slashing horizontal
lines of the skinfold over the deepset sixty-one-year-old eyes
that needed no glasses for reading, and beneath, two darkish
puffy semicircles. The eyes sought Rumsfeld's. The strong
impression I got was of total relaxation: the hand guided the
pipe as if the pipe were free of gravity.

Rumsfeld was explaining something. His hands, held out
before him on a plane parallel to the desk top, chopped

sharply thumb to thumb, then cut away from each other, the fingers fanning. Ford listened, puffed, said, "Let's get them in here and talk about it."

9:05 A.M. Jack Marsh was in the chair where Rumsfeld had sat. "You saw the letter," the Counselor asked, "from thirty-seven Democrat freshmen opposing any further aid to Cambodia?"

"I read about it this morning."

The pipe was clamped in the right side of the mouth. The face gave no message.

"Here's a letter from fifteen Senators" — Marsh reached it forward; said it proposed a candidate for Under Secretary of Transportation; summarized the man's record; made it clear that he had been a good political soldier.

"Give it to Bill Walker, Jack."

Beyond the Presidential desk from where I sat, a head of Harry Truman thrust its feisty challenge into the room. The bronze face looked pleased, as if saying: Who'd have thought I'd be one of three past Presidents represented here?

The third was Abraham Lincoln, who stood, slender and brooding, on a pedestal on the east side of the room, to my right. Ford had chosen this company of three: Washington, Lincoln, Truman. Mrs. Ford had found the Truman head abandoned in the White House warehouse.

9:18 A.M. Rumsfeld, Marsh, Hartmann, Nessen, and Friedersdorf entered for the daily session preparing Ron Nessen for his briefing of the press. Ever since Watergate days, reporters' questions in these briefings had been searching, prolonged, often fierce — the sum of all the questions having been: Does a President ever tell the truth?

As the men drew chairs around the desk, the President rose — what a big man he was! — stepped to a table behind him, picked up four brand-new pipes, still in their store packages, and tossed one to each of the pipe smokers, Hartmann, Marsh, Rumsfeld, and Nessen, who had just switched from cigarettes. "Someone gave me these. I don't much care for that type of pipe," he said. Bright-colored pipes with meerschaum or plastic bowls and elaborate cooling stems. Marsh and Rumsfeld, knowing each other's color preferences, made a swap. The steward was passing coffee again. The President, who had drunk tea at breakfast, now took his second cup of coffee.

NESSEN (*glasses parked on top of his head*): On Cambodia. I think I'll be getting flak from some things Humphrey said on "Face the Nation" yesterday — that aid wouldn't help the situation even if it got there. Hubert said he'd seen some C.I.A. cables that came to the same conclusion.

The Plexiglas-covered globe of the earth beyond the President's desk suddenly seemed to jump up into full scale. Cambodia. I was all ears. The President, who had in recent days seemed to be completely out of touch with the mood of the country on the everlasting suffering of the Asian wars, was in a tight struggle with Congress — yet again — over emergency funds for both Vietnam and Cambodia. I could imagine Truman's explosion if he had been crossed on a conviction of his in this way by an old friend. No — Ford's tone, when he spoke, was exactly the tone he used when he was talking earlier about a prospective Under Secretary of Transportation: his utterance was slow; he paused long at his mental commas; he almost never said "uh"; he spoke as if he meant just those words and no other words would do.

FORD: What I've said was that if no aid was sent, it would be inevitable that the Government would fall; if it was sent, there'd be a fifty-fifty chance of survival till the rainy season, or roughly that.

RUMSFELD: In the senior staff meeting, Brent Scowcroft said he knows what Humphrey saw, and it did not say that even if aid were sent the Government would fall. But I cautioned Ron about being too blunt here. There are bound to have been differing interpretations.

FORD: I agree. Point One (*he raises a straight right forefinger*), whatever Hubert saw, there could have been a phrase or a sentence that could have led him honestly to believe what he was saying, and Point Two (*his right hand comes up again, the forefinger and middle finger raised but bent; the hand is loose*), we don't know for sure everybody Hubert saw, or for that matter exactly what cables he saw.

HARTMANN: We do know that the public believes the President gets all the information and others only partial information. Don't call Hubert a liar. Say something like, "The President's best judgment is . . ."

MARSH: It's significant that he did tip his hat to you for supplying more information than in the past.

FORD (*leaning back in his shiny black leather swivel chair*): We made a conscious decision that Henry would go before Congress, or maybe a subcommittee, and give as much information as possible. That led Sparkman to come to his conclusion, which was to support the whole package, and it led Clifford Case to support substantially the whole package. Even in that group, though, who got a lot of facts, you have differences of opinion.

RUMSFELD: Ron, use Bob's point that we have all the information, and various people using the same information can come to different conclusions.

NESSEN: Then I'll say, based on the facts you have, Mr. President, you've concluded that there's a fifty-fifty chance of the Government's being able to carry on till the rainy season if aid is sent —

FORD (*holding up an arresting hand*): — in time. Ten days or two weeks.

NESSEN: What do I say to questions about their dickering for a lower figure?

FORD: In our discussions they suggest a lower figure. We believe our figure is right. They have the authority to set the figure. Henry made the point to the group that we want no part of giving too little. Better an adequate figure and an honest effort than too little.

MARSH: Wasn't it Churchill: "Too little and too late"?

HARTMANN: The Sudeten Plan. It was when Hitler . . .

9:50 A.M. The Nessen group departed.

Behind the President's big black seat at the desk, between it and the tall south windows, stood a wide table, on which, backed by two delicate silver Argand lamps designed for

tubular wicks that once burned whale oil but were now
equipped with tiny, flame-shaped electric bulbs bravely glim-
mering in a sea of light, there were color photographs of
Betty Ford; of all the Ford children at their father's
swearing-in, with Jack in the foreground; of Mike and his
wife, Gayle; of Steve and his bright jeep; of Susan and her
cat, Shan; and of the family's golden retriever, Liberty, on
the White House lawn. Papers that the President must read,
most of them in separate blue folders, were stacked in front
of these pictures on the table, and Mr. Ford swiveled now to
pick up the pile and lift it to his desk.

He took a fresh pipe from the top right-hand drawer of
his desk, packed it and lighted it. The steward came in to
remove cups and rearrange chairs. The President read a
personal communication from Secretary of State Kissinger,
who was away, in the Middle East, and a long briefing paper
for a meeting the President was to have before lunch with
Dr. Arthur Burns, Chairman of the Federal Reserve Board.

After a time, Mr. Ford rang for Terry O'Donnell, the
keeper of the staff door, and asked him to have some photographs delivered to Mrs. Ford, for her to autograph for
friends. Later O'Donnell came in with some commissions to
sign, among them the certificates of appointment of Carla
Hills, the new Secretary of Housing and Urban Development, who was to be sworn in at noon that day, and of John
Dunlop, the new Secretary of Labor, who was to be installed
the next week.

The President began reading again.

I felt that, no matter how still I sat, I was a distraction, and
I left the Oval Office.

I listened to Ron Nessen's briefing on a monitor in his office. It turned out that after all the time spent with the President on Hubert Humphrey and Cambodia, there was not a
single question from reporters on the war. Instead there was
a ferocious grilling that started with a question whether the
President had been informed at any time by William E.
Colby, Director of the Central Intelligence Agency, or by
any other C.I.A. official, "that the late Senator Robert Kennedy had told two associates that he had vetoed or been able

to veto a plan — this question takes a long time to ask because it is a complicated thing — the C.I.A. plan to contract with the Mafia to assassinate Prime Minister Castro."

NESSEN (*after a pause for thought*): I am not going to say anything about that, Jim.

Q: Will we ever find out anything about that, or the previous story about the C.I.A. assassination allegations which were asked about last week; that is, is the White House ever going to have anything to say about those stories?

NESSEN: Right now, I am not going to say anything about it, Walt.

Q: Last week you said a number of things. Why are you not going to say anything about it?

NESSEN: I can't.

All during the press conference, reporters kept coming back and back to this subject, and fourteen more times Nessen said, in one phrasing or another, "I am just not going to talk about that."

11:51 A.M. During the meeting with the Nessen group, the President had asked to see "the latest go-round on the Carla Hills thing," and now Bob Hartmann, who was in charge of speechwriters, and Bob Orben, one of them, brought in the final draft of the President's remarks for the swearing-in.

It suddenly seemed that Cambodia and the C.I.A. might as well be on the moon.

"I thought I might have a little fun with Carla to disavow my male chauvinism," the President said.

"You have to be careful there, Mr. President," Orben said. "That's suddenly a *verboten* area. In no part of the speech do we refer to her as a woman."

"Betty's been out in front on this Equal Rights Amendment business, and I'd like to get something in. Can't we do something with the budget side of it? You know, like a household budget. Let's see." He looked at the text. "The budget gives her a lot more than was given to Jim Lynn" — her male predecessor, still in the Cabinet as Director of the Office of Management and Budget. "That doesn't sound like male chauvinism to me. Why don't you fool around with that?"

12:07 P.M. He stood at a lectern on a podium in the East Room of the residence, alongside Secretary-Designate Hills and flanked by her husband, her children dressed to the nines, the Vice President and a ceremonial delegation of senators and Congressmen. The room was murmurous with standing guests. Television lights were on. The President placed his speech on the lectern and a respectful silence fell.

"I am in very good company," he started out, "welcoming Carla into the Cabinet as Secretary of Housing and Urban Development. Carla; Mr. Justice White, who is about to administer the oath; HUD Under Secretary Jim Mitchell; and I are all graduates of Yale Law School.

"Maybe I better not say that too loudly. I can imagine a dozen other prospects starting to practice the 'Whiffenpoof Song.' (*Half-hearted laughter*) . . ."

This voice was different from the relaxed one I had been hearing all morning. Of course, it was amplified; perhaps the amplifier had wooden parts. I had heard that Gerald Ford loved to make speeches. That he loved to sit for hours at luncheons eating bad food and listening to worse speeches than his own. That for years he had been flying here and there across the country carrying the Republican word. Recently he had hired a former producer for CBS News, Robert Mead, to give him pointers, and Mead had been trying to help the President loosen up. He had urged speechwriters to provide texts early, so the President could read them out loud several times to get his mouth comfortably around the written words. "It's hard to vocal some of those long sentences," Mr. Mead said. He had been trying to stamp out some of Mr. Ford's Grand Rapids pronunciations: "guahrantee," "judgament." But Gerald Ford had very likely uttered five million words in speeches on and off the floor of the House, and as Vice President and President, and he was, I was beginning to see, a man of intransigent habits. Right now, introducing Carla Hills, he was his old speaking self. Besides, his arms and hands, which all morning had been glid-

ing as gracefully as the smoke that played games around
them, had gone rubbery — though it must at least be said
that his gestures, unlike Mr. Nixon's, had some connection
with what he was saying.

Now he praised Mrs. Hills, referred to the Housing and
Community Development Act of 1974, and said, "One of
Carla's major jobs will be to implement this massive and, I
believe, progressive program. Incidentally, Carla's budget
for fiscal 1976 will be $7.1 billion. That is $1.6 billion more
than was given to her predecessor, Jim Lynn. Now if that
does not dispose of male chauvinism, nothing will." (*A pretty
good laugh.*)

12:19 P.M. The President walked from the East Room along
the brilliant red carpet of the cross hall, past the flags, past
the aggressive Houdon bust of Joel Barlow, under the twinkling Adam chandeliers, past the proud Hoban columns like
marble guardsmen — beyond whose picket line crimson-
coated musicians of the United States Marine Band, their vi-
olins soaring to salute the chief, were playing from the score
of a moving picture called *Villa Rides* — past black ushers,
past uniformed aides, past Secret Service operatives with
radio wires dribbling down from their right ears under their
jacket collars, past notables and bureaucrats and toadies,
breasting all the pomp with his brisk stride, which was loose-
haunched and shoulder-floating, like that of a fettlesome
quarterhorse.

In the State Dining Room he received guests beside his
new HUD Secretary, and he chatted without haste with
those who pushed their faces close to his.

12:36 P.M. He was back in the Oval Office, at his desk, his
chin resting on his left hand. Dr. Arthur Burns, Chairman
of the Federal Reserve Board, whose gray hair seemed not
to be receding but actually to be advancing down his forehead, leaned over the end of the desk to the President's
right, shuffling papers. David Kennerly, the President's personal photographer, who was bearded and brassy, and who
well knew that the most abashing eye on earth to men of
power is the camera's winking lens, came in to snap some

shots. Kennerly, or one of his four assistants, made a record of every appointment the President had, except for those with his closest staff. Perhaps these were "for history" in lieu of the Nixon tapes. Mr. Ford pleased many of his visitors by seeing that they received photographs, later, of themselves in easy intimacy with the President of the United States.

The President had a number of questions he wanted to ask: How soon would there be signs of economic recovery, and how strong would it be? Was the money supply going to continue to rise? Fast enough to promote recovery? Not so fast as to reignite inflation? Inflation was slowing down — was this a permanent reduction or was there still an underlying problem of inflation that would reappear when the economy began to turn around? What would be the effects of larger-than-budgeted Federal deficits?

Dr. Burns, in a quiet, rather high-pitched voice, gave the President a thorough explanation of monetary and economic trends; the meeting, scheduled for thirty minutes, lasted sixty-five. Dr. Burns had brought several charts; on some of them there were encouraging signs.

1:41 P.M. Enter, breathlessly, Miss Shirley Cothran, of Denton, Texas, Miss America of 1975, who had had to cool her nifty heels for forty minutes while the President and Dr. Burns were having their *tête-à-tête*. Miss America was accompanied by Doris Kelly, a young lady who was described as her chaperone; by her Congressman, Ray Roberts; and by Major Joseph A. Bradway of Atlantic City, where she had been crowned.

The President, apparently bucked up by what he had heard about money, now seemed to have no difficulty whatsoever wrenching his attention away from the economy.

FORD: Nice to meet you, Shirley.

MISS AMERICA (*memorization straining every sweet muscle of her face*): I have presents here, sir, for you, and also one for Mrs. Ford.

FORD: My wife and I watch the Miss America contest all the time. We really enjoy that on TV.

MISS AMERICA: I sure hope you saw it this year. That was the best year.

FORD: It sure was!

ROBERTS: My most famous constituent, Mr. President, and, I may say, my most beautiful one.

FORD: I thought all the girls down there in Texas looked like this, Ray.

Now came a stampede of pool photographers with still and motion-picture and TV cameras, and with hooded lights on long wires. The President and his little party were herded toward the east side of the room. David Kennerly, who had grown familiar with his boss, said, "Would you mind putting her in the middle, please?" "Not 'her,' David," the President said. "Her name is Shirley. Where are your manners?"

Miss America ran off to the side to put down her purse, which might not look nice in the photos. While cameras clicked, the President, taking advantage of a briefing, which had informed him that Shirley had studied at North Texas State University and planned to be an elementary-school guidance counselor, was chatting with her in a low voice. "How long will that take? . . . That's wonderful. . . . Fine new buildings you have there. . . ."

"Thirty seconds, please," Assistant Press Secretary Bill Roberts called out to the photographers. Then: "Lights, please. Thank you." And out went the pool.

MISS AMERICA (*in haste, sensing that she herself is being eased toward the door*): As I travel around, people ask me about all kinds of things, Mr. President, and I'm only twenty-two years old, but I really can say that I support you in every single thing you do.

FORD: I really appreciate that, Shirley. Going back to school next fall?

MISS AMERICA: In January.

FORD: I'm certain that after a hard year it will be welcome.

MISS AMERICA: Sure hope you have a chance to visit North Texas State again, sir.

FORD: Real nice to see you, Shirley. Congratulations and good luck.

Miss America looked flustered and puzzled. The President realized why, before anyone else in the room did, possibly even before Miss America herself. "Hey," he said. "Better not leave your purse, Shirley. We've got some real bad characters around here."

1:45 P.M. The President had fifteen minutes for lunch before the next scheduled appointment. He ducked into a small private room off the Oval Office that Betty Ford had been fixing up for him as a kind of hideaway.

I retired to the staff anteroom. So far I had had a sense of rushing after the President from one isolated fragment of administration or ceremony or politics or planning to another and another. I realized that I was still slightly agog, and that I had suddenly cut across the grain into a continuous timber of the Presidential process. But I wondered: When was policy made? When was thinking done? How had I missed scenes of the tense struggle over Cambodian funds? I had seen so many new faces; perhaps in time I could sort them out. I felt hurried. But here in the anteroom Terry O'Donnell, the young man who juggled people and papers in and out of the Oval Office, and Nell Yates, who kept the logs and assisted O'Donnell, were calm. Come to think of it, everyone I had seen that day had been calm. And the center of the calm, its essence and source, had obviously been the President. With Truman, it was all nervous energy, moral intensity, emotion in harness, history clamoring for expression. Here the strongest impression, so far, was of relaxation.

1:55 P.M. The President, it turned out, had taken only ten minutes to eat. He called me in and told me that it would not be appropriate for me to sit in on the next meeting, which was to be in the Cabinet Room. "This isn't really my party," he said. "The Chief Justice asked if he could come in to see me, and we've got the leaders of Congress, too. This is a historic get-together. I don't know as there's ever been a summit meeting of all three branches of Government in the White House like this in recent times — certainly not in my memory since I became Minority Leader." He motioned me to a seat. "Let me tell you about the meeting."

I was impressed in those few minutes by the President's courtesy and trust; with one or two exceptions, members of his staff had been far more cautious or manipulative than he in dealing with me.

"We have a tough decision," he said. "There hasn't been increased compensation for the Judiciary since '69 and there has been a 44.5-percent increase in the cost of living since then. This is particularly serious in the court system, because most real fine lawyers get more than the $40,000 District judges get, or the $42,000 that Appeals Court judges get, or even the $60,000 that Supreme Court Justices get, or the $62,500 the Chief Justice gets. The Chief Justice thinks the courts aren't getting, or else they're losing, their best judges on account of this. We have the same problem in the Executive Branch, where the ceiling is $36,000. We're losing top people both in the military and the State Department. Congress is having similar problems. The Chief Justice strongly feels that Congress ought to separate out the Judiciary from Congress and the Executive, but I doubt if this will be possible. The political environment is not right for increases. Congress isn't in the mood for them. I myself have suggested a 5-percent one-year cap on all Government increases. Under the present system the cost-of-living increase would amount to something like 9 percent. If you coordinate that with 5-percent increases in all three branches, the first-year cost would be $1,159,400 for the Congress, $1,039,250 for the Judiciary, $1,496,725 for the Executive, and — l was astonished at this — $27,450,000 for the military. An arrangement like this wouldn't catch the Judiciary up, but it would give some relief and then keep them current. I don't know. We're going to have to work something out to keep our best people in Government."

2:01 P.M. He took me into the Cabinet Room for the opening moments of the meeting, when the pool cameramen would in any case be present.

Chief Justice Warren Burger, Speaker of the House Carl Albert, Senate Majority Leader Mike Mansfield, Senate Minority Leader Hugh Scott, House Minority Leader John

Rhodes were waiting for Mr. Ford. The warmth of the greetings was abounding. Cambodia, energy, taxes — all quarrels seemed to be forgotten.

FORD: All three branches —
A SENATOR: A three-ring circus.
BURGER (*seeing the other two branches in such intimate embraces*): I feel as if I ought to be on the other side of the table.
FORD: In judgment?
BURGER: In the dock!

Re-entering the Oval Office alone, I felt its great force.

This room was an egg of light. I had seen that each person who came into it was lit up in two senses: bathed in brightness and a bit high. I had clearly seen each face, to the very pores, in a flood of indirect candlepower that rained down from a pure-white ceiling onto the curving off-white walls and a pale-yellow rug and bright furnishings in shades of gold, green, and salmon. But there were also dazzling parabolas of power here; authority seemed to be diffused as an aspect of the artificial light in the room, and each person who came into this heady glow seemed to be rendered ever so slightly tipsy in it and by it — people familiar with the room far less so, of course, than first-time visitors, some of whom visibly goggled and staggered and held on tight as they made their appeals; but even the old hands, even the President's closest friends, and even the President himself, sitting in a bundle of light behind the desk of the chief, semed to me to take on a barely perceptible extra shine in the ambiguous radiant energy that filled this room.

Gerald Ford wanted, and was entitled to, an Oval Office in his own style. His wife helped him achieve it. Only a few traces now remained of the Nixon Oval Office, with its ostentatious expense-account taste: the Peale Washington; a picture by an unknown artist of the mid-nineteenth century, called *The President's House;* the vulgar gold curtains behind the President's desk; the desk itself; and a few chairs. The vile bugs that had fed the tapes were gone; when President Ford learned that a device, though dead, was still embedded in the desk, he had it rooted out. Mrs. Ford, assisted by the tasteful Curator of the White House, Clement E. Conger, planned a thoroughgoing redecoration, and during the President's trip to Vladivostok the transformation was made.

Some exquisite pieces were brought into the room — a Massachusetts Hepplewhite-style chest of drawers, for instance, on which the Truman head now stood, with a serpentine front and fan inlay quadrants on the drawers; and a Federal card table made in Salem, Massachusetts, about 1810, whose top was supported by a large, carved, gilded, spread-winged eagle — the only known table of its kind in America. Most beautiful of all, to my mind, was a grandfather clock, designed by John and Thomas Seymour of Boston in the early nineteenth century, with fluted columns at the corners and beautiful satinwood inlays; its forceful ticking inexorably marked the moments of history — and of nonhistory — in this room of light.

And so the room now was elegant, but the President's own territory, on and around his desk, was simple, and was comfortable for him. Centered on the desk in front of him was a metal football, raised from a penholder base, with a plate inscribed SOUTH HIGH FOOTBALL CLUB. It was from the teammates with whom he still had occasional reunions. To his right, next to the desk, was a side table with shelves for smoking things. Next to that, on the floor, was the brown suitcase in which he carried papers back and forth to the residence each evening and on weekends. His whole family was on the table close behind him.

3:19 P.M. The President was back. Secretary of Health, Education and Welfare Caspar Weinberger and Rumsfeld entered.

The President and the Secretary had been to the same party the night before.

WEINBERGER: Thanks for last night. That was fun.

FORD: Barbra Streisand's a real good entertainer.

WEINBERGER: She is. I'd never known much about James Caan. . . .

The President, leaning back at ease in his big chair, and placing his hands together, fingertip to fingertip, praised the job that Cap, as he called the Secretary, had been doing in H.E.W., and asked him to stay on in the Cabinet.

FORD: Every President has to have his own Cabinet and his imprint on a Cabinet, but I never agreed with those demands for wholesale resignations in 1973.

WEINBERGER: That first Cabinet meeting after the '72 election was the most shocking thing I've ever been through. Such a contrast to your first meeting, Mr. President. There wasn't a person who'd been at that earlier meeting who wasn't impressed with the difference.

Secretary Weinberger thanked the President for the great honor of his invitation to stay. He said he was fifty-seven years old, and for seven years he had been away from "an income-production situation." His wife, he said, had had a great deal of discomfort from osteoarthritis and was anxious to get back to California. . . .

"I didn't know Jane was that adversely affected," the President said. "I'm sorry, Cap. Betty has something like that, I guess you know. She's been having some trouble again this week. She has this pinched nerve, you know — gives her a whole lot of discomfort. She has a great deal of fortitude, though. She bounces back."

After some further exchanges the Secretary again thanked the President for the great compliment, and said he would give an answer very soon.

3:48 P.M. The President received Bob Hartmann and three speechwriters, Theis, Friedman and Orben. Two speeches were in the works. One was to be a light affair at a dinner of the Radio and Television Correspondents Association. "It's a fun occasion," Orben said. "Nothing serious. They're going to have Charlie Byrd, a jazz musician, then Bob Hope for fifteen or twenty minutes; then you'll follow."

FORD (*with a laugh that is not altogether comfortable*): Why do I always have to be hooked up with Hope and these pros? (*Starts reading a preliminary draft. He again laughs: this is his infectious boomer. Then, after a pause*): What's this about Judge Crater? Who's Judge Crater?

ORBEN: That's a milking laugh after the big one —

HARTMANN: Judge Crater was a prominent judge of the thirties who disappeared, and —

FORD: Why don't we leave that one out? . . .

A serious speech was scheduled for Notre Dame the next week, and the President read several pages of a draft. Then he broke off.

FORD: The only problem I have with this — and maybe I misinterpret the attitudes of college students today — but I think they're moving away from the views of the last five years. I'm concerned about building rather than tearing apart. We don't want to repeat the mistakes of the sixties — or of the thirties. We want them to prepare themselves to avoid those mistakes. We need a subject that's meaningful — I'd think a foreign-policy topic. Not condemning the generation that ran things the last ten years, but looking back to the mistakes of the thirties and fifties.

THEIS: Father Hesburgh, who was a leader of the antiwar movement, strongly suggested we avoid Southeast Asia. The subject of hunger —

FORD: I'm not talking about Vietnam or Cambodia. I'm talking about a positive approach — that this generation of college students shouldn't fall into the trap of the college students of the thirties, of being oblivious to Europe's problems and those of the rest of the world.

HARTMANN: The timing's bad. Cambodia is going to be coming to a head, and anything you say is going to be read by the press as another plea for aid.

The President had put his feet up on his pipestand side table. Suggestions from the speechwriters began to swirl around him, but even I could see that an idea had lodged itself in his mind, and was there to stay.

"Higher education in the private sector . . ." "Office of liaison in the White House for higher education . . ." "College presidents . . ." "A quasi-governmental agency, where kids can buy tuition bonds . . ." "Going without dinners, eating rice in the dining halls . . ." "Notre Dame prides itself on bringing students from abroad . . ." "Peace between generations . . ."

The Presidential feet came down.

FORD: O.K. Let's think about the theme of staying involved in the world. You know, Kennedy made the Peace Corps proposal at Ann Arbor. I think the Peace Corps, with all its critics, has been a good program. The U.S. has had a great record of being humanitarian. The first foreign policy I voted for in Congress in 1945 was on the Marshall Plan — that was a great humanitarian one. If you go back to the post–World-War-II period — the Marshall Plan was nonmilitary. The best commencement speech I ever gave was at Mike's commencement at Wake Forest. I didn't want to lecture them but wanted them to be better than we had been. Disciplined freedom — here (*reaching for his brown suitcase*), I have it right here. *My* files are the only ones I trust. Here. (*He reads:*) "Of course, the young generation knows perfectly well that we senior citizens were never your age, that we were born on the threshold of senility, and that whatever we think we remember about our youth is inaccurate and irrelevant. . . ."

4:40 P.M. Rumsfeld, Marsh, and Counsel Buchen talked with the President on sensitive matters of personnel. I was not present.

6:05 P.M. I sat by while Rumsfeld went over a wide range of matters, many of which were ready for the President's initials. Mr. Ford wrote with his left hand, the hand curving above the writing. My thrilled agitation of the morning had given way to dazed exhaustion. I was still profoundly disturbed by what seemed to me the aimlessness of the speechwriting session — though I realized there would be another round on the Notre Dame speech, perhaps several more rounds. I kept thinking, however, of a speechwriting session of Harry Truman's, at which most of his principal advisers, including Dean Acheson, were present, and during which policy was really and carefully shaped through its articulation. But now Rumsfeld, with his endless vocabulary of hand signals — stabbings, long-fingered rounding out of abstractions, flat-handed layering of relationships, squarings off, chops, slaps, flicks, pinches, punches, piano playing and a bit of harp work — gave concise and brisk explanations of items he raised, and President Ford, in no hurry, made decisions as they were needed.

7:20 P.M. After eleven hours and forty-four minutes of work in the West Wing (this did not, of course, include reading done in the residence between 5:30 and 7:30 in the morning, nor reading to be done there later that evening), the President went "home."

9. TUESDAY

A Hard-edged Conservative Voice

7:40 A.M. The President, accompanied by two Secret Service men and a valet carrying the brown suitcase, arrived from the residence. He was dressed in a flashy suit of bold vertical stripes of shades of gray; he looked a bit drawn. It was raining again.

7:42 A.M. Brent Scowcroft went in to show the President dispatches from Henry Kissinger and intelligence messages that had accumulated overnight. I was not invited to join them; the President, in setting the ground rules for my access to him, had specifically excluded these daily foreign-policy and security sessions.

Lieutenant General Scowcroft, who was fifty, was Deputy Assistant to the President for National Security Affairs. This meant — though you would never have known it to look at him — that he was Henry Kissinger's administrative *alter ego;* when the Secretary of State was away, and he was often away, the general alone spoke for him to the President on foreign and national-security matters. Short, wiry, rooster-quick, with sparkling eyes, he seemed a living model of a sprite that must surely have dwelled in Dr. Henry Kissinger, who could not possibly have been as heavy and lugubrious all the way through as he looked and sounded on the outside. As to point of view, Scowcroft did in some eerie way actually seem to inhabit Kissinger. The general was a rarity — an intellectual soldier. He had a Ph.D. from Columbia in international relations; he had studied at West Point, Lafayette, Georgetown, the Strategic Intelligence School, the Armed Forces Staff College, and the National War College; and he had been an assistant professor of Russian history at West Point and professor of political science at the Air Force Academy.

8:30 A.M. Robert Trowbridge Hartmann, with whom I now entered the Oval Office, was one of the President's two Counselors; he was fifty-eight. His explicit areas of responsibility were speechwriting and, vaguely, politics, but he was a long-standing friend of Mr. Ford's and had been his Chief of Staff during the Vice Presidency, and he talked about all sorts of things with him now. Hearty, bluff, gray-haired, ruddy, he had once been Washington bureau chief for the *Los Angeles Times,* and he was shrewd and accurate in assessing how the press would respond to whatever the President did. He had a mischievous look in his eye as he handed the President a strip of teletype, saying, "You'll be happy to see that Martha Mitchell is against you."

The President read and laughed. "That's a cheery note at eight in the morning," he said.

Hartmann handed him another item, some not-so-cheery news about conservative Republicans, and an announcement that the Senate was planning to recess for Easter in just ten days — which allowed a very short time for the struggles over taxes and Cambodian aid.

He told the President that a delegation from the Gridiron Club — "the Privy Council of the Press" — sought an audience with him to present a formal invitation to this year's dinner.

He gave the President a speech Ford had made at William and Mary, as possible background for an interview he was to have later in the day with the editors of *Fortune,* on the development of American institutions.

Then Hartmann said that Jack Stiles, a Grand Rapids newspaperman who collaborated with Ford on *Portrait of the Assassin,* a book that had been a by-product of Ford's service on the Warren Commission, wanted some information from the President's personal files.

Now I had a moment of seeing the President as an author, with the look on his face of one who might have a deal in the works.

THE AUTHOR: M-G-M contacted me about taking *Portrait* and making a documentary of it. Buchen turned them down. Then M-G-M contacted Jack, and he went to California for a day or so. They want to make three two-hour documentaries, using *Portrait* as a theme. Our book took the testimony of witnesses from the report, and it backed up the commission's finding that Oswald did it alone. Simon and Schuster's thinking of republishing it. Jack wants to find out how the radio and television rights stand. With all these charges of assassination plots against Castro and everything, there may be some interest. I still think the way we used the witnesses' testimony was: Number One (*the forefinger rises to the count*), more readable than the report and than the other books that were critical . . .

The President did not get beyond Number One.

8:35 A.M. The senior staff meeting was apparently lasting somewhat longer than usual this morning, and Rumsfeld's deputy, Richard Cheney, filled in for him while he was delayed.

Right away, Cheney brought up a sticky item. In his first State-of-the-Union Message, in January, urging "energy independence," the President had asked Congress to authorize full-scale commercial development of the naval petroleum reserve at Elk Hills, California. Out of the blue, a few days later, without having notified the Administration, the Standard Oil Company of California announced its intention of pulling its drilling rigs out of Elk Hills in order to avoid possible criticism of its role there. (Elk Hills was one of the reserves involved in the Teapot Dome scandal of 1923.) The Navy, Cheney said, had not yet found a new operator and he raised the question whether the reserve should be transferred from Navy to Interior Department control.

FORD: I'm more interested in getting action, getting production, getting oil, than I am in what agency runs the place. On my next trip West I want to go out there and see firsthand what Elk Hills looks like. I'm disturbed nothing's happening there. I'd like to get some action. We're interested in substance, not jurisdiction!

8:50 A.M. Donald Rumsfeld, who came in now, was by far the most equal of the theoretically equal top members of Mr. Ford's staff. He was also, at forty-two, the youngest of them. His gift was for organization. He was the only member of the staff frequenting the Oval Office in whose eye I thought I could see, now and then, behind his fashionable "aviator" glasses with their delicate black rims, a glint that seemed to say, "That big leather chair on the other side of the desk looks comfortable. I wonder if it would fit me." He was bright, jealous, crafty, and fiercely combative; he had once captained the Princeton wrestling team. He had served four terms in Congress, representing the wealthy North Shore above Chicago, and his voting record had been almost identical with Gerald Ford's. He was a Nixon holdover — had campaigned for him in '66, run the Office of Economic Opportunity for him awhile, and in 1970 had entered the White House as his Counselor and Director of his Cost of Living Council. To Rumsfeld's credit, he eventually had been given the shudders by Haldeman and Ehrlichman, and he had had himself shot out as far away from them as he could be — to Brussels, as Ambassador to NATO. President Ford had called him home from there. His active hands moved as if blown by every gust in his mind — always shaping, shaping, grasping bits of form out of the chaos of power.

Now, taking over from Cheney, he reviewed the senior staff meeting and helped the President plan the rest of the day.

9:07 A.M. As Jack Marsh was about to enter the Oval Office, someone handed him an urgent cable for the President's eyes. Marsh read it. He said to Terry O'Donnell, "Get General Scowcroft. The President's going to want to ask him some questions about this." He entered and handed the paper to the President. It was from Ambassador Frank Carlucci in Lisbon, and it informed the President of an uprising against the Portuguese Government by air-force units. Scowcroft was soon at attention before the big desk.

FORD (*unflapped*): Do we have any information that their air force has been unhappy?

SCOWCROFT: Not particularly, as a whole. Two or three weeks ago there were some rumors of a possible coup, primarily, it was thought, in armed forces guarding —

FORD: Any philosophical differences between the air-force group and other army units?

SCOWCROFT: Not that we know of. As a practical matter, it would be difficult for the air force to mount a coup.

FORD: Keep me posted, Brent.

SCOWCROFT: I will, Mr. President.

FORD: I'm glad we've got Frank Carlucci over there. He's a good man. Any further word from Henry?

SCOWCROFT: Yes, sir. I'll bring it in later. From Turkey. Not particularly encouraging. (*He leaves.*)

John O. Marsh, Jr., who was forty-eight, and who, as Counselor, was in over-all charge of the President's relations with Congress and with various sectors of the public, including businessmen, women, minorities, and consumers, had a way of pointing at a photograph over the mantel in his office of his farm in the Virginia hills and, with a slanting look just above and off to one side of his interlocutor's forehead, saying, "That's my little shanty in Strasburg. I'm just a country lawyer." Roughly translated, this meant: "Watch out, my friend — take a good grip on your credit cards." Jack Marsh had been in Congress with Gerald Ford — as a Byrd Democrat. Now calling himself an independent, he was ideologically much the most conservative man in the inner circle on the staff (in the 90th Congress, Gerald Ford had voted 63 percent of the time with the so-called conservative coalition of Republicans and Southern Democrats; Marsh had voted with the coalition 98 percent of the time), yet he seemed personally the most sensitive and humane man in the group.

MARSH: Did you see that they've got this $6-billion bill up there to create jobs? They apparently put it together quietly in committee. . . .

By now I had noticed that whereas the Nixon insiders had

used the word "they" when speaking of hostile forces, the press, demonstrators, enemies, all who were considered threatening, this Administration had it exclusively for a single, solid, and frustrating entity — the Democratic majority in Congress.

FORD: Let's get some more information on the bill. . . .

MARSH: I've been talking with some folks from Chrysler, and they feel there's maybe too much bad news about the economy coming out of here. They were talking about boat shows. They've been doing real well, selling lots and lots of big craft. Sales are down on the blue-collar lines, the small boats, but they're real happy over-all. Chrysler boat sales are up and auto sales are down. Maybe we ought to take hold of some signs. . . .

Now Marsh brought up a sensitive matter. The *Washington Star-News* had carried a story that Representative John Rhodes, the man who had succeeded Gerald Ford as Minority Leader of the House and an old friend of his, had announced that House Republicans were going to develop a legislative program of their own, separate from the President's. He had been quoted to the effect that "the days Republicans can get elected on somebody else's coattails are gone, gone forever."

MARSH: I'm not that upset about it, Mr. President. . . .

The President's face was a mask. I could see no surprise, no hurt, no anger.

9:20 A.M. The Nessen group came in.

NESSEN: I had a big go-round on the C.I.A. in yesterday's briefing. I'd like to ask you this: What are your personal views on the use of assassination?

Here I did see a moment's flash of the Truman style. Mr. Ford's answer was an immediate reflex.

FORD (*leaning forward, striking the edge of the desk repeatedly with a forefinger*): I've been assured it's not going on, and I don't want it to go on.

Nessen gave a full account of the ferocity of the questioning in yesterday's briefing. The range of allegations, he said, was widening, to the point of speculation that the C.I.A. might have been involved in one of the Kennedy assassinations, or both. What was he to say about all these things?

A long discussion ensued, about who was, or should be, checking out allegations of past plots by the C.I.A. The question was not settled; it would be taken forward.

And I had seen one way in which policy was spurred, if not engendered.

The Rhodes embarrassment was discussed. Rumsfeld bitterly said he thought the Republicans on the Hill had been watching the President slide in the polls and "are trying to put some light between them and you. Wait till the polls go up again: then they'll come running."

FORD: John's all right. I don't worry about him.

HARTMANN: It's like when I was writing papers for the Republican Policy Committee — remember, Mr. President? — and we called them Constructive Republican Alternative Proposals. It didn't take those clever Democrat lads long to find out what the initials spelled.

Hearing this, I suddenly remembered the parentheses marking deleted expletives marching like an army of ants across the Nixon transcripts, and I realized that I had yet to hear — except in Hartmann's acronym, to cheer the President up — a single four-letter word in this room.

Max L. Friedersdorf, Assistant to the President for Legislative Affairs, gave a report on how the President's request for $222 million in emergency aid for Cambodia stood in a Senate Foreign Relations subcommittee and in a House Foreign Affairs subcommittee, and how the dickering on the tax-cut bill was coming along in the House Ways and Means Committee. Friedersdorf, a tall blond Hoosier, a former newspaperman, was in complete command of his material; he had preliminary counts on how the votes would go in various committees. The President, thoroughly at home with Congressional give-and-take, talked zestfully, predicting how this man and that man would finally come down. He named some who were dead set against him; he spoke their first names with fondness.

The prospects were bleak. It was hard to understand why the President, who had made so much of the need for this aid, was not upset.

10:50 A.M. The President received a young lady who had been designated Maid of Cotton for 1975. This stunt was a replica of the previous day's reception of Miss America, except that it had more crassly commercial overtones.

At his press briefing a few minutes later, Ron Nessen told the mediamen about the visit to the Oval Room by the Maid of Cotton, who in real life was Miss Kathryn Tenkhoff, of Sikeston, Missouri.

NESSEN: Secretary Butz also attended the meeting.
Q: Did Butz come over just for that?
NESSEN: Cotton is his area of responsibility.
Q: How much cotton do they grow in Missouri?
NESSEN: They grow cotton queens in Missouri. They grow cotton somewhere else.

11:01 A.M. The first sharp shock of the week was in store for me.

Assembled in the Cabinet Room were all the Administration's big guns on the economy and energy: the President himself; Vice President Nelson Rockefeller; Secretary of the Treasury William Simon; the President's Cabinet-rank Assistant for Economic Affairs, William Seidman; the new Secretary of Labor, John Dunlop; James Lynn of the Office of Management and Budget; Chairman Alan Greenspan of the Council of Economic Advisers; Chairman Frank Zarb of the Energy Resources Council; Dr. Burns of the Fed; Rumsfeld, Hartmann, Scowcroft, and some staff assistants.

The President asked Secretary Simon for a report on the status of a tax-rebate bill which was under consideration.

SIMON: Mr. President, we're attempting to keep this to a temporary, one-shot thing. As you know, the House has proposed a $21.3-billion rebate using more or less our method, but lowering the income allowance. No one in his right mind believes that when they get going on this it'll be temporary. On the Senate bill, I went up and testified before the Senate Finance Committee, and I guess a ball-park figure of where they'll come out would be $25 billion, and you can bet your hat the House won't be able to resist matching those goodies. . . .

FORD: Any chance of lifting the $200 ceiling on individual rebates?

SIMON: There's a fair shot of getting $500. Mr. President, this whole deal of theirs is more of a welfare thing than anything else. They're making the assumption that low-income people should get more than their share of the giveaway. It's just a welfare thing, Mr. President.

FORD: Let me ask you this: I have two sons who worked last summer and earned about $1,500 each. Would they get $100 rebate?

SIMON: In my judgment, absolutely.

FORD: That's ridiculous.

SIMON: If they're typical of young people who work in the summertime —

FORD: It's ridiculous.

SIMON: I couldn't agree more, Mr. President.

SEIDMAN: Essentially it gives them back their Social Security tax.

SIMON: That's exactly what it does.

HARTMANN: But if they go out and spend it —

FORD: They'll spend it, all right! (*Laughter.*)

A little later:

FORD: What's going on about the oil-depletion allowance?

SIMON: I think they're cutting a deal up there right now. . . .

FORD (*after more discussion*): Our position should be that we do not want a Christmas-tree bill, with a whole lot of favors and gifts attached to it, and we've got to attack the whole issue of including cutting out the oil-depletion allowance in the tax-stimulus bill.

This was the first time I had seen the President and the Vice President in the same room. They now faced each other on opposite sides of the center of the long Cabinet table. The President, as usual, was still, controlled, imperturbable. The Vice President, by contrast, was as active as a two-month-old kitten. He slumped, shot bolt upright, leaned to one side, then to the other, whispered, nodded when he agreed, shook his head when he differed. Now he spoke up.

ROCKEFELLER: Is it too late to propose an excess-profits tax on the oil companies with an allowance for plow-back?

SIMON: It is, sir. We've proposed a windfall-profits tax in preference to that.

FORD: I'm not sure I understand the difference between a windfall and an excess-profits tax.

SIMON: Sir, the windfall tax aims like a rifle at crude oil, as opposed to an excess-profits tax, which would cut across the whole range of an extremely complex system of profit calculation.

GREENSPAN: Trying to audit through the profits system of the multinationals would lead you into a hopeless maze.

The Vice President subsided like a baloon with the air escaping.

FORD: The main thing is to attach as few amendments as possible to the tax bill, so as to get the stimulus as soon as we can. . . .

The meeting lasted for an hour and fifteen minutes and went into great detail on issues that were quite technical: an intention to impose countervailing duties on European Community dairy products; proposed Export-Import Bank financing of liquefied natural-gas facilities abroad; negotiations with Chairman Albert Ullman of the House Ways and Means Committee on the energy bill, and what to do about "their" $5.9-billion Emergency Employment Appropriations Act.

Mr. Rockefeller with belling tones interrupted the Ex-Im discussion with a warning that supertankers carrying liquefied gas were extremely dangerous. If one blew up in an American port, he said, the whole city would go up. He painted a vivid picture of urban devastation.

The President's interventions were minor, until the discussion of the Democrats' big bill to provide jobs. Here his only interest was in keeping spending down. He proposed the preparation, as quickly as possible, of "an updated scoreboard" on the budget, reflecting Congressional proposals to spend more and more, and Congressional refusals to rescind or defer spending already authorized. He stressed more than once the need to dramatize "their" additions to the deficit.

Why was I shocked? Because in this discussion I had seen a first glimpse of another side of the man who had been so considerate, so open, and so kind to me as an individual — what seemed a deep, hard, rigid side. Talking here, he had seemed a million miles away from many Americans who had been hardworking people all their lives and were now feeling the cruel pinch of hard times. What was it in him? Was it an inability to extend compassion far beyond the faces directly in view? Was it a failure of imagination? Was it something obdurate he was born with, alongside the energy and serenity he was born with?

12:16 P.M. He took Rockefeller into the Oval Office with him. To my regret, I was not invited to join them — I would have loved to see the Immovable Object and the Irresistible Force collide.

I gathered they talked about two things. First, the Domestic Council. This body, originally conceived as a planning unit in the Executive, had devolved under Nixon and Ehrlichman into an operational clearinghouse that kept things moving. Ford and his staff early saw a need to restore its predictive function, because it was obvious that the President was not by nature a planner. Ford had had a long habit of juggling a multiplicity of problems in the Congress that demanded instant attention; everything was always on a day-to-day basis. And he succeeded to the Presidency, as his Counsel Philip Buchen puts it, "under a tyranny of urgency." And much as he would have liked to emulate Truman, he lacked Truman's sense of history — lacked a feel for how a decision would look five — or fifty — years hence. The thought was that Rockefeller, having put a Commission on Critical Choices to work after he resigned from the Governorship of New York, might bring a planning competence to the council. Ford had appointed James M. Cannon, long a political adviser to Rockefeller, as director of the council, and the two men talked now about the early stages of Cannon's and the council's work.

Second, the C.I.A. Who should investigate?

12:35 P.M. The President called in Alan Greenspan to fill him in on the conversation yesterday with Dr. Burns. Alan Greenspan was a devotee of Ayn Rand (*The Fountainhead, Atlas Shrugged*), the Objectivist philosopher, and, like her, he advocated pure laissez-faire capitalism and "rational selfishness."

12:46 P.M. General Scowcroft went in for two minutes — presumably with the latest word from Dr. Kissinger.

12:48 P.M. Mr. Ford received Frank Stanton, former vice chairman of the board of CBS, who for a year and a half had chaired a panel, set up jointly by the U.S. Advisory Commission on Information and the U.S. Advisory Commission on International Education and Cultural Affairs, reviewing the operations of the U.S. Information Agency, the Voice of America, and the Bureau of Cultural Affairs of the Department of State.

Before each appointment, the President was given what was formally called a briefing paper; informally, a talking paper. It had three parts: a statement of the purpose of the appointment, background, and "talking points" — actual language the President might appropriately use.

In this instance, Mr. Ford had been given the following talking points:

"(1) I understand that your panel has addressed some of the long-standing issues. . . . These activities play an important role. . . .

"(2) There have been a number of proposals in recent years for restructuring our information and cultural activities. . . ."

Mr. Stanton was then to be given a chance to make his recommendations — which, in the event, were that U.S.I.A.'s information functions be transferred to the State Department, that the long-range cultural functions of U.S.I.A. and State be combined within State and that the Voice of America be set up as an independent entity under a Government-and-public board.

"(3) The scope of your study and its recommendations are very impressive. I will want to have it studied very carefully. . . .

"(4) Thank you for your efforts. . . . You have made a most needed and timely contribution."

Actually, the exchange was far freer and a little less grammatical than this, but, all the same, so it went.

1:10 P.M. The President retired for lunch, I joined him for a few minutes in his two-room hideaway. One room was a small study, the walls of which were covered with mementos, including a huge Presidential seal which was actually a rug, hooked for the President in Grand Rapids by his half-sister-in-law, Mrs. Richard Ford; in one corner there was a luxurious stuffed-leather Barcalounger, into which the President occasionally settled to read.

His lunch was served on a tray on a small table beside a desk in the other room.

Day in and day out, Mr. Ford ate exactly the same lunch — a ball of cottage cheese, over which he poured a small pitcherful of A-1 Sauce; a sliced onion or a quartered tomato; and a small helping of butter-pecan ice cream.

"Eating and sleeping," he said to me, "are a waste of time."

I told him that it appeared to me that he liked being President.

"I do," he said. "It's mainly the challenge, John. I always have enjoyed facing up to problems; it's always been a sort of way of life with me — and you certainly have them here. I really enjoy getting up every morning, looking at the sched-

ule, seeing what the problems are. I don't long for the end
of the day."

2:03 P.M. Secretary of Defense James Schlesinger and General Scowcroft were closeted with the President, to report on
the deteriorating situations in Cambodia and Vietnam. After
about half an hour, I was admitted.

They were talking about G.I. Bill education, which the
President apparently wanted to cut back, or perhaps cut out
altogether. The tall, rugged-looking Secretary held the line
as well as he could.

FORD: You do get into a paradoxical situation. You have
an all-volunteer service, but these benefits give an incentive
to get out.

SCHLESINGER: They give an incentive to get in, sir. But
many will stay. We're attracting a different sort of person.

FORD: Ever thought of offering a greater educational opportunity if they stay in?

SCHLESINGER: We do some of that now, Mr. President, but
we're going to cut back on it. English grammar but not bas-
ket weaving, for which they've gotten credit in the past.

FORD: There are things I can do to cut off certain benefits.
But we'll have to go to Congress sooner or later. There has
to come a time when we end the so-called Vietnam war and
all its extras.

SCHLESINGER: We'll get up an options paper on the whole
thing.

The two now discussed several other subjects — officers'
pay, certain personnel decisions, Thailand, Diego Garcia,
Turkey.

Suddenly the President leaned forward, and with a vigor
far surpassing any I had previously seen him show, his voice
rising almost to a shout, his forefinger pounding on the edge
of the desk, he adjured the Secretary to get the Navy going
on the Elk Hills petroleum reserve.

FORD: Get up there and get the legislation, or we're going
to give that whole deal to Interior. Tell 'em to get off their
cushions up there at the Navy. The Navy damn well better

get moving. I want you to get action. It strikes me the Navy likes the cushy little deal they've got out there. I'm going to go and see Elk Hills, and when I come back I'm going to be one of the few people who's actually seen the place, and I'm going to be in a position to tell 'em what's what. Now you get going.

SCHLESINGER (*to his Commander in Chief*): Yes, sir.

3:08 P.M. Rumsfeld, Cheney, and William N. Walker, Director of the Presidential Personnel Office, came in to talk about some prospective appointments.

4:20 P.M. Marsh, Cheney, Cabinet Secretary James Connor, and Dr. Robert Goldwin entered to warm Mr. Ford up for the *Fortune* interview. Dr. Goldwin had recently been appointed a consultant, with a mission of bringing intellectuals in to see the President. So far, he had exposed Ford to people like Irving Kristol, of the Department of Urban Values, New York University; Gertrude Himmelfarb, historian, of City College, New York: Thomas Sowell, an eminent black economist, of U.C.L.A.; Herbert Storing, a political scientist, of the University of Chicago; and Edward Banfield, an urban specialist, of the University of Pennsylvania.

In preparation for this meeting, Dr. Goldwin had provided Mr. Ford with the *Encyclopedia of American History,* edited by Richard B Morris *et al.,* and the *Encyclopedia of American Facts and Dates,* edited by Gorton Carruth, with certain pages tabbed. Mr. Ford had done his homework. There was a meandering conversation on history — one which Mr. Truman would never have needed; or, had he heard it, would have called just too damned highfalutin.

4:55 P.M. *Fortune* editors in. Went pretty well, Mr. Ford reported afterward.

5:40 P.M. Marsh, Friedersdorf, Cannon, Cheney, Lynn, Lynn's O.M.B. deputy, Paul O'Neill, and a couple of other staff members met with the President to discuss the possibility of sending a message to Congress on a consumer-protection bill.

Once again, as the group reviewed a long options paper, I

heard in the President's comments the distant, hard-edged, negative voice I had heard that morning in the economy-energy meeting.

FORD: Is a consumer-protection bill in any form a violation of our new policy of limited spending?

LYNN: You're going to get a new law, no matter what you put in this. It's almost a certainty they'll have a law.

FORD: Then you get a question: Is it wise for me to go with a message?

LYNN: Well — to get out in front with the consumer. . . .

FORD: On page two, we ought to hold this for further study. . . . I'd be very hesitant about establishing a consumer-representative office in every department. Your agency head is going to lose control. . . . We ought to get better titles for things. The Democrats come up with titles like Model Cities, and we come up with the Ocean Dumping Act. . . . *(Considerably later, after discussion of nineteen of twenty-four options:)* I must say, on the basis of what we've been talking about, I can't see justification for sending up a message on consumer protection. . . .

In the end, Marsh suggested that at a Cabinet meeting the President might "mandate the departments to concern themselves with consumer considerations." The President added that he might then also write letters to the chairmen of the appropriate committees, on the need for certain reforms in the regulatory agencies.

So much for the faraway consumer.

6:55 P.M. Rumsfeld and Cheney came in together for the evening cleanup. At one point:

RUMSFELD: This is just something to think about. It occurred to me after our meeting this morning with Ron [Nessen] that began as a session where he could get guidance from you, and then the Congressional side came in, so Max [Friedersdorf] could get guidance, then other voices were added, so that now it has become a kind of senior staff meeting. This morning it was scheduled for fifteen minutes and lasted an hour.

FORD: This morning the circumstances were rather special.

RUMSFELD: That's true. That's true. But what I'm wondering is whether there shouldn't be a regular senior staff meeting in place of that. And whether we shouldn't get in a somewhat different cast of characters — Jim Lynn, Brent, Jack, Bob. It's fine for Ron to come to you and get your position on things, beyond which he wouldn't go.

FORD: As long as he could get some input from you and others besides myself —

RUMSFELD: Sure. He does that all day every day. . . . Maybe the senior staff meeting should be followed by a smaller group in here with you.

CHENEY: Or perhaps you should preside over the senior staff group.

FORD: Always remembering that I get more out of a meeting with several people than just one.

RUMSFELD: I'm just thinking of the most efficient use of your time.

FORD: Why don't you think it through and come up with a plan?

7:20 P.M. Mr. Ford left for the residence. That day he had spent four minutes less in his office than the previous day.

10. WEDNESDAY

Politics: "That's How It Works"

7:38 A.M. Here he came along the walkway through another soggy dawn. He stepped through a tall door into the brightness of the office in a newish three-piece suit, middling brown with a faint check, trousers cuffless, and when he bent down over the brown suitcase for some papers and then swung quickly toward his desk chair, coattails flying, you could see that the pattern of his silk foulard tie, riding a sliver of a tie pin, was repeated in the lining of the jacket. He had no less than three pens clipped in the vest pocket over his heart. The Presidential seal helped link his white cuffs.

Like everyone else in the vicinity, I was energized by the zest of this arrival. I felt the need of a lift. Some bad questions had been building in my mind. Whatever became of the motto of "communication, conciliation, compromise and cooperation" with the Congress that the President had promised on the Monday after his swearing-in? Why did everything here seem to present itself in terms of a contest with "them"? Yet when he lost and "they" won a round in that struggle, why was he so quiet, so unperturbed, as if nothing really had been lost — suggesting that nothing would have been gained, either, if he had won? What was the source and nature of the deep, hard sound I had heard in this kind man's voice yesterday, the sound that had troubled me so?

7:42 A.M. General Scowcroft and David Peterson, of the C.I.A. White House Support Staff, went in for the daily briefing.

8:02 A.M. Counselor Hartmann went in for his daily appointment.

But that morning I went to the senior staff meeting in a sort of mini-Cabinet room, where Teddy Roosevelt glared down exultantly from over the mantel at the bully young chaps he saw at the long table. Ford's staff, befitting his constant yearning to be with friends, was horizontal in form. Nixon's had been pyramidal; urgencies mounted the slopes to Haldeman at the apex, and then went in, maybe. Nine men of Ford's staff could walk into the Oval Office at any time—though there were obviously heavy constraints on their doing so: Assistant Rumsfeld, Assistant Kissinger (or Scowcroft), Counselor Marsh, Counselor Hartmann, Press Secretary Nessen, Counsel Buchen, Assistant (Economy) Seidman, Assistant (Budget) Lynn, Assistant (Domestic Council) Cannon. The senior staff comprised these men, and they or their deputies, and some others, like Frank "the Energy Zarb") Zarb, Greenspan, and Friedersdorf, attended. Secretary Simon was sometimes present, though not today.

Rumsfeld sat at one end of the long table, and he called on one man after another. Whoever had something on his mind that he thought the President either should know or should act upon spoke his piece; others took passes.

Budget's Lynn said that he had taken the liberty of telling some reporters the previous day that the Democrats' $5.9-billion emergency spending bill would overstimulate the economy and swell the deficit, and that he would urge the President to veto it; perhaps some of the staff had seen the story in that morning's *Post.*

Several had. There was some talk about "how high a profile" the President should have on vetoes at that stage of delicate bargaining. Up to that morning, he had vetoed twenty-five bills — had been the most veto-prone President since Grover Cleveland, the all-time record holder. Most of his vetoes had been standing up recently, however, and, indeed, Friederdorf now reported that Tuesday the Democratic leadership had decided it did not have the troops to override Mr. Ford's veto of the ninety-day oil-tax delay.

"Just thought I'd toss out a signal to them," Lynn said.

Friedersdorf told the staff he had some other good news, too, for a change — that the Senate Foreign Relations subcommittee dealing with emergency aid to Cambodia had voted 4 to 3 Tuesday in favor of giving the Cambodians

$125 million, and a House Foreign Affairs subcommittee split 3 to 3 on a proposal for somewhat less aid; the Cambodian proposition was not dead. . . .

8:40 A.M. In the Oval Office.

RUMSFELD: The slot situation. As you know, we've been keeping periodic book on how we're doing on the 10-percent reduction in the White House staff. We now have 533 permanents. We're aiming for 490, although we budgeted 500 for some leeway. It's very hard; there's constant pressure to add people. Last month we had seventeen departures and thirteen arrivals. We have a sizable percentage to reduce between now and June.

FORD: You'll just have to keep the pressure on.

RUMSFELD: We should be thinking about the problem of coordinating domestic and foreign policies. This has been a problem in our Government since the forties, at least. On that business yesterday of the countervailing duties on European cheese and so on, Simon went ahead on the basis of domestic pressures — no contact with State, which has to deal with the repercussions in the European Economic Community. Something to think about. . . .

9:00 A.M. One of Counselor Marsh's many duties was as White House overseer of plans for the Bicentennial in 1976. On the way in to his appointment, Marsh, a Virginian chauvinist, whispered to me that he thought of the whole forthcoming celebration not as Bicentennial but as Tercentennial — on account of Bacon's Rebellion against the Virginian colonial authorities in 1676.

MARSH (*to the President*): They're getting ready to go with a Wagon Train, a Freedom Train — all sorts of national programs, some O.K., some awful. The workload on the Bicentennial is getting pretty fierce, Mr. President, and I wonder if we could set up a task force on it? I'd suggest [Human Resources Assistant] Marrs, Cheney, Goldwin, [Cabinet Secretary] Connor, [Domestic Council Director] Cannon.

FORD: Good idea.

MARSH: Each state will have one week of national observance, with one night each in the Kennedy Center. With fifty states, that'll take just about the whole year. It's an idea that might suit me, but it sure might not suit you. Once a week!

FORD: The only thing that would suit you would be a thirteen-week celebration, for the original thirteen colonies. Right?

MARSH: Of which Virginia, sir, was the first. Do you know that until 1937 Virginia was a colony longer than she was a state?

FORD: Some think longer than that.

MARSH: We've got to work out a role for you that won't pull you apart. . . . The 1876 Centennial theme was technology. Alexander Graham Bell introduced the telephone, up in Philadelphia, I think it was. There was the reciprocating engine. New processes. Men came on from St. Louis and Akron and Council Bluffs, and there was a great outward burst in technology. We need to get some sort of logos built into our planning.

FORD: Jack Stiles [co-author of *Portrait*] was talking to me about the idea of getting an American electronic and aviation and space-industry show set up at Cape Canaveral. They've got a lot of unused space down there since the cutbacks.

MARSH: A sophisticated Disneyland. That's a good idea.

FORD: I think it's a meritorious idea. . . .

9:19 A.M. Most of the discussion in the Nessen group that morning was political. Max Friedersdorf's slightly encouraging news from the Hill raised questions: how to push through as much Cambodian aid as would survive; how to get Congress to move on the tax bill; how to get "their" big-spending bill recommitted.

The President stirred with pleasure — it almost seemed as if he had suddenly walked through a door into his real self. Familiar names: the old horse-trading routines. Even his hands seemed independently to enjoy themselves now as they settled into the little enactments of bargaining they knew so well — counting, weighing, arresting; a finger encircled a thumb (We have that man), knuckles rapped the desk (Try again), the whole hand flapped (He's hopeless). He reminisced about motions to recommit, as if remembering great football games. The names like candies in his mouth: Frank, Gale, Hugh, John, Al, Herman, Gaylord, Barber, Mike. . . .

FORD: That Gale McGee is a stanch guy. I remember when Gale and I used to fight tooth and nail for foreign appropriations. In those days, old Passman was adamant against anything foreign. . . . What's the next step, Max?

FRIEDERSDORF: Well, the House subcommittee will vote again, of course, and the full Senate committee will vote, I believe, on Monday.

FORD: Anything I can do?

FRIEDERSDORF: Our present count on the probable vote in the full Senate committee is seven to seven, with Senator Percy undecided. I think a call to the Senator would be most helpful.

FORD: Sure, I'll call Chuck.

JACK HUSHEN (*Nessen's deputy, who was going to have to take the briefing that morning, because Nessen would be sitting in on a scheduled Cabinet meeting*): What am I to say about this Republican loyalty oath, to you and the principles of the party, that Representative Anderson and Senator Percy are circulating? A kind of pledge of allegiance to the party.

FORD: Haven't seen it. I only saw the news story.

FRIEDERSDORF: John Anderson mentioned it Monday night.

RUMSFELD: A value it does have is that it brings people out into the open, and it offsets that Rhodes stuff about a program independent of yours.

FORD: Let's say I'm grateful for this show of strong support —

HARTMANN(*always the realist*): You don't have that yet.

FORD (*trying again*): I'm grateful for the support, and I hope as many as possible —

MARSH: "Loyalty oath" is not what it is.

FORD: I wouldn't use that term at all.

FRIEDERSDORF: Or even "vote of confidence." . . .

HUSHEN: Jim Lynn came out in the papers urging you to veto the big emergency jobs bill. Do you want to say something about that?

FORD: I do feel an inclination to veto a bill for $5.9 billion. But I don't want to get too far out in front on that, because some of these smart politicians up there might tack onto the bill something we want a lot — this Cambodia and Vietnam aid. This word of warning from Jim Lynn, Director of O.M.B. — that's a pretty strong signal. That's as far as I'd want to go just now. . . .

9:46 A.M. Mr. Ford read some briefing papers — Cabinet meeting coming. Across the room, the Seymour grandfather clock uttered, uttered, uttered. . . .

10:17 A.M. The President went to the Cabinet Room to greet fifty-three state and national winners of the twenty-eighth annual Voice of Democracy scriptwriting contest, sponsored by the Veterans of Foreign Wars and its Ladies' Auxiliary, for which, that year, half a million competing tenth-, eleventh- and twelfth-grade students across the country had written short broadcast scripts on the theme "My Responsibility as a Citizen."

As the Chief Executive entered, these young presences filled the Cabinet Room with a vibrant energy, like that of a ravenous school of fish breaking water to feed. They surged forward, winked flashbulbs, blurted out heartfelt encouragement and advice. The President's cool soon quieted them.

Mr. Ford's talking paper had offered him some bland suggestions on how to greet these winners: "I want to thank . . . congratulate . . . I would like to hear each one of you. . . ."

Instead he struck out on his own with a brief and basic civics lesson — so basic as to be, it seemed, quite a few grade levels below those of his audience; yet he delivered the central passage of this simple lecture with an intensity of emotion that I had not heard in anything he had said up to that time:

FORD: I think this is a wonderful thing for the V.F.W., of which I am a member, and its Ladies' Auxiliary, to have done. You've been here for a week? Then I trust you've seen all three branches of the Government. This Government of ours has three coequal branches. First we have the Supreme Court, that's the first branch. Then the Senate and the House of Representatives, that's the second. And then we have the President and the Executive Branch, that's the third. We have a system of checks and balances. The founders of this Government, those who drafted the Constitution, had very strong feelings that the best way to protect individual freedom and to meet the challenges from day to day was to keep this system of checks and balances in each branch strong — and also to leave substantial powers in the hands of state and local governments. I hope you'll go back to your states and sooner or later you'll take some part in one of these branches, whether in the Judiciary, or as a Senator or Congressman, or maybe right here as President. Have a safe trip home, and we'll see you back here one of these days, hopefully, running things.

10:22 A.M. General Scowcroft and Rumsfeld conferred with the President in the Oval Office.

10:45 A.M. Mr. Ford spent a quarter of an hour preparing himself for the Cabinet meeting. 11:04 A.M. — The President entered the Cabinet Room. 11:05 A.M. — "Camera Opportunity": Photographers bustled and shoved. 11:07 A.M. — Exit press.

11:08 A.M.

FORD: We have a very full plate today, and we should get started.

He greeted two new Secretaries, Carla Hills of HUD and Bill Coleman of Transportation, and reserved time for a departing Secretary, Peter Brennan of Labor, to speak at the end of the meeting.

He told the Cabinet that with the extension of the Clemency Board's period of activity, there had come a sudden

flood of 11,000 new applications for clemency from draft
evaders and A.W.O.L.'s, with 4,000 to 5,000 more cases expected before the deadline. To save money on the huge load
of clerical work this would entail, he asked all the departments to lend staff personnel to the Clemency Board.

Now he called on Vice President Rockefeller to give the
Cabinet an account of the recent drama in the Senate over
the filibuster, during which the Vice President, in a handsome display of Rockefeller gall, had faced down the Southern bloc and brought about a long-needed and historic
change in the rules of procedure, under which 60 percent of
the Senate, rather than, as in the past, two thirds, could
henceforth vote to limit debate — thus curbing the power of
a regressive minority to resist change simply by talking a bill
to death. "I might add," Ford says, "that Rocky handled
himself brilliantly."

The Vice President rose, brimming with joy, and Dick Par-
sons, a towering assistant of his, propped up a large chart on
an easel at the end of the room, and handed Mr. Rockefeller
a wooden pointer.

ROCKEFELLER: . . . On January 10, I asked the President
how he wanted Rule 22, which regulates filibusters, handled.
The President decided that as the presiding officer of the
Senate, it was my responsibility and that I should handle it as
I saw fit. As you can see by the chart, there are essentially
two strategies, referred to as the Northern and Southern
routes. . . . Mondale put two motions in one during this
period, which is incorrect, and that was disallowed. Then
Senator Allen put three motions in one, which was also disallowed. Senator Byrd and Senator Griffin finally agreed on
the wording of the motion, but Mansfield objected. . . . As
we moved through these series of steps outlined on the
chart, alternating between the Northern and Southern
routes and various motions, we reached a point where I
asked for the clerk to call the roll. Senator Allen objected
and raised a point of parliamentary inquiry. The Vice President again then asked for a roll to be called, and again Senator Allen raised the point of question of parliamentary in-

quiry and again I asked for the roll to be called. This is where the controversy really became a public feud. The Senators at that point gave me a very bad time. But according to Rule 19 in the Senate, on a point of parliamentary inquiry the Chair is allowed, at his discretion, to recognize or not recognize the Senator. At any rate, we finally reached an agreement. There was a two-hour recess during which a compromise was worked out, and the final agreement was the Southern route, which is the way the majority wanted to go. Everyone was happy — the conservatives, the liberals, the Republicans and the Democrats have all generally turned out to be fairly happy about it. I have arranged a series of small dinners with various members of the Senate to make certain that there are no hard feelings. . . . I might add, Mr. President, that I am grateful for the support that you gave me during this period, both publicly and privately. I appreciate it, and I believe and hope I did what you wanted. . . .

FORD: At this time, I would like Earl Butz to tell us what has been happening to farm and food prices, and what we can expect for the rest of the year. Earl?

BUTZ: Well, Mr. President, it looks like this. There has been a 14-percent increase in price of food in 1974 over 1973. Eighty percent of that increase has come after the product has left the farm. This can be accounted for by higher wages, higher transportation costs and higher fuel costs. While the increase has slowed down some, it has not stopped during the first quarter of 1975. It appears that food prices will be up 1½ percent to 2 percent over the last quarter of 1974. So the increase has slowed down markedly. It is interesting to note that the index of prices paid by farmers is up 12 percent, but the index of prices received by farmers is down by about 15 percent. The statistic that you will find interesting is that 17 percent of the take-home pay of the average American will go for food. This is down slightly over 1973, and also interesting to note is that only Canada and the United States are nations below 20 percent of take-home pay going for food. This can be attributed to several things. One-third of the meals are currently eaten outside of the home. Looking toward 1975, we anticipate a leveling off or decline in food prices. There will be more beef eaten by Americans this year by about seven pounds per capita for the year. However, Americans will eat less pork and poultry per person, and the beef will be relatively cheap. Fruits and vegetables will generally be less expensive, and of course, Mr. President, you know about our peanut problem. We have had one for years. We are up to our ears in peanuts. The area where we will be shortest in everyday diets will be on grain-fed beef. Mr. President, you can expect a record wheat crop. Since 70 percent of all wheat in America is winter-grown, that crop is already in. We have had a 6-percent increase in acreage, and 400 million to 500 million bushels of grain above last year's crop, so we will have a record crop. We currently have four million acres in soybean cultivation. So we hope, as we look toward 1975, the escalation of food prices is behind us.

FORD: Are the farmers happy, Earl?

BUTZ: No, sir, they aren't.

Now the President introduced Administrator Russell Train of the Environmental Protection Agency to explain a controversial decision Mr. Train had made the week before giving the automobile industry until 1978 or even — if Congress will approve — until 1982 to meet final antipollution standards.

TRAIN: Thank you, Mr. President. As most of you know, it was a very complicated and controversial issue. . . . As you know, autos using catalytic converters cut down pollutants, give low operating costs, better gas consumption and have fewer maintenance problems; but it has been found that they also give sulphuric-acid mist, which is dangerous. So the decision was whether to hold the line and continue with the interim standards, or to go with the higher standards and run the risk of putting the sulphuric-acid mist in the air. Our research indicated that the sulphuric acid was a very real and dangerous problem. While it isn't a national problem yet, it soon could be, and we really can't afford to play the numbers game. Through our research we found that desulphurization was not a good solution, for it would take some two years of research and testing to be prepared to do that on a regular basis. We also found that sulphate traps aren't a solution, and not something that our technology is readily able to produce. The real concern we had was if we moved to the new higher level of standard, which is the .9 California standard, we would actually be doubling the amount of sulphuric acid in the air. Therefore, after much thought and a lot of advice, the decision was made to stay with the 1975 interim standard, 1.5 percent hydrocarbons as opposed to .9 percent, the California standard. This of course caused considerable problems. The health-services industry was not happy, the auto people were not happy, and the mayors and governors were not happy.

There was considerable discussion of the catalytic-converter issue. Vice President Rockefeller, having had a nice chance to talk, was relatively unbouncy today, but soon he did sound another of his alarms.

ROCKEFELLER: Mr. President, I fear that this could really become a serious political problem and perhaps a liability next year. I know we will have examples of garages catching on fire and people burning to death; cars catching on fire, gas stations exploding — all because of the catalytic converter. If someone wanted to make this a political issue in 1976 and brought out these gruesome details and stories, they would put the burden on your back, and they would be asking why you didn't tell them that this was a problem. . . .

TRAIN (later): Mr. Vice President, what you say is true, perhaps, to a certain extent, and if one carried it to the extreme, it could become a political liability. However, the reports about fires, explosions and death are very fragmented at best. We simply don't have adequate information at this time to prove that this is true. If we do pull the catalyst off the automobile at this time, we will have an increase of three times in the level of pollutants.

ROCKEFELLER: I would really like to see the President take the public into his confidence and include them in this information, so they feel like they are sharing in the decisions, and we can assist them in making their determinations, and this therefore will not become a political liability at a future date. . . .

FORD (*after twenty minutes' discussion*): Last October we decided that an inflation-impact statement should be made about all new legislation which we were proposing and the Congress was proposing. Maybe we can do the same thing here. It says something about my basic philosophy of government. I think that we have to implement this philosophy, and the consumer has a right to know what the exact impact, both pros and cons, will be of decisions which his Government is making. It's not just environmental regulations that raise this issue. There are literally thousands of examples. I recall the problem we had with the truckers' regulation issued by the Department of Transportation before you arrived, Bill. I had to make a decision on New Year's, when I was on vacation, to let a regulation go forward because we were so far down the road on it. To hold it up would have imposed economic hardship on the industry, which had geared up to implement the Federal rule. As a result, we are increasing the cost of trucks and trailers 5 to 7 percent — it's some very large sum like 200 million dollars. I now understand that this regulation might force some companies out of business. I have no doubt that many energy regulations create the same kind of dislocations. Therefore, when we submit legislation and proposals, we must make certain that we know both sides of the story and what the total impact will be, so we can inform the Congress and the public about everything to do with that particular problem.

Next the President called on Secretary Schlesinger to brief the Cabinet on the situation in Cambodia and Vietnam.

The Secretary unwrapped maps; there was some joshing, to the effect that he might simply use Rocky's filibuster chart, which was still on the easel, to make his case.

The Secretary's briefing, the discussion that followed it,

and Secretary Brennan's swan song, uttered in the street-hardened tones of Hell's Kitchen, Manhattan, concluded the meeting.

12:44 P.M. The President returned to the Oval Office for a chat with Secretary Morton. They discussed Morton's imminent transfer from Interior to Commerce.

12:58 P.M. Mr. Ford was joined by Congressmen John Rhodes and Albert H. Quie for a short prayer meeting. Mel Laird usually joined the group in these habitual devotions, which had continued intermittently for about seven years; he was unable to be present that day. The three talked awhile, then each prayed aloud and alone for about a minute, asking for guidance, giving thanks, weaving in his largest concerns, praying not only for his own interest or for those of the President, but also for the good of Congress and the country. Then the three intoned the Lord's Prayer together.

1:10 P.M. Lunch: cottage cheese drenched in A-1 Sauce, and so forth. 1:20 P.M. — Mildred Leonard, Mr. Ford's executive secretary for twenty-three years, came into the hideaway to assist him with private correspondence. 1:35 P.M. — Other paperwork. 1:57 P.M. — Major Robert E. Barrett, one of the President's military aides, in for three minutes on a personal errand.

2:03 P.M. For the third time that day, the President entered the Cabinet Room, this time to receive the United States Commission on Civil Rights.

Chairman Arthur Flemming, former Secretary of Health, Education and Welfare, had asked for this meeting to discuss the current state of Federal enforcement of civil-rights law. The President had done his homework, and showed his familiarity with many of the questions Chairman Flemming and other commision members raised. It did not take him long to start talking about Congress:

FORD: Of course you know that I have recommended a five-year extension of the voting-rights law. We may have a problem up there on the Hill. You know the present act expires August 8. I've noted that several interested and influential members of Congress think something ought to be added to the act for the benefit of Spanish-speaking citizens; others want to extend the act to some pockets in the North where you have alleged discrimination; others want to extend it to the whole country. I don't know what the impact will be, but these are knowledgeable and influential Senators and Congressmen. There could be a delay. There are some people who don't want any voting-rights law at all, and there are some who want it amended. If those two groups got together fortuitously, you could have trouble — you might not have the present law extended. . . .

2:42 p.m. The President made his telephone call to Senator Percy.

FORD (*leaning back*): Hi, Chuck . . . I'm fine, how're you? . . . No. Say, I appreciate the initiative you and John Anderson and Bill Milliken have taken to support me up there, trying to get a few signers here and there. . . . Oh gee, that's good, I hadn't heard that. . . . You know, it's good to have a policy, but if you don't have 51 percent of the vote! (*Laughs.*) . . . Chuck, the reason I called, in addition to thanking you, was because of the vote that's coming up Monday, I believe it is, on Cambodia in the Foreign Relations Committee. You know about the four-to-three support we got in the sub-committee for a $125-million drawdown for economic and military support. . . . I'm hoping that if, after you've looked at it, you can see your way to help out in the full committee. It would be extremely appreciated. . . . Chuck, I can't ask for anything more. . . . I have not talked to — say, while I have you, I'm sure you're cognizant of the thing Jim Pearson and Frank Church . . . Yes, the three-year program, with termination, *vis-à-vis* South Vietnam. If we could satisfy both Frank as well as Jim, this might be a way of, if we can get them to agree . . . You're a friend of Jim Pearson — could you see if you can . . . Let us know, and we'll do our best to cooperate. . . . (*Big laugh.*) I can't disagree with that under any circumstances. . . . O.K.,

Chuck. Right. . . . Right. . . . That's good. Many, many thanks. Good-by.

He hung up. He turned to me and said: "That's the way it works."

I remarked that it sometimes sounded to me as if he missed the good old days in Congress.

FORD: When you've worked in a place twenty-five years you can't help missing the people — on both sides. It's different. Up there you're only one of 435. Even if you're a leader, you have to work with 434 very independent people. They can tell you no, and you can't do anything about it. Down here, the President is the final decision maker on a few things, but you still have to work with those people — in a different relationship. My only ambition in all those years was to be Speaker of the House. Obviously that was not going to be. So now I'm here. I liked that, and I like this. I'm adaptable, I guess.

"That's the way it works." Suddenly, after this phone call, I had a sense of links — of a kind of chain that had been there all morning. Nostalgia about votes to recommit. "Strong feelings" about checks and balances, in the homily to the kids. "My philosophy of government" — in the Cabinet meeting — which seemed to come down to making sure the consumer understood "both pros and cons." Offering up prayers with his old friend John Rhodes — the very man who had just announced the plan for a House Republican legislative program independent of his. Doubts about survival of the voting-rights act in the give-and-take of the Hill — "knowledgeable and influential men." And now the phone call: "Chuck, I can't ask for anything more."

The adversary process of checks and balances in which Mr. Ford had become chained as President, all the more starkly because he dealt with a Congress dominated by the opposition party, merely added new links to old ones. He believed in this process. He had a long habit of playing the national poker game, it was of his essence. "I liked that, and I like this."

I went back to the press room, and someone dug out for me the text of the President's statement that Monday after the swearing-in, and I found the catch. The full sentence read: "As President, within the limit of basic principles, my motto towards the Congress is communication, conciliation, compromise and cooperation." Now I was beginning to realize the weight of the reservation.

What were the basic principles? This morning I had heard the first name Barber in passing in the Nessen session. Who was Barber? He was Barber B. Conable, Jr. And who might he be? He was the Congressman from New York who, in the last full year of Nixon's Presidency, had distinguished himself by casting the greatest number of votes in favor of Nixon-backed bills of any member of Congress. For some reason Barber B. Conable, Jr., was not now President of the United States. And what about the man who *was* President? When all the ayes and nays were counted, he had been the second most faithful to Nixon of all the 435 members of Congress.

The basic principles were couched in the voting record over the years: *against* Federal aid to education (1956, 1961, 1963, 1965, 1969, 1970); against Federal support for water-pollution programs (1956, 1960); against creation of the Office of Economic Opportunity (1964); against mass transit (1973); against ending the bombing of Cambodia (1973). *For* defense spending (consistently); for revenue sharing (1972); for cutting off aid to students who participated in campus disruptions (1968); for the Civil Rights Act (1964) and the Voting Rights Act (1965) — but only after the failure of weaker substitutes, which he favored; for watering down of the Voting Rights Act (1969). In 1967 he gave a speech on the House floor entitled "Why Are We Pulling Our Best Punches in Vietnam?" He supported Vietnamization. In 1970 he advocated the impeachment of Supreme Court Justice William O. Douglas.

Classical Republican conservatism was deeply implanted in Gerald Ford. The hard sound I had heard the day before was perhaps less a matter of coldness of heart than of glacial caution. Wariness in a world in which change was rampant. The aggressiveness of the defensive center.

And, above all, I realized was there was this: ever since he had entered public life in 1949, Gerald Ford had been on the losing side. He had always been a member of the minority. He had a firm habit of losing — of shrugging off each setback and of turning to the next day's hopeless task.

"I'm adaptable, I guess." Now I wondered, how adaptable? In form or in substance? In ways of working or in the set of the mind?

3:23, 3:34, 3:49, 3:55, 4:09 P.M. The President interviewed a series of candidates for replacement of his military assistant. At the end of the session Dick Cheney, Rumsfeld's deputy, asked him his preferences.

FORD: Who-all on the staff interviewed them?
CHENEY: Jack, Don, Brent, [Staff Secretary] Jerry Jones, Jim, and I.
FORD: I'd rather wait and get your recommendations. (*After a pause:*) I don't want to prejudice you.

4:25 P.M. The President called me to his desk.

FORD: I want to tell you about Bob Orben, who's coming in next. In '68 I had to represent the Republicans at the Gridiron dinner. You're supposed to be funny for ten minutes and serious for two, you know. I'd been to several of those dinners, and I'd heard two top people misjudge badly — Soapy Williams made a political speech, and John Lindsay told off-color jokes. So I thought I'd better get some help. I went to George Murphy, and he went to Red Skelton, and he got me Bob Orben, who'd been writing for TV comedians for years. Well, the speech turned out to be well received. Of course, my opposition was Hubert, and he talked for twenty-four minutes. But Bob comes in nowadays on a consulting basis. He has an excellent style, and he's broadening me out in speech work.

4:30 P.M. Orben came in with the text for a speech the President was to make at a Gridiron-like dinner of the Radio and Television Correspondents Association the next night.

FORD (*reading aloud from the text*): "I have only one thing to say about a program that calls for me to follow Bob Hope: Who arranged this? Scoop Jackson? It's ridiculous. Bob Hope has enormous stage presence, superb comedy timing and the finest writers in the business. I'm standing here in a rented tuxedo — with three jokes from Earl Butz!"

ORBEN: I've been playing the tapes of your speeches. Your timing at the Alfalfa Club was fine — conversational. But other times you tend to be a little slow. Whenever you're doing humor, don't pause in a sentence. Watch Hope. You'll see he really punches through a line. Don't pause.

(*The President tries again.*)

ORBEN: That's better.

FORD: Is it moving?

ORBEN: You're moving right along. Put a slash in after "ridiculous." You could pause there. . . .

FORD (*a little farther on*): "And so far, this has really been a very exciting week in Washington. Particularly in the Congress. On Monday, Carl Albert picked up Bella Abzug's hat by mistake . . . put it on . . . and disappeared for three days!"

ORBEN: Very good.

FORD: If I get a laugh — would it be a good idea to gesture, as if I'm putting on a big hat?

ORBEN: I don't think it's necessary. They'll be getting a visual picture. But if you're more comfortable doing it that way —

FORD: It's a little demonstrative.

ORBEN: It wouldn't hurt.

5:00 P.M. Rumsfeld in the evening roundup. The astonishing range of an hour's business: the Cabinet meeting that morning; the C.I.A.; the meeting yesterday with Chief Justice Burger; the decision of the staff aides on the candidates for military assistant, and the roles, desired ranks, number and responsibilities of military aides in the future; a candidate for a Federal post; some procedural questions; the possibility of some time off for a staff member; tomorrow's schedule; a half-dozen schedule decisions for the future; some administrative questions concerning the President's secretaries; the recruiting of a new deputy for a Cabinet officer; the need for some guidance on management of an agency; Cambodia; trips that had been planned; details of an imminent visit to the West Coast; attendees at Cabinet meetings; urgent details of planning on the economy; some non-Government views on the economy; two personal matters. The President also "signed off on" the retirement of an admiral and the promotion and reassignment of two other admirals, and gave Rumsfeld three notes on matters that had come up in meetings he had had during the day, on which he wanted action.

6:00 P.M. Paperwork.

7:13 P.M. To the residence.

11. THURSDAY

Where, Deep Down, Did the Poor Boy Lurk?

6:00 A.M. He was grinding out a mile on his exercise bike. It was a long mile, an uphill mile, because the brake screw was turned down tight. He was in navy-blue pajamas and a light-blue, short-sleeved, karate-style kimono.

"Henry exercises on one of these things," he told me, "but while he's riding he props a book on the handlebars and reads."

We were in what could only be described, amidst the lavish décor of the rest of the White House, as the Fords' real home within the home. Mr. Ford, pumping away, told me, "The Nixons had separate bedrooms; this used to be his." But when the Fords moved in, Betty said she and Jerry had shared the same bed for twenty-five years, and she wasn't about to let that be changed. She was still asleep now in the big bed in the next room.

The President had been up since 5:30, as on most mornings. He had read part of the *Washington Post* before I arrived. He was chugging away now, his inner motor fully engaged, as alert and calm as if in a Cabinet meeting. He said he fell asleep at night in ten seconds, slept soundly for five hours and waked up fully refreshed. "Oh, very occasionally," he told me, "Betty will say, 'Gee, you had a bad night,' but I'm not cognizant of it. She'll complain I was restless. Maybe it woke her, but it didn't wake me. I sleep very deeply, and I come back easily."

He dismounted the bike and moved to a machine for strengthening thigh and knee muscles; this stood between the bicycle and a tall corner cabinet, which held the trophies of a lifetime of competition. He sat on the red leather platform of the machine and did forty knee-lifts with each leg; on his left foot was a weight of forty pounds, on his right, twenty-five pounds. "This knee" — a hand indicated the right — "I favor a bit." Both knees had suffered football injuries, and the left knee had been operated on in 1932. "The other one gave me problems for thirty years," he said. "It would begin to lock on me on the fairway, or it would go weak when I was skiing. So in '72, after I got back from China, I had it operated on, too. The usual cartilage-and-ligaments thing."

He got down on the floor and did twenty push-ups and, prone, twenty lifts of his torso, with his hands behind his head, to harden his gut.

Then, a trifle winded, he dropped into a blue leather lounge chair, an old favorite of his, made in Grand Rapids, and he lifted his slippered feet onto a matching footstool and resumed reading the *Post*. "In the evenings," he said, looking over the edge of the paper, "I'll sit here, Betty'll sit there" — in an overstuffed chair close by — "and we'll read or watch television. It's just family in here." Resting on the spines of three photo albums in a magazine rack to his right, between the two chairs, was a remote-control pushbutton box for changing the channels on a television set and, under it, a paperback copy of *Plain Speaking: An Oral Biography of Harry S. Truman*, by Merle Miller. The television set was in a huge console built into the corner next to the fireplace, which was to the President's left. Beside the President's feet on the footstool was a looseleaf notebook inscribed in gold letters: *The President's Daily News Briefing*. The brown suitcase for his official papers was propped open between the footstool and the fireplace.

I left him while he read the rest of the paper and the staff news summary; and got dressed.

6:55 A.M. He joined me, in shirtsleeves, and we walked into an overpowering ambiance of history in the President's dining room. The walls were papered in huge, lush, and wildly inaccurate scenes of the War of Independence — Washington in command at the Battle of Niagara Falls, the capture of Wechawk Hill by Lafayette, the surrender of Cornwallis at Yorktown and Washington's triumphal entry into Boston — printed in France in 1854 by Jean Zuber. A tiny television set was on the dining table, off to the left of the President's place-setting. A scooped-out half pineapple served as a bowl for chunks of its flesh; a tall glass of orange juice and a Thermos carafe of tea waited for him; a butler brought him a single toasted muffin with margarine. The *New York Times* was on a side table to his right, but that morning he did not read it. We ate and talked.

"I get my energy," he said, "from my mother. She was a tremendously energetic person, just fantastic. She probably had more friends than any woman I ever knew. Everybody loved her. She was a human dynamo in a womanly way. She wasn't a great career type. But she was the most thoughtful person, always writing to people — a note on a birthday — or calling on some who were in the hospital. She just had great compassion for people, plus this almost unbelievable energy. . . ."

"My very young years, I had a terrible temper," he said. "My mother detected it and started to get me away from being upset and flying off the handle. She had a great knack of ridicule one time, and humor the next, or cajoling, to teach me that anger — visible, physical anger — was not the way to meet problems. But then adversity in athletics also helped teach me. Adversity in my personal life; I thought I was madly in love with a very attractive gal. It didn't work out. One time, I thought that was the greatest catastrophe in my life. It just didn't turn out to be that way. But going back to my mother's input: she taught me that you don't respond in a wild, uncontrolled way; you just better sit back and take a hard look and try to make the best decision without letting emotions be the controlling factor. . . ."

He spoke deliberately, without emotion, sometimes pausing in midsentence to gather his thoughts, and using my first name often. He was concerned about whether I was getting enough breakfast. Dr. Lukash was very strict with him about his intake of calories, he said. . . .

"Sometimes I do get angry," he said. "People feuding — and I guess this goes back to experiences I have had in athletics. A feuding football team never got anyplace. A feuding staff in the White House is never going to get anyplace. It's so senseless. Anything that's senseless is frustrating and upsets me. . . . Nothing is more frustrating to me, John, than to have staff jealousies. Nothing gets my mind off what I want to think about more than to have petty jealousies in staff people. I just can't tolerate it, and it's more disturbing to me than anything. But competence, loyalty, hard work — I do think I get those things from the people on my staff. . . ."

We talked quite a lot about football.

". . . The last game we played was with Northwestern, and I had a very good day against a darned good Northwestern guard. Rip Whalen. I just gave him fits. I knocked him all over the field. . . . And on the way back from the Shriners game, Andy Kerr and Curly Lambeau spent a good share of time trying to talk me into playing for the Green Bay Packers. And then Pottsy Clark, who was the head coach of the Detroit Lions, who had seen some of the Michigan games, tried to get me to play for the Lions. . . . I'd learned a little about sitting on the bench. . . . In those days, the center had to pass the ball, not to a quarterback, but to a tail-back. You really had to pass the ball; you had to lead the runner, and had to block at the same time, and you played defense, too. . . . The people that I met. . . . I had some good teammates and good coaching, and I've kept those associations. . . . The actual competition is a pretty good character builder. . . . And football is as good a training ground from the team-operation point of view as anything I can think of. . . ."

And now he told a strange tale. I had known that Gerald R. Ford, Jr., was not born with that name — that his mother and his actual father, then a Nebraska wool trader, were divorced when he was two years old and that not long afterward he was adopted by, and renamed for, the Grand Rapids paint salesman his mother married. The story: "I was, I think, a junior in high school in the spring, 1930. I worked at a restaurant across from South High called Skougis's. It was a 1929, 1930 hamburger stand with counters — a dilapidated place. Bill Skougis was a shrewd Greek businessman, and he hired as waiters the outstanding football players. He hired me my sophomore year. He paid me two dollars plus my lunch — up to fifty cents a meal — and I worked from eleven thirty to one, through the noon-hour class periods, and one night a week from seven to ten. I waited on table at one of the counters, washed the dishes and handled the cash register. My working place was right near the entrance. It was a long, narrow restaurant. You came in, and I was on this side washing dishes, checking people out. There was a candy counter on my side that went right down the room. There were tables and another counter. I was standing there taking money, washing dishes, and I also had to make cheese sandwiches behind the barrier. This man came in, and he stood over there. And he was a stranger. Strangers didn't come in often. This man stood over there against the candy counter. I was busy, yet I couldn't help but notice that he stood there for ten minutes. Finally he walked over to where I was working. Nobody was bothering me. 'Leslie,' he said. I didn't answer. He said, 'I'm your father.' He said, 'I'm Leslie King, and you're Leslie King, Jr.' Well, it was kind of shocking. He said, 'I would like to take you to lunch.' I said, 'Well, I'm working. I've got to check with the owner.' He said, 'I haven't seen you for a good many years. You don't know me.' So I went to Bill Skougis, and I said, 'I've got a personal matter. Will you excuse me?' And he did. My father took me out to his car, which was parked in the front — a brand-new Cadillac or Lincoln — and he introduced me to his wife. So we went to lunch. He was then living in Wyoming with his wife, and they had come out to buy a new Cadillac or Lincoln, which was a beautiful car for those days, and they had picked it up in Detroit and were driving back to Wyoming, and they wanted to stop in and see me. Which he did. And after he had finished lunch, he took me back to the school. I said good-by. He said, 'Will you come out to see me in Wyoming?' I said I'd think about it. . . . The hard part was going home that night, and how to tell my mother and stepfather. That really worried me, because I had grown up, since I could remember, with my stepfather. It was only a year or two before this that I'd learned I was not living with my real father. My relationship with my stepfather was so close that it never entered my mind not to tell him. It was real hard. That was the difficult part. . . ."

"My junior year at Ann Arbor," he said, "which would be '33–'34, when my stepfather's business had long gone to pot, he was hanging on by his fingernails, my father — my real father — had been ordered at the time of the divorce to pay my mother child maintenance, and he never paid any. I was having a terrible time. Sure, I was earning my board, and I saved some money working for my stepfather in the summer. But it wasn't enough. I wasn't able to pay my bills — the fraternity, the room where I lived. And I wrote my father and asked him if he could help. And, as I recall, I either got no answer or, if I got an answer, he said he couldn't do it. I felt that, from what I understood, his economic circumstances were such that he could have been helpful. I had that impression. From that Lincoln or Cadillac I'd seen that he'd bought. And then after I graduated from Michigan, I went to Yale, of course. And then one time, out of the blue, I got a letter, a phone call, or something, saying that he was coming with his wife, the woman I had met, with his son by the second marriage — he was really my stepbrother. And they were trying to find a school in the East for him, and could they stop by and maybe I could give them some advice. So they stopped. I did meet the son. And I went to dinner with them and gave them some thoughts about schools in the East and never saw them again. . . ."

"My stepfather," he said, "was the only boy in a family of three girls. His father died at a very young age, I think of a train crash. So Dad Ford quit school, or had to — never went beyond the eighth grade. And he really lifted himself up by great effort, going step by step. He was probably one of the most respected people in the community. for his civic-mindedness, his integrity, hard work. . . . He always saw something good in somebody, even people who had nothing in common with him. We got into a discussion about somebody one time, and I said, 'Oh, he's no good. He does this, or he does that.' And he said, 'Well, but he also does this, which I like — and you ought to like.' . . ."

"At one stage," he said, "when I was eight or nine, I had a slight tendency to stutter, very infrequent, and yet it did appear once in a while. Some people alleged at that time that my being left-handed also being partly right-handed, that the ambidextrous situation contributed to the stuttering tendency. I either outgrew it or it wasn't well founded. But this is an interesting thing: I never noticed it in myself until one night I was sitting at dinner in Washington about six months ago, and this woman noticed I ate left-handed. She said, 'What else do you do left-handed?' I said, 'I write left-handed.' And she said, 'Do you throw, kick, play golf left-handed?' I said, 'No.' She said, 'You're one of the few odd people who do things left-handed when you sit down, but you're right-handed when you stand up.' I've never gone into it, but this woman really perked my interest. . . ."

"I spent a great deal of time for a period of about four years as a Boy Scout," he said. "I think scouting had a great deal to do with getting me on, and helping me stay on, some of the character attributes that I think I have, and that are important. Again, it was good associations — with leaders, with troop members. I was just very fortunate to get into a stream of athletics, student groups — a stream of people that was good, clear, strong. . . ."

He told me another story: "As assistant navigator, I stood officer-of-the-deck watches. You had four hours on and then usually eight hours off. But it just so happened that about December 16 or 17 of 1944 we got caught in that terrible typhoon off the Philippines. We had spent the day before refueling and helping in the over-all task-force refueling operation. I had had the midnight to 0400 watch, and that was at the very high point in the typhoon. I was relieved and went down to hit the sack. And that morning I got about forty-five minutes' sleep before we had our regular morning general quarters, a half-hour before sunrise. I then went back to bed, and I had gotten back to sleep again. I don't know how long. Not very long. All of a sudden, general quarters rang again. And I woke up, and several people were dashing down the passageway yelling, 'Fire, fire, fire!' — which I later learned had been caused by a plane breaking loose, not adequately tied down, and slamming against another, and that broke loose another. And pretty soon they were all rolling back and forth as the ship rolled at the height of the storm. And, unfortunately, somebody had left some gasoline in one of the planes, and friction sparked it, and the gasoline started a fire, and these planes as they were going back and forth bashed into the air intakes, so instead of fresh air going down to the boiler room, they took in smoke from the hangar deck. So we lost ten or twelve people down in the boiler room and engine room who just never knew what hit them. . . . I woke up and I was down in officers' quarters. And I started up — have you got a pencil there? Here's the carrier, and here is the island of the carrier, right here. My stateroom with another fellow was down here. When I heard general quarters, got out of the sack, saw people running, smelled the smoke — I always went out of my stateroom up to a ladder here and then went out a door there onto the flight deck and climbed up another ladder onto the island structure to my job as officer of the deck. Well, this time, the moment I stepped out on the deck, the ship rolled way over, and I lost my balance. I went sliding just like a toboggan. Couldn't have lasted more than two or three seconds, 'cause it was only one hundred and some feet wide. But anyhow, I spread out as much as I could. There was nothing to grab on to. But fortunately around a flight deck there's a little raised metal rim so that tools won't roll over the side. And I hit that with my feet, and it spun me around, and I dropped, half in and half out of the catwalk that goes all the way around just below a flight deck. I fell halfway in and halfway out. If I'd gone another foot, I'd have gone over the side. We lost about five men overboard. For me, it was just one of those quirks. Pure happenstance. If I'd had a different angle, different speed. . . ."

"You know," he said, "I wasn't married until I was thirty-five. Basically, two reasons. One, I was always so busy, never really had enough time to get involved, and I always had sort of a focus on, concentrating on something careerwise — focused in that area. And second, I had only one serious romance, other than the one I had with Betty, with this girl from Connecticut College, very superior girl — but it didn't work out. So I just forgot being too much interested in marriage. Then I met Betty, and she was very attractive. She added a sense of stability and serenity. And by the time I was thirty-five, I was pretty well on course and wasn't preoccupied. I knew where I was going — at least where I wanted to try to go. And so our lives sort of fitted at that stage, plus a very excellent, broad, broad relationship. And she has done a super job, because in Congress, which our married life coincided with, she was strong, self-reliant, ran the family, gave me a chance to do things that broadened my relationships. And I think she contributed very substantially in the opportunities that materialized in my becoming President. Very loyal. She also has the capability of bringing you down to earth, once in a while, when you get some illusions. . . ."

"My gracious," he said, looking at his watch. "They'll be waiting for me."

7:42 A.M. He emerged from the family room, followed by a valet carrying the brown suitcase. In the elevator, I noticed — since he now had a jacket on — that he was wearing a dark-gray double-breasted suit with peaked lapels and a hairline pinstripe. A Secret Service man was waiting at the elevator door to the ground-floor corridor. The President briskly stepped out onto the dazzling crimson carpet that tied together the tunnel-like chain of Hoban's massive groined arches, which seem designed to bear all the weight of the history overhead; in the recesses of these arches, first ladies hung. Claudia (Lady Bird) Johnson was right across the way as we started along.

Standing in an open doorway on the left, opposite Caroline Scott Harrison on the right, was Rear Admiral William M. Lukash, the President's physician, who, with his almost hairless head all tanned, his figure slim and lithe, seemed to have the health and poise of a hungry leopard. A specialist in gastroenterology, he was named Assistant Physician to President Nixon in 1969, and, being a Michigander with a wife from Grand Rapids, he suited Gerald Ford to a T.

"Good morning, Bill," the President said, in a tone of voice that would have made it absurd to ask how he felt. The concern, at the moment, was all for Betty, who had been suffering pain that week from the mysterious pinched nerve in her neck, which had bothered her off and on for years; and for Susan, who had had a touch of bronchitis.

FORD: How's Susan? Seen her this morning?

LUKASH: Not yet. She had a little fever last night. She won't be going to school today. I'll be checking up soon.

FORD: Let me know how she is, and Betty, will you? Give me a call.

LUKASH: Yes, sir. (*Seeing me with him:*) Did you do your exercises this morning?

FORD: Yes, Doctor. Yes, Doctor.

7:44 A.M. We paced along past Edith Galt Wilson and Sarah Childress Polk, and then out into the open air — the fourth rainy day in a row — along the covered walkway beside the former swimming pool, and around into the Oval Office. Fifteen minutes late.

7:47 A.M. Scowcroft and Peterson. 8:12 A.M. — Hartmann. 8:30 A.M. — Rumsfeld. 9:07 A.M. — Marsh. 9:22 A.M. — Nessen, Hartmann, Rumsfeld, Friedersdorf. All the words the President had spoken at breakfast hung like a veil of gauze over these conferences. I kept looking closely at this man who had such an energetic, compassionate mother and two fathers — or none. Were there any traces at all of the temper tantrums? Where, deep down, did the poor boy lurk, to whom two dollars a week earned at Skougis's dilapidated joint had made such a difference? Nessen asked what he was to say about Scoop Jackson's proposal that Mike Mansfield go to China and negotiate with Sihanouk. This was an insolent suggestion — that the Democrats should simply take over foreign policy from the President. "The way it's being phrased," Rumsfeld said, not soothing the sting, "is, 'Why aren't you willing to try anything at this stage to get peace?' " But Gerald Ford sounded, as always, totally serene. "I frankly haven't had a chance to talk with Brent about that," he quietly said. Friedersdorf mentioned the bad setback Wednesday in the House, whose Democratic caucus had voted 189 to 49 against any additional military aid to Cambodia. "You can say," the President calmly told Nessen, "that my reaction was tremendous disappointment" — which did not show at all — "that such an action would be taken despite the advice of the Congressional delegation that went out to Cambodia, onto the scene."

9:57 A.M. The President left for a courtesy tour, long overdue, of the East Wing, where Mrs. Ford's staff, the President's Military Assistant and aides, his organization for liaison with the Hill, and those who handled White House tours and visitors had their offices. On the way through the residence, he went upstairs to see how Betty and Susan were feeling. When he reached the East Wing, he shook sixtythree staff hands, ranging from that of Nancy Howe, Mrs. Ford's personal assistant, to that of the young lady who answered the not inconsiderable number of letters addressed to Shan and Liberty, the Fords' Siamese cat and golden retriever.

On the way through the open hallway to the Legislative Affairs office, he suddenly came on a group of about fifty students and teachers from Brady Middle School, which, I was soon told, stands on Chagrin Boulevard in Pepper Pike, Ohio; this happened to be the next batch, lined up behind a barrier, for a White House tour.

"My God, it's the President!" a teacher gasped.

Mr. Ford, smiling benignly, unexcited, taking his time, walked into the group and shook almost every hand, and asked earnest questions as he moved from one to another. The teachers were losing feathers in their flutter, but the kids took the whole scene just as calmly as he did. The news would spread like wildfire, first through Pepper Pike, then through all of Ohio, that President Ford personally greeted every tour of the White House.

10:26 A.M. Back to the Oval Office. With all his leisurely motion through the morning, the President had made up the fifteen minutes of tardiness and was now five minutes ahead of schedule.

10:30 and **11:30 A.M.** The next two meetings were related to each other. The common situation was this:

The cost of postal operations had been going up. To get into the black, the Postal Service either would have to reduce its services and increase postal rates again in a few months, or would need to receive larger Federal subsidies. Wages accounted for 80 percent of postal costs, and one reason it had been so hard to get the Postal Service out of politics was that nearly 1 percent of the entire working population of the country was in the Postal Service; there were 700,000 votes there. Postal unions would soon begin negotiating a new contract; there was talk of a possible strike, even though it would be illegal. Would the National Guard be used in that case?

The President met first with the chairmen and ranking minority members of the House and Senate Post Office and Civil Service committees, Representatives David Henderson and Ed Derwinski, Senators Gale McGee and Hiram Fong.

McGEE: There's no way that the 30,000 post offices in this country can pay their way. We have to support them.

FORD: Could you justify a 10-percent subsidy for those communities that have post offices? . . .

McGEE: Congress doesn't think it can stand for another first-class rate increase, because we get so much mail on it. . . .

FONG: Would you designate someone on your staff for liaison with us on this?

FORD: We will do that. . . . I'd like to give the signal that we don't want a strike, we'll do everything we can to reach an equitable labor contract. But if there is a strike — well, we must move the mail. . . .

McGEE: Nobody loves us.

FORD: I'm learning that fast down here, Gale.

Meeting next with Postmaster General Benjamin F. Bailar, William J. Usery, Director of the Federal Mediation and

Conciliation Service, and some others, the President got his message across more explicitly: he believed the users of the mails should pay for the service; he did not favor larger subsidies, which, he said, would transfer costs from postal users to taxpayers at large.

Myron Wright, Vice Chairman of the Postal Board of Governors, quietly pointed out that more than 80 percent of all mail is "business-oriented," and suggested that the general public shouldn't have to subsidize that. . . .

FORD (*toward the end of the meeting*): I want to say very firmly, we want equity, but we can't afford to have the inflation re-exploded. I expect the mails to be delivered. We hope the contract will be solved, but the mails (*strong emphasis*) will be delivered.

During these discussions which had been long and intricate, three shadowy images had been hanging like smoke in my mind: of the junior in Deke at Ann Arbor, unable to make ends meet, driven to begging for money from his non-father of a father; of the assistant navigator shooting across the tilted deck of the *Monterey* and very nearly flying into the sea; of Michigan's center giving Northwestern's Rip Whalen fits, knocking him all over the field. . . .

12:20 P.M. The President received five-year-old Pamela Jo Baker, the model for that year's Easter Seal poster — a curly-haired child who had been crippled with cerebral palsy since birth, and who had learned to walk and talk through Easter Seal services. She wore braces on her legs; she tottered; and she seemed — understandably — very frightened. With her was Peter Falk, star of the TV show *Columbo,* who was honorary national chairman of the Easter Seal drive, her father, and her two Senators, Randolph and Byrd.

FORD (*to Falk*): My wife and I watch your program a lot. I get very concerned about your personal security and safety from time to time.

FALK: Don't worry about me. I'll be all right. I have to come on the next week.

FORD: How many handicapped children do your services help?

FALK: Children and adults. Nearly 300,000 this year.

The President took Pamela Jo up in his arms, and he talked to her softly. Then he asked where Liberty was. Somebody ran for the dog. Liberty romped wildly around the Oval Office, then suddenly lay down on her back at the President's feet.

FORD (*to Liberty*): That's not a very nice position for a lady to get into!

The President carefully pinned a little brooch, with a Presidential seal on it, on Pamela Jo's dress.

When she left in her father's arms, the President called, "So long, Pam." Her eyes were fearless now. She had obviously liked that quiet man who was holding her. With an effort, she waved.

12:44 P.M. General William C. Westmoreland, former commander of U.S. forces in Vietnam and former Chief of Staff of the Army, paid a call which had been deferred since early in the year because the general had had a heart attack on January 5. He came in, as it was decorously put in a briefing paper from Henry Kissinger, to "discuss his opportunities for further Government service."

FORD: I was real sorry to hear about your heart attack, Westy.

WESTMORELAND: I was the lowest-risk sort of person. No weight problem. Low cholesterol . . .

FORD: I've been trying to get Betty to go along with me on buying a place near you down there at Hilton Head, but I'm not making much progress. How's that Kuwaiti project doing? Aren't they trying to develop the shoreline near you there?

WESTMORELAND: There was some opposition from environmentalists. But now the Jews have gotten into it — some highly respected people — and I believe several houses are under construction.

FORD: Like Hilton Head?

WESTMORELAND: Smaller and more exclusive. Something like Seabrook Island.

Now, for the first time, I had noticed something: there was a certain urge toward mimicry, an echoing effect, in Gerald Ford. He seemed anxious always to please; one assumed that as a basic drive in all politicians. But the hint I was getting now was of something more, some sort of protean need and knack — some part of him became the person he was talking with. Westmoreland sat ramrod-straight; Ford was upright now. Westmoreland talked in cranky, clipped tones; Ford was growing more spare in his speech.

FORD: I'll keep my eyes and ears open, Westy. Some part-time commission.

The President mentioned one possibility — on which it was obvious the general had had his eye — but Mr. Ford said there was no vacancy. He had just replaced one person in that group.

WESTMORELAND (*taken aback*): I was given to understand there was no statutory limit on the number of members —

FORD: Well, its chairman doesn't want it to get too big. I can understand that. We'll definitely keep you in mind, though.

WESTMORELAND: I've been decorated in sixteen foreign countries. I know something about . . .

They began to talk about conditions — about inflation and recession and energy and:

FORD: I've been having a hard time getting Congress to act responsibly on Indochina, Westy. I just learned a few minutes ago that the full House Committee on Foreign Affairs rejected the Cambodia package by a vote of eighteen to fifteen.

WESTMORELAND: It's reminiscent of the early days of the German military threat. The North Vietnamese are the Prussians of the Orient. . . . Sihanouk has no clout.

FORD: That's my impression, Westy.

WESTMORELAND: This Jackson proposal that Mansfield go out there and negotiate with Sihanouk — it's ridiculous.

FORD: Westy, they're all trying to find some way to do something that won't be enough to save the situation but'll avoid political blame. That's all there is to it.

WESTMORELAND: There is only one language that Hanoi understands, and that's force. If we'd just send our B-52's in there to bomb the supply trails and mine Haiphong harbor for a month, this whole atmosphere would change.

FORD: Unfortunately, the law says we can't do that, Westy.

2:18 P.M. Personnel Director Bill Walker and Phil Buchen in on a personnel matter.

2:35 P.M. Jim Cannon in to talk about the Domestic Council.

3:03 P.M. The President, Secretary of the Interior Morton, Lynn, Zarb, Cannon, and O'Neill were disposed in sofas and chairs at the fireplace end of the Oval Office, talking about what the President called "the politics of oil." In this case, of eking oil from the outer continental shelf, from under the sea off our shores. The question to be discussed that day was not whether to drill the shelf for oil; the question was who was to get the revenues from the oil when it had been found. Maine and several other states had sued the Government, claiming they owned the offshore shelf and any oil in it. Secretary Morton was to testify before the Senate Interior and Insular Affairs Committee the next day and wanted guidance on what to say.

What interested me in this meeting was its big-business boardroom tone — one that I had heard several times in those days. The options sounded strangely corporate: "we" could take all the revenue; or, if "we" were forced to, "we" could share it with the coastal states; or, at worst, "we" might have to share it with all the states. But the Supreme Court was probably going to decide that "we" owned the whole shebang.

MORTON: O.K. Let's ride this out till the Court decides.

LYNN: Let's wait, and move from a position of strength.

We'd want to see what we want to buy from the states with a sharing formula.

The whole style of an Administration is revealed in the phrases that it uses. Need we hear more than "take the hang-out route" and "twisting slowly, slowly in the wind" to conjure up the entire nightmare of the Nixon decline? The style of the Ford Administration was different — it was the style of Middle American businessmen's in-group fast talk. Its root stock was Adam Smith *laissez-faire* wheeling and dealing, onto which was grafted, to produce strange fruit, the tone of voice of Eisenhower's Defense Secretary Charlie (What's good for General Motors is good for the country) Wilson. All week long I had been noting bellwether words and phrases, spoken by Cabinet members and top advisers, and I had just added three new specimens there in the outer-continental-shelf meeting. Listen:

We're going to be nickel-and-diming the multinationals. He can bring most of his Indians along. Appearancewise. Programs coming down the pike. Down the road. Downstream. Ball-park figure. They won't be able to resist matching those goodies. Paint a bigger picture. Public posture. Big go-round. Signed off on. Shopping list. They're cutting a deal up there right now. We don't want a Christmas-tax bill. That aims a rifle straight at crude oil. Afraid that'll tilt the industry toward the foreign car. They're trying to put some light between themselves and you. We're kind of salami-ing it. That's just putting a different gown on the same doll. Consumerism, Naderism, clean-airism. He's John Dunlop's honcho. He's going to waffle it. Pick of the litter. God-dog it. Time to get our socks pulled up on that. This could get pretty antsie-dancie in the next few weeks. I'm not married to the 5-percent figure. I'm not in glue on how far we should go. Let's be stupid, if necessary — and I find that very easy, Mr. President. A game plan and a sound signal. Let's let Hollings and Jackson fight each other till they lie down. I think I can punt tomorrow. That's one frontier that's out of the ball game. That just won't fly. Maybe you can get that under the tent. Roll it around in that direction. That's a modification I think you could hang your hat on. We'll try to screw the thing down so that it doesn't come leaking out of the basement windows.

4:07 P.M. A young Congressman from Florida named Lou Frey came in to talk with the President about the possibility of locating a new solar-energy research program at the Kennedy Space Center, to offset recent NASA cutbacks. Frey bitterly opposed a recent 730-man cutback in personnel at Patrick Air Base; unemployment in the Cocoa Beach area was running about 11 percent. Frey was considered a Republican comer; he was Chairman of the Republican Research Committee in the House, and he was thinking about running against Democratic Senator Lawton Chiles in 1976. The President, after hearing his appeal, said he couldn't make any promises, Lou. As to the cutbacks in Lou's constituency, they'd been a response to Congressional bites out of the defense budget.

Frey suddenly started talking with flashing eyes about something called "ocean thermal gradient research," a plan for getting endless amounts of energy out of differences in temperatures in the sea. He would like to start this going in a big way off Florida, in the Gulf Stream.

FORD (*taking Frey's fire calmly*): Very interesting.

4:30 P.M. Hartmann, Theis, Friedman, Orben, Casserly came in for another session on the Notre Dame speech — into which, in the long run, the old domino theory made its weary way.

5:25 P.M. Mr. Ford went downstairs for a haircut; he had one every ten days or so. As Milton Pitts, the White House barber, went to work in the brightly lit shop, the President glanced at the afternoon *Star-News* and then read over once again his gags for that evening's Radio and Television Correspondents dinner. The texture of Mr. Ford's hair was extremely fine; Mr. Pitts tried hard to give it the dry look, full on the sides. A quirky coincidence had brought these two men together. One afternoon about five years before, Mr. Pitts, who operated four Washington barbershops, one of

them in the Sheraton-Carlton, had been approached in his
Georgetown shop by a young, well-dressed man who did not
sit down in a chair but asked to speak privately with him.
They went into a back room. The young man said President
Nixon needed a new barber — would Pitts be interested? He
was. The young man was Alexander Butterfield — who,
some three and a half years later, blurted out to investigators
for a Senate select committee, in apparent inadvertence, that
everything that took place in Richard Nixon's Oval Office
was recorded on tape. It could be said that Alexander Butterfield had made possible the haircut that was now taking
place.

6:07 P.M. Back to the Oval Office for some paperwork.

6:15 P.M. Major General Richard L. Lawson, who was about
to be replaced as the President's Military Assistant, brought
his family in to say good-bye.

6:24 P.M. Rumsfeld's roundup.

7:07 P.M. To the residence. Mr. Ford took his supper on a
tray on a small table in the bedroom, to be with his wife.

9:00 P.M. The President boarded a motorcade on the curving driveway of the South Grounds. At 9:03 he arrived at
the Statler-Hilton, where he was greeted by William W. Win-
pisinger, President of the Institute for Collective Bargaining,
and by Postmaster General Bailar and by others. At 9:04 he
paused in a holding area outside the hotel's Congressional
Room, waiting to be announced. At 9:05 he went to the head
table, where the famous labor negotiator Ted Kheel presented him with a sculpture entitled *Collective Bargaining: Out
of Conflict, Accord* by George Segal, a representation of two
men at a small table in head-to-head parley.

9:15 P.M. The President again boarded the motorcade and
rode to the Washington-Hilton Hotel. At 9:27, in the Cabinet Room of the hotel, Charlie Shutt, Washington bureau
manager of Hearst Metrotone News, presented him with a
can containing a sixteen-millimeter film entitled *Forward
Together: Gerald Ford Assumes the Presidency.* At 9:32 the Presi-

dent stopped by at the Jefferson Room to pay his respects to
a dinner party being given by the Storer Broadcasting Company for the wives of the radio and television correspondents who were concurrently banqueting in the International Ballroom — to which, at 9:42, he proceeded. He
went to the head table. At 9:45, President Marya McLaugh-
lin of the Radio and Television Correspondents Association
introduced Bob Hope, who spoke for half an hour and was,
fortunately for Mr. Ford, rather peevish and dull. At 10:23
the President began speaking:

> FORD (*he has listened carefully to Hope; he now really punches
> through his sentences*): I have only one thing to say about a
> program that calls for me to follow Bob Hope. Who ar-
> ranged this? Scoop Jackson? (*An encouraging explosion of
> laughter.*) It's ridiculous. (*Slash — slight pause for comedy tim-
> ing.*) Bob Hope has enormous stage presence, superb com-
> edy timing and the finest writers in the business. (*Slash.*) I'm
> standing here in a rented tuxedo — with three jokes from
> Earl Butz. (*Laughter and applause!*) . . .

10:31 P.M. Remarks concluded, 10:37 P.M. — President left
head table, went to motorcade. 10:48 P.M. — Motorcade arrived at South Grounds.

About 11:15 P.M. The President was seated in his blue
chair, feet up on the footstool, reading a long and extremely
complicated briefing paper from the Domestic Council on
higher education; another, also complex, was on land use.

About midnight. The Iron Man went to bed, and — if we
can believe his own account, and I, for one, can, knowing at
first hand that he had started that day under a full head of
steam 18½ hours before and hadn't stopped once since —
dived into deep, dark waters in ten seconds.

12. FRIDAY

But on Foreign Policy, Only Kissinger

He came in half an hour late that morning, in a dark-blue pinstripe. The fifth rainy day in a row. He explained that he had had a dental appointment on the ground floor of the residence at 7:15, and that cleaning his teeth had taken longer than expected. He smoked eight pipefuls of tobacco a day, he said, and that caused a lot of staining; sometimes he wished he could cut down.

8:10 A.M. Scowcroft and Peterson went in.

I suffered now, more than the President ever seemed to suffer, from a feeling of having got behind. My week as a watcher was drawing to a close, and so much that I had seen had flashed past me, as if in a speeded-up motion picture. I had a feeling of having missed many glimpses I should have been able to catch — and now, as Brent Scowcroft went into the Oval Office, I was suddenly sharply aware of one of the unseen scenes; I had not had a single direct view, all week long, of a foreign-policy discussion, to say nothing of a foreign-policy decision.

Again that morning I attended the senior staff meeting, where I heard two suggestions put forward that exemplified the staff's efforts to grope their way, from day to day, toward efficiency.

LYNN: Every proposal to the President from a department should be tabbed with a run-down of the situation on the Hill with respect to the issue involved, and with a clear indication of what the department would intend to do on the Hill, either absent a decision from the President on the proposal, or with one. . . .

RUMSFELD: Big issues that are going to be around, and that should come before the President, should be isolated, so we make sure he has a chance to see them well ahead of time. . . .

8:55 A.M. Rumsfeld in for his morning conference.

RUMSFELD: You have meetings scheduled for the afternoon to discuss policy on land-use and higher-education legislation. O.M.B. has been trying for a long time to get the Domestic Council to prepare option papers on these areas, but with the transition in the Domestic Council to the Rockefeller crowd, it's been a bit chaotic over there, and I'm afraid they got the papers to you very late.

FORD: Do I know it! I had to wait till after the Radio-TV dinner last night to read them. Eleven thirty at night ain't a time to read up on this very complicated higher-education problem.

RUMSFELD: I'd be for no decision. Let's get an orderly look at those issues. I'll put a stop on the two meetings, and I'll set up the meeting Jim Lynn has been wanting, to talk about the no-more-spending question. . . .

9:15 A.M. Marsh went in; after him, walking haltingly with a cane, went the President's Counsel, Philip W. Buchen: I was uninvited to follow — and I realized that another direct view I had missed that week (because everything the Counsel touched seems to be sensitive) was that of a talk between Jerry Ford and Phil Buchen. Buchen was Ford's oldest friend and closest confidant in the White House. Three years younger than Ford, Buchen, while he was an undergraduate at Michigan, had met the famous athlete at one of the house parties Delta Kappa Epsilon held each New Year's Eve in Grand Rapids; later he roomed with Ford while they both took summer courses at the Michigan Law School; later still, he became Ford's first law partner in Grand Rapids. He limped from a childhood attack of polio; seated, he lifted the weak leg over the strong one to cross them. His rheumy eyes blinked, and the muscles around them moved with a remarkable rippling effect, under a thin slanting hedge of white eyebrows. When he spoke, it sounded as if he had BB shot rattling around in his larynx, and what he said was conservative, commonsensical, decent; the President listened to him. Something Phil Buchen had said to me one day, in talking about the coming to power of his friend, stuck in my mind as a kind of motto for the Administration: "This is not an era for change."

9:35 A.M. The prebriefing session, with Nessen, Rumsfeld, Marsh, Hartmann, Friedersdorf.

NESSEN: Where do we go now, as far as legislative strategy on Cambodian aid is concerned?

FORD: Without knowing the details, I think we have to keep the pressure on. I strongly disagree with the position taken in the two Democratic caucuses. I hope that wiser heads will prevail in the end. . . .

Nessen tested the President on several other positions.

Suddenly there was a bad moment; it came up from nowhere like a sudden whirling desert dust spout. Nessen had been reading from a newspaper column; "a White House source" had said something that Nessen said he thought might need clarifying or correcting. The President seemed to shrug it off.

RUMSFELD (*sharply*): Mr. President, I think you should read what it quotes Bob Hartmann as saying.

Nessen passed the clipping to Mr. Ford. He started reading it. He did not light his pipe, did not lift his unlit pipe to his mouth. Hartmann's flushed face slowly turned to the right; his lips were pursed, and the habitual twinkle in his eye was replaced by something dangerous, something that could scratch; I remembered that he was rather proud of having a paperweight of carborundum, which is used in abrading steel, on his desk. The President handed the clipping to Hartmann without comment. Hartmann glanced at it.

HARTMANN: This is what we used to call in the trade "thumb-sucking." When a reporter doesn't have any facts, he sucks his thumb awhile and then he writes down whatever comes out of his thumb.

But Hartmann was crossing and recrossing his legs. Rumsfeld's eloquent hands had a delicate tremor. I watched the President closely, mindful of what he had told me at breakfast the previous morning: "It's more disturbing to me than anything. . . ."

This was where I really saw the scope and influence of his self-control. I was so fascinated by his face, which was perfectly peaceful, perfectly serene, that I did not catch the exact words he spoke to Don Rumsfeld, but I could not miss the equable, firm, unreproachful quality of his voice. Then:

FORD (*in silky tones*): Anything else, Ron?

NESSEN: What do I say about the conservatives who are calling Rockefeller a liability?

The nasty little twister had already passed; one could hardly believe it had ever been there; the air was as still as glass. The next time Rumsfeld spoke, his voice was completely normal. Hartmann rubbed the bag under his right eye with the back of his right hand, and when he took his hand away the benign look had returned.

10:15 A.M. Nessen group out. Paperwork.

10:52 A.M. The President went into the Cabinet Room to receive a delegation of Soviet officials, led by (it should not be incredible that stereotypes sometimes actually do show up) a simulacrum of a bear, a great hugger of a Russian man, State Minister of the Food Industry Voldemar Lein. With him were the ministers of food production, all looking well fed, for the Ukraine, Belorussia, Estonia, Armenia, Kazakhstan, Uzbekistan, and the Russian Republic. These men had just completed a delicious tour. They had been invited by Donald M. Kendall, chairman of PepsiCo — which had established a bottling plant in the Soviet Union and distributed Soviet vodka here — to see how food was processed in the United States, and from sea to shining sea they had visited plants of Hershey chocolate, Heinz soups and canned foods, Sara Lee frozen cakes and pastries, Kraftco cheese and margarine, Coors beer, Sun Maid raisins, Roma wine, Valley Foundry (winery equipment), Bird's Eye foods, Maxwell House coffee, Frito-Lay potato products, Tropicana orange juice, Pepsi-Cola bottling and Philip Morris cigarettes.

While waiting for the President, the various national food ministers had been taking turns popping in and out of the chair with the little brass plate on the back which said THE PRESIDENT while a pal across the table took snapshots of them in the highest seat of power. On the President's entrance everyone cooled it and took a Cabinet member's chair.

Of all the establishments the Russians visited, the one Minister Lein talked about with the most ursine joy was Disney World.

FORD: Did you go in the Haunted House?
LEIN (*rolling his eyes in terror*): *Da! Da! Da!*

The President made a set speech, which was Russianized by an American translator: ". . . helpful and beneficial . . . General Secretary . . . Vladivostok . . . expansion of trade . . . détente relationship. . . ."

Then Minister Lein made a speech, which was Englished by a Soviet translator. Minister Lein, it seems, was accustomed to good long feasts of talk. He did not spare the courses. We learned a great deal from him about food processing, as practiced both in the Union of Soviet Socialist Republics and in the United States of America. He grew expansive on the benefits of mutual visitation, trade, friendship, cultural exchange, and détente.

Mr. Ford, maintaining firm eye contact even during translational interludes, was growing larger and larger, his chin was jutting out farther and farther. At last the State Minister sprang to his feet, and Mr. Ford sprang to his feet. The State Minister snapped open a large suitcase of gifts — a huge buffalo carved from a root by a peasant, a scarf with ПЕПСИ-КОЛА   (Pepsi-Cola) and МИР (peace) printed on it, an exquisite miniature samovar, a very large pipe, a cup and saucer, an ancient ruble and a bottle each of Ambassador and Stolichnaya vodka. By the time he got around to mentioning the vodka, Minister Lein's arms, elbows bent, were flapping.

LEIN (*as translated*): When you are tired, President, drink a little from these two bottles and (*flap, flap*) you will be STRONG!

FORD (*elbows bent, but not quite flapping*): I WILL!

11:20 A.M. Secretary Schlesinger and General Scowcroft went into the Oval Office; I was not invited.

Once again, seeing Kissinger's deputy's back recede as the door closes, I began thinking about what I had missed during the week.

Why, I wondered, had this candid President opened the door so wide to me on domestic-policy meetings, and on appointments of all sorts, yet excluded me from every consideration of foreign affairs?

One answer, of course: Dr. Kissinger was away. Another: it had been a bad week — Cambodia, Vietnam, frustrations by the Congress.

But now I remembered that when Mr. Ford had first met with me a month before to discuss this project, he had told me (not then knowing that the Secretary would be in the Middle East that week), "The only meetings I can think of that you won't be able to sit in on are my talks with Henry." After that appointment, Ron Nessen had softened the blow of this exclusion by explaining to me that nobody, but nobody — excepting the Secretary's other self, Brent Scowcroft, and occasionally Secretary of Defense Schlesinger — went in with Henry to discuss foreign policy with the President. General Scowcroft had later confirmed this to me.

And now this idea suddenly bothered me, and even alarmed me — not the idea of my own exile, I mean, but that United States foreign policy should have been transacted man-to-man between Henry Kissinger and Gerald Ford. I had seen endless meetings of six, eight, ten advisers sitting with the President to hammer out policy on the economy and energy and Congressional tactics and everything else under the sun; there the President had heard numerous advisory voices. But foreign policy was apparently of a different order. Of course, Dr. Kissinger had the whole weight of the State Department behind him, and I was told that he did occasionally appear at senior staff meetings to brief the President's advisers; but in the formulation of settled policy, this President, who had had a minimal exposure to foreign affairs before he came to office, heard, I was told, only one voice, and a mercurial voice it was, Henry Kissinger's. Yes, this was the most alarming thought I had had all week.

But that was not all there was to it. General Scowcroft was in there now with the Secretary of Defense; I could only speculate that they were discussing with the President the deteriorating military situation in Indochina. Earlier that morning General Scowcroft had been in with David Peterson of the C.I.A. These couplings forcefully reminded me of Dr. Kissinger's dual role — as Secretary of State and Assistant to the President on National Security Affairs.

General Scowcroft had told me that the National Security Council — which consisted of the President, the Vice President, the Secretary of State and the Secretary of Defense, with the Director of the C.I.A. and the Chairman of the Joint Chiefs as attendant nonmembers — did not meet on a regular basis and did not set policy when it met. Final policy, Scowcroft had told me, was set by the President in consultation with the council's chairman, who was Henry Kissinger.

Diplomacy, security, foreign intelligence — one daily voice for all? To advise a President with virtually no experience in those areas? Why were the President's domestic advisers, civilians, not present as a matter of course to speak for the citizenry on every occasion when foreign affairs and national security, with their horrendous potential for economic commitment and even armed conflict, were discussed?

Schlesinger and Scowcroft were in with the President for an hour and a half.

1:05 P.M. The Gridiron Club delegation, eight Grand Panjandrums of the Washington news corps, waited on the President with an invitation to their dinner. Photographs, standing with the President.

1:10 P.M. Winners of a White House Press Photographer's Contest in to stand beside the President and have their photographs photographed.

1:15 P.M. Lunch. That good old cottage cheese, drenched in that good old A-1 Sauce.

2:03 P.M. The no-more-spending meeting. Lynn, Seidman, Marsh, Hartmann, Buchen, Nessen, Scowcroft, Greenspan, Cannon, Friedersdorf, Cheney, O'Neill.

In his State-of-the-Union Message two months before, the President had said, "I have also concluded that no more spending programs can be initiated this year, except for energy. Further, I will not hesitate to veto any new spending programs adopted by the Congress." Aware, for some time, of all sorts of proposals, major and minor, some of them meritorious or even obligatory, that were "coming down the pike," James Lynn of the Office of Management and Budget had been trying to get a precise interpretation of these two sentences.

This was an uncomfortable meeting for the President, who found himself on the spot for having given Congress a firm commitment which his advisers had obviously not thought through. He was pulled and pushed, in this discussion, by dissonant voices — humane, goading, "realistic."

O'NEILL: If you go all the way with this, you're going to have to be against all kinds of things you may not want to be against — new medical devices, regulation of toxic substances. . . .

LYNN: Do you want to celebrate National Peanut Day?

GREENSPAN: The real problem is that there's no way, as an exact matter, to resolve this. . . . A substitute program isn't a "new" program. . . . Let's say that large spending programs are out, even if they have a future date on them — '77 or '78 — but that you could get small programs under the tent. Of 1,000 programs, 950 would be small ones you don't care about. . . .

Ever since breakfast Thursday morning, I had been looking for signals of stress under the calm exterior. I had seen all week that it was not easy for Gerald Ford to be in the presence of contention; and that, by the same token, it was not easy for him to make what he referred to, in the language of umpires, as "a tough call." Yet once he had made such a decision, he did not agonize over it; rather, he became convinced of its rightness and was stubborn in its defense, even when, as with the Cambodian-aid request, it was unpopular, politically hopeless, and of most improbable efficacy.

I was beginning to be able to tell when the pressure was on. He had three laughs: a radiant, healthy and catching outburst of real mirth; a hesitant laugh, expressing slight embarrassment or uncertainty; and, rarely, a mild, monosyllabic utterance of a manly giggle, delivered as the immediate preface to speech — which, when I had heard it, had seemed to cover flickering anger. Also, when he touched his face in one of two ways: thumb under chin, index and middle fingers up along the cheek, ring and little fingers bent down across the mouth; a grasping of chin between thumb and forefinger.

2:56 P.M. He returned to the Oval Office with General Scowcroft, who was in for twenty minutes.

3:16 P.M. A few spare minutes, time to rehearse alone a speech he would have to make during his next appointment.

4:00 P.M. Mr. Ford went to the residence — first to the East Room, where he delivered the speech, which was pleasantly bantering, to 250 editors and publishers of small-town and rural weekly and daily newspapers, convened in Washington for the Fourteenth Annual Government Affairs Conference of the National Newspaper Association; and afterward to the State Dining Room, where drinks and a spread were furnished, and where he chatted — he really did seem to enjoy these occasions — with some of the newspaper people and their families.

As he started moving to leave, a moblet closed around him. He was besieged for autographs. The hallway was soon choked. He signed and signed, smiling and asking friendly questions. In a very few minutes, miraculously, he was swallowed by the elevator, off to the side of the cross hall.

"The secret in that kind of crowd," he said to me on the way back to the Oval Office, "is to keep your feet shuffling all the time. You get to your destination that way without offending anyone."

4:45 P.M. Personnel Director William N. Walker brought his staff of about a dozen into the Oval Office to meet the President. This was one small episode in Mr. Ford's obviously genuine drive toward accessibility and openness. He was charming to these staffers, each of whom, in his or her way, worked hard for him.

I had an opportunity to ask him whether his accessibility, of which I had been a beneficiary, had drawbacks.

FORD: It does in some respects. Don Rumsfeld and I are trying to do something about it. I really should have more time during the day just to totally concentrate without listening. My tendency is to be more open. Don's tendency is, thank God, to start closing doors. We've made headway. I think after another few months we'll squeeze down the system, so to speak, so that I can have more time to actually think and contemplate. On the other hand — and I've argued this with Don — in many respects I think I'm a better listener than I am a reader. I have learned to read fast and to absorb, but there are certain things you can't do quickly, without talking them out — at least, I can't. I need more time. We have to find time to study, to think.

5:00 P.M. To the Cabinet Room, to meet with retiring Secretary of Labor Peter Brennan and a group of leaders of the building-trades unions, to talk about the lamentable rate of unemployment — almost 20 percent — among the members of some of those unions. These were big, hearty, tough men, and, as always, the President vibrated to strong chords struck near him.

FORD: Peter . . . Like to welcome your colleagues . . . loyal, dedicated fellows. . . . What we've tried to do — we think it's a better way, though not necessarily for the building trades, I realize — is with a tax cut, if we could just get the Senators and Congressmen to move on it.

BRICKLAYERS' INTERNATIONAL PRESIDENT THOMAS F. MURPHY (*on the President's left, slamming the table with his hand*): Why don't you just send 'em home?

FORD: Sometimes I wish I could, Tom.

Here, as I watched Mr. Ford gradually rise to the level of intensity and decibels of these former hodcarriers and masons and plasterers and bricklayers, I also saw them quieted by his final imperturbability. Thus, I was aware of a principle of reciprocating influences always at work with this man. He yielded, but only to a certain point; beyond that point, he tranquillized.

5:56 P.M. Former Governor William Scranton of Pennsylvania, an old friend, into the Oval Office to talk. This was the only strong advisory voice Mr. Ford would have heard all week long expressing views even slightly more liberal than his own. All the rest of his advice had come from people either as conservative as he, or more so.

6:24 P.M. Rumsfeld's deputy, Dick Cheney, and the Cabinet Secretary, Jim Connor, took the evening roundup.

6:42 P.M. Paperwork.

7:11 P.M. The President emerged in his anteroom, ready to go home. But he was waylaid there by one of his military aides, who had been downstairs at a farewell party for General Lawson.

AIDE (*putting an arm around the President's shoulders*): Be a good guy, Mr. President, and listen to just one song from this Air Force bunch we've got down there.

The President was willing to be a good guy.

The aide ran off and soon reappeared with a quartet that called itself The Winning Hand, belonged to the Arlington, Virginia, chapter of the Society for the Preservation and Encouragement of Barbershop Quartet Singing in America, and came in several shapes and sizes of the same light-blue suit.

FORD (*pointing to Nell Yates, at the desk by the door to the Oval Office*): Sing a serenade to Nell there.

Out popped a pitch pipe. Then:

> *They say that it's a woman's world,*
> *and I believe it's true.*
> *For women like to better men*
> *in everything they do.*
> *In politics, science and industry,*
> *the girls are always right.*
> *So I concede they're better than we —*
> *they've earned the right to fight.*
> *And I'll be standing on the pier*
> *handing out doughnuts*
> *When we send the girls*
> *over there. . . .*

7:17 P.M. The President left for the residence, taking me with him.

We went up to the family quarters on the second floor, and he settled me in the "living room" and excused himself; he said he wants to check in with Betty. He went into the bedroom.

This "room" I was in was really just a grouping of furniture — a sofa covered in bright flowered cotton quilting, some easy chairs, a brass-railed oval coffee table, superb porcelain lamps, four fresh flower arrangements, no books lying around — at the end of the long, long second-floor central hall; it seemed a cozy room with one wall missing.

After a few minutes the President emerged and said he'd like to have me come in and meet Betty.

The bedroom was a cheerful place; it was in the northwest corner of the mansion, and it must have filled up to the brim with sunlight, as with sweet cider, in the daytime — though, come to think of it, there had not been a moment of sunshine all through that week of Mrs. Ford's having suffered with neck pain. She was in the wide bed. She looked frail. Her head rested on a small cylindrical pillow. I had an impression of a sea of whiteness and lace.

Susan was standing beyond the bed, in jeans and a Norwegian ski sweater.

Mrs. Ford raised her shoulders with difficulty to reach and shake my hand across the expanse of the bed. I was really glad to meet her; I had admired her straightforwardness and courage, and I had had a sense that just as Bess Truman stood close behind her Harry's backbone, so this woman fanned up the warmth in her Jerry. She had been watching television. The President snapped off the set as we talked.

MRS. FORD (*to her husband*): Say! Lynda Bird Johnson Robb is writing a book, and she wants me to name the person I think is the most important American of all time. How about helping me?

The President seemed about to make a suggestion, when she went on:

MRS. FORD: I thought of Lincoln, and Jefferson, and of course old George —

SUSAN: What about Hamilton? Adams? John Hay?

MRS. FORD (*looking up at Susan*): No, I was thinking only of the top people — the giants. (*She turns her eyes — mischievous now — back to the President's.*) Would you buy Susan B. Anthony?

FORD (*with a peal of his good laugh*): There you go again!

The President, Susan, and I were seated now in the living room. He was on his second Beefeater martini on the rocks. The delicate subject of intellectual competence had come up.

FORD: Well, you know, it's an interesting thing, John. I don't know whether grades are the way to say somebody is bright or dumb or otherwise. But I've often thought — when I was in high school, where the competition was mediocre, I got a little over a B average. When I went to Michigan, I did the same.* I think at law school — the same.

I said that Myres McDougal, a professor at the Yale Law School, had told me Mr. Ford had fared pretty well there — had ranked about one-third of the way down from the top of his class.

FORD: Great guy. He was the Law School faculty member who was assigned to interview me as an applicant.† He — or somebody — told me that in the class I entered with, which had about 125, there were 98 or 99 who were college Phi Betes, of which I was not one. And they were extremely bright. Very able guys. . . . So I seem to have had a capability of competing with whatever competition there was at each level; and yet I could have enough outside activities to enjoy a broader spectrum of day-to-day living than some of them. But I must say I worked damn hard. And I happen to agree with people that grades are very important, but I don't think that's the final criterion by which to judge people.

SUSAN: Well, that's news!

FORD (to Susan): Yeah, I've been pushing you, beating you to get good grades, haven't I?

SUSAN: You put restrictions on, if my grades go down. . . .

---

* In his four-year Michigan career, Mr. Ford earned A's in Decline of Rome to 1648, Civilization from 1648, Labor I and American Government. He received C's in English Composition I and II, second-year French, Finance, Geography, Money and Credit, History of the South Since 1860 and Psychology of Management. He got B's in everything else.

† Professor McDougal's notes on that interview were: "Goodlooking, well dressed, plenty of poise, personality excellent. Informational background none too good, but he is interested, mature and serious of purpose. Intelligence reasonably high. I should predict a 74 or 75 average with us. I see no reason for not taking him." The professor's academic prediction was remarkably accurate. Ford's average in all subjects was 74.8. He got 78 in Constitutional Law, 74 in Federal Jurisprudence, 79 in Public Control of Business.

We were at dinner. The table was lit by candles; dusk had fallen on the bold scenes from the Revolutionary War on the walls around us.

FORD: You watch, John. When they bring the dinner in, Susan's plate and mine will be all served — rations. But they'll pass things to you, and let you take as much as you want. You watch.

SUSAN: I've taken off thirty pounds.

The President's prediction was soon borne out.

Susan had been writing articles for *Seventeen,* and she and I talked awhile about Being Writers.

SUSAN: My second piece was about Mother's Day — really about the great job my mother has done all these years. Then they wanted me to do Father's Day for June. I said, "That's too much."

FORD: It's good discipline — writing for deadlines.

HERSEY: Yes.

SUSAN: The August issue is going into the works already. They want me to write about my summer. How do I know what my plans will be? . . .

Mr. Ford talked about clothes. He bought about three suits every two years, he said. The one he had on, he said, was made by Lloyd's, a tailor in Grand Rapids to whom he had gone for years — it was out of style, the lapel was too narrow, he pointed out. He could never throw anything out. The blue shirt he was wearing, he said, was new — had just got it from a Washington tailor, Harvey Rosenthal. The President was now getting his suits from Rosenthal's, he said; they came into the White House for fittings. One of the luxuries . . .

We had butter-pecan ice cream for dessert. After it, Mr. Ford took tea. He started talking again about enjoying the Presidency:

FORD: I like meeting with one group to discuss this, and the next meeting to discuss that. I don't really object to anything unless it interferes with our family relationship. And

that hasn't been too bad. Probably the major test was at Vail
this Christmas, it wasn't — . . . I suppose somebody who is
hypersensitive might say, "Gee, I couldn't do this, or that."
But if you just relax and enjoy it, it doesn't make you tense,
it doesn't make you irritable.

SUSAN: Just like when we were in Vail. Even though you
did have the Cabinet meetings — when they were over, it
was like you were back on your vacation.

FORD: It worked out very nicely.

SUSAN: Secretary Simon stayed, and we had a good time
with him. He couldn't have been nicer.

FORD: The only thing that is disappointing — I guess any
President has this. The President thinks he has the right answers. The facts of history are that he doesn't always — but
he thinks he does. And he would like to implement, he'd like
to execute — to get things done. But under our system, the
Congress has a very definite partnership. Right now we are
going through an extraordinary trauma in the relationship
between the Congress and the President. I understand that.
I've been on the other end of it. But if there was one part
which I would really like to change, it would be the speed
with which you could make decisions and carry them
out — in foreign policy, particularly. . . .

We were in the family room now, he in his blue chair, I in
the overstuffed chair next to it, and the time had come for
me to ask him some direct questions.

*Harry Truman seems to be much in his mind. What are the things
he admires about him as President?*

FORD: Well, he came from relatively humble beginnings.
He obviously was a man who knew people, understood people and worked with people. He had a lot of courage, was
forthright, didn't hesitate to make decisions. Those are the
things I admire.

What attributes does he feel he brings to the Presidency?

FORD: I don't like to talk about it. Maybe what I say is what
I would like to have brought, but . . . I think I bring a

responsible decision-making process, based on a great deal of fundamental knowledge of how things work in our Government. I consider myself very lucky that I bring this to the White House, that I have acquired, that I have retained, a great deal of background in the political process. I know I'm conscientious. I know I'm a person who can listen. I believe I bring out in people I work with their best qualities. I think I have a knack of picking people who have talent.

What would he like to be remembered for?

FORD: I think that America went through one of the most unbelievable periods in the last two or three years that we'd ever want to. And I found myself in a situation where somebody had to take over — internationally, domestically, governmentally — and handle circumstances such as had never transpired in this country before. And if I can be remembered for restoring public confidence in the Presidency, for handling all these transitional problems responsibly and effectively, for achieving decent results domestically as well as internationally, regardless of how long I serve, whether it's two and a half years or six and a half years, I think that's what I'd like on my tombstone.

He was restless. Maybe he was as dissatisfied with this last answer as I had been. He rang for a butler and asked for more tea for both of us.

Can he give, in a capsule, the essence of his political philosophy?

FORD: I happen to think that we should have great opportunity for people in this country to get ahead. Hard work should be rewarded. I don't think people who have had bad breaks should be penalized, but I don't think you can reward people who don't try.

Where does his conservatism come from?

FORD: I think it was the upbringing in my stepfather's family — he was a sort of a Horatio Alger in a limited sense. It was my upbringing in a family that had to live, not an austere, but a moderate life.

How conservative does he see himself as being?

FORD: Well, I'm conservative in that I believe in saving — I'm talking personally, now — I believe in saving, I believe in building through effort. On the other hand, I enjoy material things. This is a nice place to live, and there are many conveniences that are made available here. I enjoy belonging to Burning Tree. We were talking about clothes — I enjoy nice clothes, not flamboyant or extravagant. I enjoy doing nice things. But I enjoy these things because I worked for them.

Does he think that the material side of the Presidency, and its conveniences, won't get to him?

FORD: I don't think I've shown any evidence that they have, and I don't see why they should. I've had a long sixty years without any of this, so these aren't things that I couldn't get along without in the future.

What about the sense of power that comes with an office like this?

FORD: I don't enjoy it. I think I accept it as part of the responsibility. I recognize that it is there, and that I have to use it judiciously. I don't shy away from it.

Does he think of himself as a Middle American?

FORD: I do see myself as a Middle American. I have a Michigan background. I went to school in Michigan from kindergarten through college. But I've been fortunate enough to have exposures that broadened the spectrum, broadened the horizon.

How would he describe a Middle American?

FORD: A person who is moderate-to-conservative, philosophically; who yet has compassion for people less well-off than himself; who wants to have his country do what is right for everybody; who is concerned with the national security; who is willing to make sacrifices; who is willing to work; and who is a lot smarter that most politicians give him credit for being.

How can he use the word "compassion" so much — and ask for higher prices for food stamps?

FORD: The trouble with a lot of these programs, where compassion ought to be the main thrust, is that they get well beyond the properly intended scope. And the net result is that when you try to bring them back to focus on the people who need and deserve help — whether food stamps or welfare generally — when you try to cut out the undeserving so you can give more to the people who are really in need, you can't be compassionate for the ones who get cut out, because they shouldn't have been in the program in the first place. And yet they're the most vocal; they're the ones who feel that because they were on something, they ought to continue. Really, the ones that are deserving of compassion are the ones that complain the least. It's the ones who are sort of the fringe people who cause the most trouble and get the issue confused.

Perhaps I had phrased that last question badly. I was thinking back to Tuesday, when I first had been surprised by what seemed to me the hard sound in his voice, the sound of distance from ordinary people — which seemed so contradictory to the direct and unfeigned kindness he was able to offer whomever he met face to face. Perhaps I could come at this from another direction — by way of another contradiction in him.

He was famous in Congress for his gift of compromise, but even some of his good friends say he is stubborn at times. How do these two things go together?

FORD: It is paradoxical. I try to rationalize that when I am stubborn, I am right, and therefore compromise seems fundamentally wrong. Now I suppose to somebody who's sitting on the other side, when I take a firm position, he says, "Well, he's just being stubborn — not necessarily 100-percent right." But there are occasions where I will be very firm, and stubborn might be another term for it.

What are his feelings when he is criticized?

FORD: When I read or listen to criticism, I try to analyze whether it's legitimate by my standards; and if I think it's unfair and feel very secure in my judgment, sometimes I'm amused by the criticism, sometimes I'm irritated, but the last thing I'm going to do is let anyone know it. But as long as I feel that what I've done is right, I'm not going to be upset about it and fly off the handle or change my course of action. If the criticism is fair — and there are instances when I might have made a mistake — then I take it and look it over. If I've made a mistake, I don't hesitate to change.

Looking back, what mistakes?

FORD: Well, there's probably one incident in retrospect I might have handled differently, and this is the famous challenge to Bill Douglas. But at the time, I was faced with a very difficult practical problem within the Republican party in the House. Bill Douglas had made some decisions, and his married life was different than most — many conservative people were upset about him, and we had a very strong small group of very conservative Republicans in the Congress. And for a period of about a month or so, they kept telling me, "You either do something about it, or we're going to offer a motion of impeachment, which is a privileged motion of the highest, and we're going to force a vote." I tried to keep them from going off the deep end, and they kept pressuring and pressuring. And then this famous *Evergreen* publication came out, a very ill-advised article by the Justice in a magazine that I think is pornographic by any standards. And that upset me, plus the pressure from these others. So I said to myself, in order to keep the irresponsibles from forcing the vote, I will make this speech, and I will not say there should be impeachment, but that there ought to be a study. Well, I did it. I never demanded his impeachment. I advocated a study. Well, in retrospect, forgetting the pressures that were existent then, I suspect it was the one thing that was a bit out of character.

What does he say to those who call him a plodder and a man without charisma?

FORD: I kind of resent the word "plodder." (*What is it that one can hear in the careful way he says these words? There is something gathering, something clotting, under the perfect control.*) I would put it another way. I'm a determined person. And if I've got an objective, I'll make hours of sacrifice — whatever efforts are needed. Some people call it plodding. The word is somewhat downgraded, but I'd rather be a plodder and get someplace than have charisma and not make it.

Now I realized that we had shared a moment of strong and puzzling feelings. Beneath the control, I could hear that he was angry with me, and I was glad of it. He had a right to be angry; I had asked him hard questions, and just now an insulting one. For my part, although I was deeply troubled by some of his policies, and by the long reach and rigidity of his conservatism, I had nevertheless come to like him as a man — he had been most kind and generous with me; his good laugh, when I had heard it, had filled me with its energy and warmth. And so I was grateful for this human moment, even though it was ugly, for I felt that at last we had really and truly met.

But it was only a moment, as I had to hurry to the next question.

Does he have any chance to talk to poor people?

FORD: In this job, I have had very little. When I was in Congress, a great deal. When I was in Congress, I made a maximum effort. I think that was helpful, both substantively and politically.

Wouldn't it be now, too?

FORD: Well, we've thought about that, and quite frankly I've been intrigued with the program Giscard has, of having gone to dinner in the homes of citizens, or having people in. I'm a little hesitant about doing it, because it looks copycat. Now that I've talked about it, I think there's some merit in it. As to how you do it . . . I don't know if you've ever heard about my trailer operation.

What was that?

FORD: That was the smartest thing I ever did. Grand Rapids was the main area of the district. After I'd been in Congress about six years, I found I was spending 90 percent of my time in Grand Rapids, and not doing much out in the smaller communities in the rural areas. I got the idea of having Jerry Ford's Main Street Office. So we rented a trailer, and I would take it to Cedar Springs, and we'd advertise that I was going to be there in the morning. I'd speak, going to the high school and the grade school and talking to the kids, and then I'd speak at the Cedar Springs Rotary Club, or Kiwanis — this wasn't just campaign years, off-years as well. I'd walk up and down the main street for an hour or so, stopping at stores. And then from two thirty to eight o'clock I'd be in the trailer. And we would have anywhere from 25 to 125 people come and see me individually in the back room of the trailer. And I had my secretary or administrative assistant out front. In the course of two months in the fall, maybe three months, I'd do it in twenty-five, thirty different places. We would have anywhere from 1,500 to 2,000 people who would stop in and see me, to criticize, to compliment, to give us problems to work on. We could always say that I had my office within ten miles of every home in the district. People could never say they couldn't come and see me. It was the greatest political asset in a nonpolitical way.

This picture excited me, and I interrupted him to exclaim how good it would be if he had a trailer like that now. I imagined the Presidential trailer in remote hamlets, on hot city streets. He was not interested in my enthusiasm, and at once I realized how silly it was — the mobs, security, a nation isn't a district. . . .

And yet, how good it would have been if in some way he could have spoken — not just with Kissinger and Simon and Morton and Schlesinger, with Rumsfeld and Hartmann and Marsh and Buchen, with importunate politicans and selected intellectuals — but also, good listener that he was, inner mimic that he was, one-to-one with ordinary men and women, his constituents, from whom he had somehow drifted so far away.

FORD (*ignoring my interruption*): On some occasions I'd be in the trailer until midnight. It was interesting in that district. It had many strong, devout, Calvinistic Dutch people. Holland, Michigan. Zeeland, Michigan. In one area of the district, 90 percent of the people were strong Protestants — not Dutch Reform, but Dutch Christian Reform, which is a group that broke off from Dutch Reform because it was too liberal. I would have the ministers from these areas in, and sit down with them before they'd talk about a problem, and they'd say, "Can we have a few moments of prayer?" And we'd pray in the trailer — sincerely, very devoutly.

Somehow, thinking about the trailer, I had lost the thread of all the hundreds of questions the week had raised in my mind. Thinking about more than the trailer, really. Thinking about what seemed for a moment possible but obviously was not; thinking about the insistent sound of caution in all that Mr. Ford had been saying that evening; thinking about the hopes that so many citizens had had for a whole new era, after the Nixon debacle, in our national way of looking at things — hopes for a time of change that was evidently not going to be fought for, or even dreamed of, by this man, because in his view, and in that of his advisers, this was "not an era for change."

The brown suitcase, full of papers, sat there like a reproach. I sensed that the President was itching to get down to work. I thanked him for dinner, and for his time, and for his openness. He considerately went all the way downstairs in the elevator with me, to make sure I would find my way back to the West Wing, where I had left my coat early that morning.

FORD: Good night, John. See you in the morning!

13. SATURDAY

The Shot Took Off for Atlanta, Georgia

Saturday morning he indulged in what he called "sleeping over"; this meant that he didn't show up at the Oval Office until 8:30. He had a light schedule — a chance to clear his desk.

8:34 A.M. Scowcroft and Peterson in. 8:55 A.M. — Peterson out. 9:35 A.M. — Scowcroft out, Marsh in. 9:50 A.M. —Marsh out.

The day had dawned with an overcast sky, but the forecast, at last, was excellent. Now suddenly a dollop of sunlight fell like a promise through a rip in the clouds and diluted with finer stuff the artificial brillance of the Oval Office. No more was needed to make the President ring for Terry O'Donnell and tell him to line up some golfing companions for the afternoon.

9:50 A.M. Cheney and Greenspan in. 10:15 A.M. — Greenspan out. 10:25 A.M. — Cheney out. 11:00 A.M. — Cheney in again. 11:35 A.M. — Cheney out again. Paperwork.

GRANDFATHER SEYMOUR: Tock . . . Tock . . . Tock . . .

1:35 P.M. A motorcade of four cars left the South Grounds: the President in a blue sedan, reading the afternoon *Star-News* as he went; a Secret Service car, which followed the sedan closely; a staff car; a car for the photographic pool, going along as far as the entrance gate to Burning Tree — just in case.

The President changed in the locker room, then went to the first tee, wearing now an old visored cap, brown-on-brown saddled golf shoes, green pants, and a blue windbreaker of the Pinehurst Country Club, which he picked up when he went there the previous year to visit the golf Hall of Fame and played a round with the famed inductees. With him were his good friend William Whyte, a vice president and Washington lobbyist for United States Steel; Clark MacGregor, once a fellow Congressman with Ford, later John Mitchell's successor as Chairman of the Committee to Re-Elect the President and now a Washington-based vice president of United Aircraft Corp.; and Webb Hayes, a Washington lawyer and great-grandson of President Rutherford B. Hayes.

Ford teamed up with Whyte; the foursome settled on a "two-dollar Nassau" — a betting deal that couldn't hurt anyone much. The men did not use golf carts; caddies carried their clubs.

On the first few holes, the President had a bit of Oval Office in his swing. His long game was very strong; his chips and putts, more often than not, were too strong. He putted with a wide stance suitable for good hard clouts. The sun was fully out now. There was a breeze with sharp teeth that bit the flags on the greens. So discreet was Burning Tree County Club that these flags didn't even have numbers on them. One was conscious of several men, carrying odd-shaped cases, ranging in the woods on either side of the fairway and far ahead. Following the foursome at a polite distance were Dick Keiser, Chief of the Presidential Protective Division of the Secret Service, who was often taken for the President in crowds; Lieutenant Commander Stephen Todd, the President's naval aide, carrying a walkie-talkie, to be in touch with the White House communications center at all times; and Dr. Lukash.

It was the seventh hole, par four.

Gerald Ford's huge tee shot took off for Atlanta, Georgia, but the ball had a mind of its own and in midair veered left toward Charleston, South Carolina; on the way there, however, it hit a tall tree and, with distinctly Presidential luck, bounced out to a splendid lie in the left rough.

There, with a No. 2 wood, the President connected so hard that one was forced to wonder what that small sphere stood for in his mind. The ball rose and rose and flew as straight and true as Air Force One nonstop to the green, to within ten feet of the pin.

The President cupped his hands around his mouth and exultantly shouted to his partner across the fairway: "Hey, Bill, is that where I'm supposed to put it?"